# A CENTURY OF INSURANCE

PLATE I

SIR HENRY WILLIAM PEEK, BART.

First Chairman, 1861-1863

# A
# Century of Insurance

THE COMMERCIAL UNION
GROUP OF INSURANCE COMPANIES
1861-1961

*A Centenary History by*
*EDWARD LIVEING M.A.*

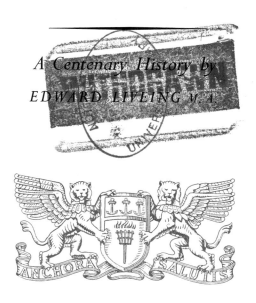

H. F. & G. WITHERBY LTD

First published 1961

© Commercial Union Assurance Co. Ltd. 1961

MADE IN GREAT BRITAIN

Printed by
WITHERBY & CO. LTD. 15 NICHOLAS LANE
LONDON E.C.4

# COMMERCIAL UNION GROUP OF INSURANCE COMPANIES

## *UNITED KINGDOM*

Commercial Union Assurance Company Limited
North British & Mercantile Insurance Company Limited
British and European Insurance Company Limited
British General Insurance Company Limited
Edinburgh Assurance Company Limited
Fine Art and General Insurance Company Limited
National Insurance Company of Great Britain Limited
Ocean Accident and Guarantee Corporation Limited
Ocean Marine Insurance Company Limited
Palatine Insurance Company Limited
Railway Passengers Assurance Company
Travellers' Insurance Association Limited
Union Assurance Society Limited
West of Scotland Insurance Office Limited

## *UNITED STATES OF AMERICA*

American Central Insurance Company
California Insurance Company
Central Surety and Insurance Corporation
Columbia Casualty Company
Commonwealth Insurance Company of New York
Commercial Union Insurance Company of New York
Mercantile Insurance Company of America
Pennsylvania Fire Insurance Company

## *CANADA*

Canada Accident and Fire Assurance Company
North West Fire Insurance Company
Occidental Fire Insurance Company

v

*AUSTRALIA*

Commercial Union Assurance Company of Australia Limited
Australian Mutual Fire Insurance Society Limited
British General Insurance Company of Australia Limited
Insurance Office of Australia Limited
Ocean Accident and Guarantee Corporation of Australia Limited
Palatine Insurance Company of Australia Limited
Union Assurance Society of Australia Limited

*NEW ZEALAND*

Dominion Life Assurance Office of New Zealand Limited

*JAMAICA*

Jamaica Co-operative Fire and General Insurance Company Limited

*AUSTRIA*

Anglo-Elementar Versicherungs-Aktien-Gesellschaft

*DENMARK*

Forsikrings-Aktieselskabet Vidar

PLATE II

*Baron Studios*

RONALD C. BROOKS, O.B.E., M.C.

Present Chairman

# FOREWORD

*by*

THE CHAIRMAN

To mark our centenary the decision was made to publish a volume giving the history of the Commercial Union during its first hundred years. The author's purpose has been to set out faithfully the development of a world-wide insurance business against the social and economic background of the times. I believe that he has been successful in a task which has been far from easy.

The Commercial Union Group of Insurance Companies is now protecting many millions of policyholders in nearly all parts of the world against a diversity of risks which would have astounded our predecessors in the nineteenth century. The present and future generations will assuredly be faced with changes in the pattern of economic affairs every bit as revolutionary as those of the past. Guided by the lessons of the first hundred years, some of which are recorded in this book, we will accept this challenge with quiet confidence and with a determination to maintain in our second century of insurance the standards, the diligence and the imagination which I feel are revealed in this commemorative history.

It is hoped that our wide circle of friends and colleagues, both at home and overseas, will find in the following pages material which will interest and stimulate them. I know that the author's only regret has been his inability to mention in one volume all the General Agents and other friends without whom progress would have been impossible.

RONALD C. BROOKS.

# CONTENTS

# LIST OF PLATES

# INTRODUCTION

S EVERAL different methods of approach presented themselves
when this history of the Commercial Union and its Group of
companies was being considered. One of the largest and, inter-
nationally, most widespread organisations in British insurance, it inevitably lent itself to varying forms of historical treatment.

As a fully composite insurance business its activities could have
been described in separate parts devoted to the contributions which
it has made to fire, accident and marine underwriting and to life
assurance. As an organisation of international status it would have
been possible, and not without considerable interest, to trace its
development in separate parts relating to the United Kingdom, the
United States, the English-speaking nations of the Commonwealth,
Europe, the Far East, and elsewhere. Equally, and though this approach would have entailed difficulties in any account of recent
years, the growth of the parent company and of its major subsidiaries
at home and abroad might, in some degree at least, have been dealt
with separately.

These and other alternatives were discarded in favour of as
straightforward a chronological account as possible. This has the
obvious advantages of spontaneity and human interest, while at the
same time the story unfolds itself in a progressive sequence of events.
Even so, the development of a complex business enterprise cannot be
told in a completely straightforward historical way. A constant *va
et vient* between the activities of one department and another
and between events in different parts of the world was one
problem that had to be contended with. Another was the introduction into the narrative of the many important companies, each with
its own individual history, that now compose the Group. The first
of these two problems has been met by dividing the work into parts
dealing with specific periods of time, but through chapters describ-

ing concurrent, yet diverse, matters in separate groupings. The second has been met by introducing into the narrative the history of each of the major subsidiary companies up to the time of its acquisition and subsequently referring to it as and when events demanded.

Throughout this history I have endeavoured to show the impact of current affairs—economic, social and international—on the activities of the Commercial Union Group and the insurance market generally. But to concentrate on the main theme, which is the growth of the business itself, I have avoided as far as possible overloading the account with too much extraneous matter; and in certain passages, especially those covering the aftermaths of the two world wars, I have been obliged to over-simplify the wide complexity of certain economic aspects.

To some considerable extent this account of the growth of one large group of composite insurance offices may be found to exemplify much that has transformed British insurance generally during the last hundred years, and especially in the present century. Some of these developments may be worth while summarising briefly.

Rationalisation within the British insurance industry has been as marked as in the other spheres of commerce and manufacturing. The period which saw the greatest number of amalgamations was the first quarter of the present century; and the Commercial Union was one of the companies that showed the largest expansion through such associations during that period. The reasons for this process of rationalisation were varied. In the early stages there was a tendency to take over moribund companies. Later, however, the importance of gaining professional expertise—and this was particularly necessary over the growth of accident underwriting from the turn of the century onwards—played its part.

The purchase by the Commercial Union, as indeed by other large composite offices, of other businesses not only augmented capacity to provide services of every kind to clients, but also widened interests to such an extent that they could counterbalance fluctuations in one field of underwriting by successful returns in another. A further effect of the mergers at home was to expand activities overseas, since most of the larger companies acquired in the United Kingdom were also well established in foreign fields. This process was taken a stage further by the purchase of indigenous foreign businesses—a process in which the Commercial Union, for instance, actively engaged itself from early in the century onwards.

Within a few years after the First World War this trend of rationalisation slowed down and came almost to a full stop. The principal reasons for this will be found to emerge clearly enough in this history. The size of the largest groups had reached a point where any further amalgamations would have entailed associations too immense at that period to offer any incentive. The time, in fact, had arrived to stop expansion and start consolidation. For some thirty years no further noteworthy mergers were to take place. The tendency towards larger groupings, however, has returned in recent years. The growing combinations in other industries, the nationalisation of public services, the advent of atomic energy, and the operation of large institutional pension schemes are among the many factors contributing to this. In particular, the problems and potentialities of consolidating and developing fire and casualty business in the United States constituted the principal reason for the recent amalgamation of the Commercial Union and North British & Mercantile Groups. In general, the demands of the modern world's highly industrialised communities require an ever increasing concentration of wealth and experience in the provision of underwriting services.

Of more interest perhaps to those within the insurance industry than to the general public has been the rise to greater influence of a professional managerial class. Many of the early offices, and also of those started in the Victorian era, owed their origins and early success to groups of merchants and manufacturers who were primarily interested in fire underwriting. The Commercial Union was among their number and it is a somewhat remarkable fact that very early in its career it also branched out successfully into life and marine business. By the turn of the century, however, its Board included distinguished men of affairs as well as merchant princes. Their value lay in the general influence and prestige that they brought to the business. But they were not professional entrepreneurs and the all-round growth in the complexity of underwriting, together with the development of accident insurance, required a General Manager, with wide executive powers and the assistance of a strong management staff, which was acceded to in 1901. This arrangement has since worked admirably and is characteristic of most of the other large-scale British composite offices existing today.

The general public may not have a full conception of the extremely important part which the British insurance industry plays in the country's economy and especially in regard to invisible exports. Its overseas revenue bulks large in our income from abroad and it is symptomatic of other elements in the insurance market that the Commercial Union Group's revenue from these sources constitutes approximately three-quarters of its entire annual income, nearly one half of this total being derived from the United States alone.

It is with some considerable regret that I have not been able to pay tribute as fully as I would have wished to the extremely valuable contribution made to the Group's development by the principal agencies associated with it abroad and in the marine market. Where particular events have brought them into this history, they have been referred to, but more than that space unfortunately would not have allowed.

I would like to take this opportunity of acknowledging with gratitude the encouragement and the wealth of first-hand information that I have received from Sir John Makins. Mr. V. E. Masters has been a constant guide and mentor, and I have also been generously assisted by heads of departments and other officials in the parent company and other companies of the Group.

I should also acknowledge the research facilities provided to me by the British Museum Library, the Guildhall Library, the Library of the Chartered Insurance Institute, and the Library of Lloyd's.

Among many published sources consulted I am particularly indebted to two recent books—Harold E. Raynes' *A History of British Insurance* and D. E. W. Gibb's *Lloyd's of London*.

Edward Liveing,

London, 1961.

# PART ONE

# Years of Growth

## 1861-1899

# CHAPTER I

---

# *Results of a Fire—1861-1863*

I

J A M E S   B R A I D W O O D, Chief Officer of the London Fire Engine
Establishment, had often in recent years looked across the
Thames with anxious eyes towards the tall warehouses on the
south bank near London Bridge. They were modern, substantial and
believed to be fireproof. On the other hand they covered a very wide
area, their bulky structures closely adjoining one another, and they
housed a vast quantity of inflammable material. Even at high tide
the level of the quays on which they abutted was nearly five feet
above the Thames and at low tide nearly twenty-five feet, so that no
water could be obtained from the river except by fire floats.

Now as he reached them on the afternoon of Saturday, June 22nd,
1861, with London basking in the sun, his anxieties were fully
realised. The ponderous, seemingly indestructible buildings were in
deadly peril, as his experienced eyes, taking in the scene at Cotton's
Wharf, quickly told him.

It was here that the fire, reported to him at his Watling Street
headquarters about ten minutes earlier, had broken out around 4.30
in a new warehouse containing hemp. By now the warehouse was
fully ablaze and the fire had already spread to neighbouring buildings. Braidwood ordered up almost the whole of his available force
and put a new steam float into action as well as one of the new land
steamers. But despite the frantic efforts of himself, his firemen and
workers in the warehouse, the fire continued to spread with unrelent-

3

ing rapidity. It soon reached Hay's Wharf and engulfed Chamberlain's Wharf filled to capacity with tallow, sulphur, oils, paint and other combustible materials.

By ten o'clock that night the whole area around Tooley Street from St. Olave's Church to Hay's Wharf was one gigantic furnace. By midnight even the great warehouses of Hay's Wharf, erected five years earlier and regarded as among the strongest and most highly fire-resistant in all London, could no longer hold out. "To mere flames", as *The Times* subsequently recorded, "these structures would have been invulnerable for days, but no building substance could withstand such tremendous heat."

Throughout the night the enormous destruction continued, watched by thousands of spectators who flocked to the scene on foot, by train, by carriage and, risking the dangers of a river covered with huge floes of burning oil and tallow, by boat.

Fortunately, a change of wind prevented the fire from invading the southern side of Tooley Street. But it took two days to get it under control and the ruins that it left behind smouldered on till the rains and frosts of winter did their work.

"The Great Tooley Street Fire", as it afterwards came to be known, was the worst conflagration London had experienced since the Great Fire of 1666. Five wharfs—Cotton's, Iron's Granary, Hay's, Daisy's and Ellis's—were completely destroyed, together with Humphrey's Warehouse. Four of the Chamberlain's Wharf warehouses and seven on Hay's wharf were also gutted. A great part of Tooley Street, with its ship chandlers' offices, its shops and houses, was wiped out. On the Thames itself an American steamer, four sailing ships and many barges were burnt to the water's edge and sank.

Strangely and happily, human casualties were very slight. Among them, however, was poor Braidwood, killed by a wall of one of the warehouses when it collapsed and buried him in hot brick and stone. The death of this gallant personality, who had led the London Fire Engine Establishment for nearly forty years with conspicuous ability, was mourned by London and the whole nation. Queen Victoria was deeply affected and sent a message of condolence to his widow. Mrs. Craik, authoress of *John Halifax, Gentleman*, composed a funeral ode. Every stationer's shop in London sold obituary cards carrying Braidwood's portrait. The bells of all the churches in the City rang their requiem as his mile and a half long cortège passed on its way.

2

No sooner had Braidwood's funeral taken place than the inevitable repercussions of the disaster started. The insurance companies found themselves in the unenviable position of having to meet losses that totalled over £2,000,000, which was a large figure in money values a century ago. To their credit none failed to meet their commitments. But they were exasperated with public criticism of the handling of the fire and appalled by the prospects of further disasters in the rapidly growing Metropolis.

Understandably enough, they decided that the time had come when they could no longer be expected to cover practically the whole costs and responsibility of maintaining London's fire fighting services and early in 1862 they sent an ultimatum to the Home Secretary to this effect. Faced with this, the Government fell back on the recourse of appointing a Select Committee. Its terms were, " to enquire into the existing state of legislation and of any existing Arrangements for the Protection of Life and Property against Fires in the Metropolis ". In this case a Select Committee's findings bore quick fruit, for they led effectively through parliamentary legislation to the establishment of a Metropolitan Fire Brigade and eventually to the municipal control of fire brigades throughout the country. This change ended a long, honourable, but out-dated association of fire insurance businesses with the protection of the community against dangers which were now continuously on the increase and more properly a matter for public control.

Less reasonable and more immediate was another reaction of the insurance companies. They tried to enforce conditions regarding storage arrangements and construction of warehouses and they raised their premiums on wharf and warehouse risks to an extremely high level. This action caused a storm of fury in the City. Some three hundred leading merchants, brokers, bankers and warehouse keepers combined together to present a petition to the Lord Mayor which was couched in forthright language that could not be ignored:

> "We the undersigned Merchants and others trading in London respectfully request your Lordship to convene a Public Meeting to take into consideration the largely increased rates of premium demanded by the Public Fire Insurance Offices in consequence of the recent calamitous Fire in Southwark; and we beg to submit to your Lordship the following brief explanation of the cause of soliciting your Lordship's compliance with our requisition.
>
> The principal Offices have for a long series of years received an extent of premium from the Insurance of Merchandise and depots thereof which we believe to have been instrumental in promoting the increase of the value of their property to a very considerable extent after payment of all claims to which losses by Fire have subjected them.
>
> The recent Fire of Southwark was of an extent never equalled in the Metropolis since the foundation of the Insurance Offices and consequently of an exceptional character. The Offices nevertheless have in their panic occasioned by so serious a loss endeavoured to establish a tariff of premiums which if submitted would render them far more than an equivalent for their risks; in fact would convert an extraordinary calamity into the basis of a permanent source of excessive profits. To exact the high rates now proposed by the Offices, who by combination exercise a practical monopoly against which at present the mercantile community is powerless, would be to encourage non-insurance and thus to stimulate an imprudent habit of trading, the evils attending which could hardly be exaggerated and which we earnestly deprecate."

Sir William Cubitt was Lord Mayor of London that year and this petition fell on ready ears, for it was his own firm, one of London's leading contractors, which had erected the massive new warehouses of Hay's Wharf for their owner, Alderman John Humphrey, to whom he was closely connected through the marriage of his two daughters to two of Humphrey's sons. He called a meeting in the Egyptian Hall of the Mansion House. It took place on July 25th and was a stormy affair. The case for the insurance companies was put by the secretary of the Globe. He argued that mercantile insurance in London had been unprofitable for the past ten years, that the late fire had incurred enormous losses to the underwriting companies and that under the circumstances the offices were justified in making some addition to their rates. At the same time he held out prospects of reduction of the rates as soon as new methods of classification of merchandise in store and future limitation of the size of warehouses were acceded to.

The speech met with a hostile reception. The proposals were declared unjust and excessive and the meeting passed a resolution to oppose by lawful means the establishment of the new rates, whether by the formation of a company or otherwise. It also appointed a committee to consider the best means to pursue these objects including consultation "with the combined Fire Insurance Offices relative to the readjustment of their greatly increased rates of insurance".

In this innocent-seeming provision for consultation lay the real sting. Acting on it at its first meeting the committee decided to intimate to the offices that it was ready to receive any communications they cared to make. The offices, with three exceptions, turned a deaf ear to the offer. The members of the committee had been holding their trump card and they now proceeded to play it with a decision on August 5th to form a new company, to be called the Commercial Union Fire Insurance Company, with a capital of £2,500,000.

To proceed with the company's formation a special committee was appointed under the chairmanship of Henry Trower, a partner in the firm of Trower and Lawson, importers of wine and spirits. This committee got quickly to work and at its first meeting on August 10th resolved that the capital issue of £2,500,000 should be in 50,000 shares of £50 each, of which £5 only should be called up. It appointed Henry W. Peek, senior partner in the wholesale grocery business of Peek Bros. & Co., as its Chairman, and Henry Trower as its Deputy Chairman, authorising them to take temporary offices at 34, Gracechurch Street. It also agreed on the wording of a Prospectus which Peek sent out from his own office in Eastcheap with a skilfully written covering letter. The Prospectus read as follows:

"The Committee of Merchants, Brokers, and others appointed at a Public Meeting, held at the Mansion House on the 25th July, 1861, to consult with the combined Fire Insurance Offices relative to the readjustment of their greatly increased rates of insurance, have decided upon the establishment of an Independent Company.

Powerful support has already been obtained from the various interests represented at that Meeting, and a Provisional Board has been formed from the leading commercial houses and others who, by their influence and extensive connections, at once secure to this Company a large amount of profitable business.

The first principles of the Company will be the establishment of an equitable classification of the risks as regards both Merchandise and Warehouses, and more liberal arrangements than are now obtainable upon Floating and Short-time Policies. A scale of rates will be adopted which, while fully remunerative, shall be sufficiently moderate to encourage a universal habit of insurance.

It is intended to reserve a percentage of profits for periodical division amongst Insurers.

The Company will undertake the insurance of Houses and their contents at equitable rates, this class of business having long proved a large source of profit to existing offices.

The Company will be strictly independent in its operations and in pursuance of the comprehensive principle on which the Board has been constituted, it will address itself to every class of Insurers.

The principle of limited liability will be extended to all insurances with the Company by the introduction of the usual clause limiting the amount of each Shareholder's responsibility.

Power will be taken in the Deed of Settlement to extend the operations of the Company to Life and Marine business should it hereafter be thought desirable to do so."

From now onwards the "Board of Provisional Directors", as it was styled in the minutes of the meetings between August 15th and October 1st, was intensely busy and, after the share list was closed on August 28th, its Allotment Sub-Committee worked up to 10.30 p.m. on at least two occasions. The constitution was established by a deed of settlement on September 28th and the Commercial Union Assurance came into existence as a joint stock company.

Scarcely more than two months had elapsed between the Meeting at the Mansion House and the formation of the Commercial Union. The need for prompt action was obviously urgent. But this does not detract from the qualities of zeal and energy shown by the "provisional directors", who now became the Company's first Board. They were an influential group of men—interesting in the businesses they represented and interesting in their own personalities.

At the head of the table sat Henry Peek, a youthful figure in the middle thirties. With his black hair, dark-complexioned face, brown eyes and long nose he looked more Gallic than English. This was understandable because, while on his father's side he was a West Country man, on his mother's side he descended from a Dieppe family, the Lemaîtres, who as Huguenots had taken refuge in England after the revocation of the Edict of Nantes.

The Peek family had been in the City since 1810, trading under the title of Peek Brothers & Co., as wholesale dealers in tea, coffee, cocoa and spice. They had connections through agencies with Europe, China, the United States and Canada, so that Henry Peek brought a wide knowledge of world commerce to the Commercial Union's board room. He was also a born leader of men, and one of his colleagues was in later years to describe him as the greatest personality he had ever known.

According to this colleague's description, he had extremely firm convictions which sometimes bordered on pig-headedness. Though a lovable character, he was also an autocrat and a martinet. Woe betide the man who failed to tell him of any negotiation that was going wrong or to consult him about appropriate action in dealing with difficult problems. He had an awkward habit, so far as his co-directors were concerned, of looking in to see the various managers on his way to board meetings so that by the time he took his seat he knew more about the work of departments than the chairmen of the committees and would ask questions that were unpleasantly embarrassing to answer. In fact, he watched his colleagues with eagle eyes and if he noticed that any of their number were not following the agenda, when the minutes were being read, would rap out a question such as, "Does it correspond with what you have on the agenda, sir?"

But the bark was worse than the bite and, as the years went by, there was not a member of the Board or an officer of the company who did not come to hold him in affectionate regard for personal kindnesses shown and an absolutely wholehearted loyalty and devotion to the company's interests.

Henry Peek remained Chairman till 1863, was re-elected Chairman for the year 1875 to 1876, and was a Vice-Chairman in 1894 to 1895. He served continuously on the Board up to his death in 1898. There can be no question of doubt that his mercurial and volatile personality exerted a profound influence on the traditions of the

Commercial Union during its formative years in the nineteenth century. How he contrived to crowd his singularly assorted activities into his life it is difficult to imagine. He was as much a countryman as a townsman and somehow managed to divide his time between his estate on the coast near Lyme Regis and his numerous business and public affairs in London.

From 1868 to 1884 Peek represented Mid-Surrey as a Conservative in the House of Commons and was created a baronet in 1874. It was during this period of his career that he built himself a tall, rambling house off St. Mary-at-Hill behind his place of business. On the grey stone lintel above its doorway was carved a sentence in French—*Le Maitre Vient*. On its outer walls were built a number of nesting boxes, the small ones for sparrows, the larger for pigeons. Each had its little platform for the alighting bird, its tunnel-like entrance and cosy brick-built interior. The lintel and the nesting boxes are still there with their testimony to the sense of humour and kindliness that mellowed a self-admitted arrogance.

"I am pleased to be a director of the Commercial Union," Sir Henry Peek once said to a friend, "because in my own business I am an autocrat, whereas at the Commercial Union I've learned that my views do not always prevail."

To Henry Trower almost as much as to Henry Peek the Commercial Union owed its foundation and early progress. He was its first Vice-Chairman from 1861 to 1863, succeeded Peek as Chairman in 1864, was Vice-Chairman again from 1876 to 1877, and Chairman once more in 1877 to 1878. The headquarters of his wine business were at 32, Eastcheap, only a few doors down the street from Peek's offices. A solidly built man, with a heavily bearded florid face, he was forty-six when the company started, and he was to remain on the board up to his death in 1899, outlasting Peek by a few months. His son, Captain P. Bence Trower, subsequently served on the Board for a number of years.

Another outstanding personality among the first directors was Jeremiah Colman, partner in the famous mustard firm of J. & J. Colman. In his middle fifties he had already built up in Cannon Street the London end of the business, whose works were in Norfolk. His appearance, with his hair curling forward over a wide forehead and his deep-set penetrating eyes, clearly showed an alert brain and the brilliant instinct for commercial affairs that marked him out as a man to whom his colleagues inevitably turned for judgment and leadership at difficult times. He was to be elected Chairman in 1870 and to be as actively associated with the activities of the Commercial Union as with those of his own firm until his death in 1885. And this, as we shall see later, was not the end of the Colman family's relations with the company.

Then there was Samuel Hanson who was to succeed Trower as Chairman in 1865 and to continue as a director until his death in 1882—a man with a kindly face and, though still in his fifties, a mien made venerable by a forked and flowing beard such as would have delighted Edward Lear. He was senior partner in the firm of Samuel Hanson & Son of Eastcheap, and father of a future Lord Mayor of London, Sir Reginald Hanson. Founded in 1747, Samuel Hanson & Son continues to this day as an eminent business in the wholesale grocery trade.

A handsome, well-dressed member of the Board was Alexander Sim, then in his early forties. A partner in the wood-broking business of Churchill and Sim he combined a talent for finance with expert knowledge of the Scandinavian timber trade, becoming in later life a director of the Baltic Exchange. Twice Chairman of the Commercial Union, in 1869 and 1878, he was to serve on the Board until his death in 1885, when he was succeeded by his son, Alexander Billing Sim.

The youngest director was Frederick William Harris, then aged twenty-eight, partner in the well-established shipbroking and shipping firm of Dixon & Harris, known today as Harris and Dixon of Gracechurch Street. He was already a man of wide interests which he was to broaden in the seventies when he became largely responsible for the development of the South Wales coalfields, heading a company that sank pits there and for many years supplied the Admiralty with the best type of anthracite. The town of Treharris was named after him, he became a J.P. for Glamorganshire, and was elected to the Council of the University of Wales. His commercial and public activities in the City were equally wide; the Mutual Steamship Insurance Association was formed under his aegis in 1885 and two years later he founded the British Steamship Investment Trust Ltd. in conjunction with his partner, James Dixon. He was appointed a Lieutenant of the City of London and in 1895 was elected Master of the Court of the Drapers Company.

Frederick Harris became Chairman of the Commercial Union in 1873 and again in 1888, and was to serve on its Board for fifty-six years until his death in 1917. This was not the end of the Harris family's associations with the company since he was succeeded on the Board by his son, Sir Austin Harris.

Shipbroking was represented by Nehemiah Griffiths, senior partner in the firm of N. Griffiths, Tate & Fisher. This was a business which he had started as far back as 1817 and which had developed valuable associations with Spain, Italy and other countries. Griffiths was to reach the age of eighty-six, when, still on the Board of the Commercial Union, he died in 1878. It is interesting to record that Griffiths, Tate (Insurance) Ltd., the successors of Griffiths and his partners, maintain their association with the Commercial Union.

Alderman John Humphrey, whose connections with Hay's Wharf have already been mentioned, was in his late sixties and his death two years after the company's formation deprived the Board of its most important figure in the City's corporate life, for he had been the City's Sheriff in 1832 to 1833, Lord Mayor in 1842 to 1843, and had represented Southwark in the House of Commons from 1832 to 1852. Incidentally, he was the last Lord Mayor to make the journey to Westminster by State Barge.

Another City alderman was Sir Andrew Lusk, Sheriff of London and Middlesex in 1861. His period as a director was brief owing to numerous subsequent associations with public life including membership of the Thames Conservancy Board and representation of Finsbury for twenty years in the House of Commons in which his Scottish characteristics earned him a name as an advocate of retrenchment and a rigid critic of the smallest details of estimates.

Then there was Francis Hicks, partner in the sugar refining and wholesale grocery business of Thomas & Francis Hicks at Colonial House, who was to be elected to the Chairmanship in 1870. His great work, as Treasurer of St. Thomas', in building its new Hospital was to earn him a knighthood conferred at its opening in 1871. And there was Smith Harrison, whose tenure of office up to 1869 was comparatively short owing to his extremely active business career in

Liverpool and London as one of the co-founders of the well-known East India merchant firm of Harrisons and Crosfield.

There were twelve others, all men of standing in the City, but those referred to were certainly the mainstay of the business in its early years. Here, however, should be added the names of two personalities elected directors very shortly after the company's foundation. One of them was John Boustead who had started life as a civil engineer, but in 1861 at the age of thirty-nine was a partner in the family business of Price & Boustead, then engaged in the coffee industry in Ceylon. He was to be the Commercial Union's Chairman in 1867 and 1868 and to remain on its Board till 1879. His resignation was due to the disaster which overtook Ceylon's coffee crop that year when the plants were so ravaged by disease that the island's output almost completely disappeared. Boustead, a man of great courage and resource, hastened out to the island and proved equal to the occasion. As one of the most influential owners of coffee estates there he turned disaster to success by securing the adoption of the tea plant in place of coffee, and this led to the establishment of Ceylon as one of the world's greatest tea producing countries. It also remade the fortunes of his business which in 1901 was amalgamated with Boustead Brothers and in which three of the present day partners are members of the Boustead family.

The other director, elected in February 1863, was Falconer Larkworthy. Here was a character such as only his period of time, perhaps, could have produced—a virile, buccaneering, yet deeply Christian type of Englishman who at the early age of thirty, after adventures in various parts of the world, though more especially in Australasia, had recently returned to his native country to take over the Managing Directorship of the Bank of New Zealand in London. His interests in finance, travel and world affairs were legion. He became a leading advocate of paper currency—an advocacy which in later years became tinged with the religious and idealistic fervour that had guided him throughout his life. After building up the finances of the Bank of New Zealand he went on to become a most successful Chairman of the Ionian Bank. He was to serve for the record period of sixty-five years on the Board of the Commercial Union until his death in 1928 at the age of ninety-five.

The company's first Manager, Henry Thomson, had been

appointed by the provisional directors in September. There followed constant additions to his staff to cope with the rapid growth of activities. Within three months the accommodation in Gracechurch Street became insufficient and larger premises essential, and towards the end of the year a move was made to 19, Cornhill. At first these new quarters were rented by the company, but a short time later it acquired the head lease for £4,500 and in June 1863 purchased the freehold for £14,050. It was in that year that the range of the Commercial Union's interests, referred to later, was expanded, and in November adjoining premises at 20, Cornhill were acquired for £26,500, a substantial sum being spent on them for adaptation to the requirements of the business.

3

Meanwhile, the older fire offices had awaited during the late summer and early autumn of 1861 their new rival's first move. They were held in some suspense because, with a nominal capital of £2,500,000 and power to double this, with the issuable shares being quickly taken up and with its powerful representation of City interests, it constituted a formidable challenge.

They did not have long to wait. Early in October the Commercial Union started an advertisement campaign in *The Times* and other dailies as well as various weeklies. The advertisements called attention to the fact that the company's "tariff for London mercantile business has been adjusted on the principle of classification, thus adopting the plan that each class of goods should be charged a premium proportionate to the risk. . . . The Directors in deciding upon this tariff have endeavoured faithfully to fulfil the wishes of the mercantile community, expressed at the influential Meeting held at the Mansion House on the 25th July last, and trust that they will receive such support as will enable them to carry out the system of rating on a classification of goods. . . . The Directors will at the expiration of five years return to insurers a percentage upon the profits of the fire business."

The main battle that followed between the Commercial Union and the older offices was fought out over the wharfs and warehouses of Thamesside, though its repercussions spread to the ports of Merseyside and elsewhere and indirectly into the textile industry. For a short period, and this is more than of passing interest, the Commercial Union had an ally in the Mercantile Fire Insurance Company—the only other company which materialised from the Mansion House meeting—but within its first year of existence the Mercantile combined with the North British to form the North British & Mercantile Insurance Company, which nearly a century later was to join forces with the Commercial Union.

Brief, but decisively important, this Thamesside struggle had its peculiar features which can only be explained in their historic context. In 1858 the majority of fire offices doing business in the Port of London had accepted a London Mercantile tariff drawn up by the newly formed Association of British Fire Offices under the leadership of the Sun, Phoenix, Royal Exchange, Imperial, and Royal of Liverpool. The "Waterside" District, as it was described under these Tariff regulations, extended from London Bridge to the Dog and Duck Stairs at the end of Russell Street. So far as this area was concerned—and it embraced practically the whole of the Port of London—the rates in force on warehouses were defined in fairly simple terms—3/- per cent on brick-built structures containing no hazardous goods and 4/- on those containing hazardous goods, while on the other buildings not constructed of brick the rates were 5/- and 7/- respectively.

Immediately after the Tooley Street Fire these rates were raised respectively to 7/6d, 10/6d, 10/6d, and 15/-. Floating Policies, to cover more than one wharf, were also greatly increased, the highest rates, for instance, being raised from 12/6d to 35/-. A new and separate classification of rates was also applied to the Docks and Up-Town Warehouses.

Alarmed by the Mansion House meeting, the Tariff offices had already begun to reduce their increased rates from the end of July onwards, and notably so in the case of the Docks and the Up-Town Warehouses. However, when the Commercial Union introduced its system of rating in October, it met with a ready response. In the main it was based on the principle of dividing warehouses and wharfs into three classes and goods into five. The permutations and combinations involved in applying these various classifications were complicated, but they offered far more equitable terms than those of the London Mercantile Tariff. Whereas, for instance, over extreme risks such as paraffin oil stored in a third-class warehouse, "a building wholly or mostly of timber", the rate was 30/-, that on tea or coffee in a first-class warehouse, "a building the external walls of which are of brick or stone", was only 4/6d.

The general effect of the Commercial Union's tariff was to under-cut almost the whole range of the London Mercantile Tariff system except over extreme risks. But it did not have it all its own way and in March, 1862, letters from influential quarters in the City, written in no uncertain terms, were arriving at 19, Cornhill. Two of these came from Lombard Street:

5 March, 1862

DEAR SIR,
          The Insurance Offices have given us a return of premium on risks lately taken to cover goods in the Dock Warehouses, improvements having been certified as satisfactory. I am told, however, that the Commercial Union declines to make a return, though they will make a corresponding reduction in their charge for new business.

I shall feel obliged by your enquiring into this, as a decision of this kind is not calculated to give customers a favourable opinion of the liberality of the office.

Yours etc.,
H. M. MATHESON.

6 March, 1862

DEAR SIR,
          You are, I think, under a misapprehension about our Policy taken out with your Company. We have £76,000 insured on the St. Katherine Dock Up-Town Warehouses at a premium of 5/-.

The old Companies have now reduced their rate for their Warehouses to 3/6d., giving a return for the difference between that rate and those charged at the beginning of the year for the annual Policies taken out at that time.

It is impossible to suppose that your Company will not put their constituents on an equally good footing.

Yours etc.,
CHARLES MAGNIAC.

What had happened was that the London Tariff Offices were now making considerable concessions over rates in Docks and their Up-Town Warehouses. They were also being more elastic in granting certificates regarding the suitability of warehouses. The rate for any one dock after receiving their certificate was now 4/6d per cent. The East and West India Docks had already obtained this and the Up-Town warehouses of the East and West India Dock Company and of the St. Katherine Dock Company were being charged at the still lower rate of 3/6d.

These letters were addressed to Alderman John Humphrey, in particular. They could not have been aimed at a more sensitive spot in the company's body. Humphrey was associated with Thamesside wharfing interests, and a director of the Commercial Union and was also a member of its Tariff Committee. He at once prepared a paper which he read to that committee a few days later and which suggested that " to meet the alterations made by the combined offices of their Tariff for mercantile insurances we also modify our rates and classification ".

Humphrey's proposals, somewhat modified, were put into effect at once. This time goods were classified under three classes only, and buildings grouped under two principal headings—(1) Docks and their Up-Town Warehouses. (2) Wharfs and Warehouses of First-Class construction. The rates offered under these classifications ranged from 3/- to 8/- in the Docks and their Up-Town Warehouses and from 5/- to 12/6d. at Wharfs and Warehouses of First-Class construction.

However, late in June Henry Thomson heard that the London Mercantile Tariff companies were on the point of capping part of them by reducing their " Tariff on the Up-Town warehouses to 3/- if taken separately, to 3/6d. if together, and their rates upon all Docks and Up-Town warehouses to 5/-". On reporting this fact he was authorised by the directors to " take risks on the collective warehouses (except the St. Katherine Dock Warehouses), at the same rate as may be decided upon by the combined offices ".

The battle continued well into the following year, 1863, but long before then it was becoming obvious that this kind of commercial throat-cutting could not go on. Early in the autumn of that year Samuel Hanson, Chairman of the Commercial Union's Tariff Com-

C

mittee, his colleague, George Brooking, and Henry Thomson met up
with the representatives of the Tariff Offices appointed to confer with
them, and on November 3rd submitted to the board an amended
London Mercantile Tariff as a basis of agreement between the company and its opponents. They recommended its acceptance on the
grounds that it contained "not only the substantial adoption of
Classification and the consequent equitable rating of risks—the two
great principles on which this company was formed—but that also
in its details it is almost without exception conformable to our own
existing Tariff".

To this recommendation the Board agreed and there now followed
a series of conferences between the Commercial Union, the Associated Fire Offices and also the Northern Offices. These were held on
the premises of the Sun Fire Office, a Mr. Hault representing the
Associated Fire Offices, a Mr. Fuchs the Northern Offices, and Hanson the Commercial Union, with S. J. Fletcher of the Sun acting as
Secretary. From these meetings there emerged on November 27th an
amended London Mercantile Tariff, suitable to all parties and
incorporating provisos by the Commercial Union regarding the
limitation of sums taken for guarantee and of commission rates paid
to the agents, as well as the expression of its desire to be represented
on the Scottish and Northern in addition to the Southern Committees. On December 8th the company formally intimated its decision
to become a party to the new Tariff system.

Had the specially appointed gamekeeper turned poacher? This
is a fair question to ask and not a particularly difficult one to answer.
Without the establishment of the Commercial Union, and for that
matter also of the Mercantile, the Tariff companies could have continued to exact high rates for the insurance of London's docks and
warehouses. This is not to say that in association they would have
used their virtual monopoly to maintain indefinitely the extremely
high rates imposed in the first panic after the Tooley Street Fire;
and, in fact, there were signs of relentance even before their new
rivals took the field.

As matters turned out, the opposition of the City of London's
merchants, embodied in the creation of the Commercial Union,
turned an unpleasant crisis into the safer channels of compromise.
While on the one hand this new company lost its full independence

of operation in fire insurance some two years after its foundation, its impact on the other hand upon the whole tariff system was of vital importance.

The immediate results of that impact were in the revision and classification of rates, but the ultimate effects were even wider and more profound. In the middle years of the nineteenth century Britain's industrial revolution was in full flood. The upsurge of new industries and resultant commerce was visible in a vast quantity of new factories and warehouses, many of them built rapidly and with little regard for durability, safety or suitability for accommodating manufacturing activities or the storage of merchandise. The chain reaction set up by the Tooley Street Fire brought about an elaborate classification of buildings and merchandise and insurance rates relating to them—developments as much in the interests of manufacturers and merchants as in those of the fire offices. The better your building, the less you paid to have it insured—the collective results of which simple axiom were to prove their value with the passage of time.

Furthermore, the amended London Mercantile Tariff of 1863 led to improvements in the practice of reinsurance, giving greater security to policy-holders in the event of serious disasters and conflagrations. It was, in fact, a turning point in the history of British insurance, for it consolidated the Associated Offices organisation out of which grew the Fire Offices Committee, established in 1868, and a year later the Fire Offices Committee (Foreign)—institutions which have since become of great importance and are today familiar to all those whose calling, whether at home or abroad, has anything to do with the underwriting of fire risks.

It is interesting to speculate on the workings of Providence as seen in the far-reaching results of a fire.

# CHAPTER II

---

## *Victorian Heyday—1862-1889*

### I

THAT tide in the affairs of men which "taken at the flood, leads on to fortune" may well be said to have attended the early years of the Commercial Union, for the company came into being at the very height of Victorian prosperity. It rode the tide well, avoiding under shrewd direction most, though not all, of the shoals and currents which brought not a few commercial houses, too impetuous and unwary, into danger and disaster.

The roseate optimism with which our forebears in the early sixties of the last century viewed the world was never to be repeated. It was then that the effects of the British industrial revolution reached their climax. Simultaneously, a decision by the United States, locked in civil war in 1861, to introduce a paper currency not convertible into gold brought a rush of the precious metal into Europe for investment. To cope with the ever increasing demands for our products at home and overseas large sums of money were constantly needed for the equipment of our industries, the extension of our railway system, and the building of new ships. These factors in their own turn created the need for further capital equipment. Money was there for the asking and money was constantly and urgently required. After the passing of the Companies Act in 1862, 300 new limited companies were founded with a nominal value of £504,000,000, and in one year alone, 1863, £145,000,000 of new shares were issued.

Well could Stanley Jevons boast in 1866 that "Unfettered commerce, founded on the basis of our coal resources, has made the several quarters of the globe our willing tributaries. The plains of North America and Russia are our cornfields; Chicago and Odessa our granaries; Canada and the Baltic our forests; Australia contains our sheep farms, and in South America are our herds of oxen. Peru sends her silver, and the gold of California and Australia flows to London; the Chinese grow tea for us, and coffee, sugar and spice arrive from the East Indian plantations. Spain and France are our vineyards, and the Mediterranean our fruit garden; our cotton grounds, which formerly occupied the Southern United States, are now everywhere in the many regions of the earth."

These circumstances explain to some extent at least the development of the Commercial Union's activities in its very early years. It will be recalled that in their prospectus the directors expressed their intention "to extend operations to Life and Marine business should it hereafter be thought desirable". Provisions for this had been written into the deed of settlement, and by resolution of the shareholders on January 20th, 1862, the directors were authorised to go ahead with both projects.

Life assurance was the first of the two to be undertaken. W. P. Pattison was appointed Actuary, Dr. J. Syer Bristowe and Thomas Smith were elected Physician and Surgeon respectively, and a Life Committee under the chairmanship of Francis Hicks was started in March, 1862.

The scepticism of an earlier age about assuring one's life had largely disappeared when the Commercial Union entered the life assurance market. Long since vanished were the days when Daniel Defoe, in deprecating the practice, wrote that he would "say nothing to it, but that in Italy, where stabbing and poisoning is so much in vogue, something may be said for it and on contingent annuities, and yet I never knew the thing much approved on any account". Scepticism of this kind had been reasonable enough because even until the late years of the eighteenth century whole-term policies were scarcely known and even short-term assurances were more frequently offered and taken out—not to cover one's own life, but those of other persons. This was nothing more than gambling, which often took the form of taking out policies on the lives of public men liable to sudden death. At the time of the Excise Bill, for instance, Sir Robert Walpole was insured for many thousands, and when George II fought at Dettingen, 25 per cent was paid against his return. Legislation in 1774 put an end to such practices, and by the beginning of the nineteenth century life assurance was becoming a more readily understood and accepted institution.

Even so, the situation in the life assurance market during the mid-Victorian Era was not unlike the early stages of a Grand National. As the vogue to assure one's life for the benefit of one's dependants gathered way, the number of companies prepared to undertake such policies increased accordingly, and the Companies Act of 1862, which limited shareholders' liabilities, not only augmented the increase, but led to the promotion of businesses which at the best were badly managed and at the worst bordered on chicanery. The figures may seem fantastic to a modern reader, but it is a fact that between 1843 and 1870, 219 Life Assurance offices were founded and 170 went out of existence. This situation was further complicated by amalgamations and transfers so that policy holders, with no control over their destinies, often found themselves being passed from one company to another, their funds being reduced by a succession of commissions, legal expenses and sheer bad management.

This was the astonishing state of affairs that existed during the first eight years of the Commercial Union's transactions in life assurance. It was brought to an end in 1870 by the Life Assurance Companies' Act resulting from a private member's bill brought forward by a Mr. Stephen Cave who, in introducing it to the House of Commons, stated that " at the present time fifty-nine life offices are being wound up in Chancery, and many of these, like Aaron's rod, have during their term of existence swallowed up several others ".

Despite these conditions the company made satisfactory progress in its new sphere. In presenting the balance sheet in 1863 Henry Peek mentioned the fact that the Life Branch's business up to the preceding December was at the rate of nearly £8,000 per annum. " To anyone familiar with first-class Life business," he added significantly, " this result will be known to be a great success." In the following year Henry Trower, the succeeding chairman, stated that " the success of the Life Branch has been almost unprecedented;

the new premiums for the year are £20,940 4s. 9d., an amount obtained by very few of the most successful Life Offices in the Kingdom".

The tale of progress continued and by 1870 the assets of the Life Branch exceeded £235,000. This was less than a year after the failure of the Albert Life Assurance and its subsidiaries, to which Jeremiah Colman, in that year the Commercial Union's Chairman, referred delicately as circumstances "creating considerable distrust in the stability of Life Assurance Institutions," adding that "the statement of new business proves that this uneasy feeling has in no way affected the position of the Life Branch".

The development of the company's life assurance activities in these years was due to sound finance and good management. The Life Tables adopted in 1862 covered Whole Life With and Without Profits, Short Term Assurance, Endowment Assurance, and also Joint Life Assurance—this last a form of insurance which has since passed out of favour except for certain business purposes. What is interesting is that the present-day premiums and those of a century ago are not so greatly divergent as might be expected. In fact, modern rates of premium can be obtained fairly accurately by deducting 12/- from the original rates of premium quoted by the Company in 1862, as will be seen from the following comparative table:

| Age next birthday at entry | 1862 rate | | | 1960 rate | | |
|---|---|---|---|---|---|---|
| | £ | s. | d. | £ | s. | d. |
| 30 | 2 | 3 | 7 | 1 | 11 | 10 |
| 40 | 2 | 17 | 2 | 2 | 5 | 0 |
| 50 | 3 | 18 | 9 | 3 | 7 | 7 |

In deciding on the Life Tables of 1862, Hicks and his committee agreed that it was "inadvisable to retain upon any one life a larger risk than £3,000". This was a sensible precaution in the first stages of establishing this type of business because early claims for very substantial amounts could not be met from a relatively small fund. Greater risks were, in fact, accepted, but only with reassurance arrangements. Some years later the company started to accept maximum risks of £5,000. Since then "maximum retention", as it is styled nowadays, has been progressively increased.

As though to give an initial shove to their new boat several of the directors took out policies with their own company. In fact, the first accepted life policy of the Commercial Union was a Whole Life for £4,000 With Profits (subject, of course, to reassurance) issued to Jeremiah Colman in April, 1862. Within a few weeks William Leask, Frederick Harris, Henry Ghinn, Samuel Hanson, and the company's Fire Manager, Henry Thomson, took out policies for considerable amounts.

Understandably enough, it was big game on the whole that the company looked for in building up its life fund at the start, and it even did some successful stalking beyond the Border, gaining Lord Strathmore and the Earl of Fife as substantial policy holders.

2

The company started to operate in marine insurance on January 1st, 1863, from an office at 5, Royal Exchange Avenue. Its first underwriter was James Carr Saunders. This was an outstandingly good appointment by the Board. From then until 1876, when he was elected a director, Carr Saunders was to make a small fortune for the business. He was, in his day, one of the most brilliant men who transacted business in the London marine market.

The expansion of world trade and, therefore, of mercantile fleets during this period was phenomenal. By 1860 the tonnage of shipping entering and leaving British ports had reached nearly 25,000,000; between 1860 and 1870 it increased to 36,600,000; in 1880 it reached nearly 59,000,000. Despite growing American competition on the high seas we were still the leading maritime nation in 1860 and by the end of the American Civil War in 1865 our lead was undisputed. "When all was over in 1865," as Sir John Clapham was to write years later, "Americans were thinking more of the prairies than of the seas." From then until 1895 Britain's share of traffic on the high seas rose to be greater than at any time in her history.

Our maritime supremacy in those years considerably strengthened the position of British marine insurance business generally, but the continuous growth in world shipping was of equal importance owing to the international character of the London market. The opening of the Suez Canal in 1860 was one of several factors in this development, and so too was the ever increasing momentum of the change-over from sail to steam which spelt greater safety and reduced risks.

Taking all these facts into account as well as the effects of the American Civil War in the sixties, which resulted in the transference of the greater part of marine insurance in the United States to the United Kingdom, the Commercial Union could not have started the underwriting of ships at a more fortunate moment. On the other hand these very conditions in themselves created a wave of speculation and the flotation of numerous marine insurance schemes so that competition was rife and the company's new venture might easily have come to grief without cool judgment and sound finance.

These were not wanting, as the annual reports clearly show. From 1863 to 1864 the premium income of the Marine Department averaged £100,000, in the next five years up to 1869, £200,000, and from 1870 to 1875, £300,000.


3


It was the success of its life and marine activities which brought the Commercial Union through its early years—and not, strangely enough, its operations in fire insurance which was its original *raison d'être*. The vicissitudes of the Fire Branch must have given the Board a great deal of anxiety. Its early administration was in capable enough hands. From the time of its formation in July, 1862, the Fire Committee was presided over for eighteen months by Samuel Hanson; Smith Harrison succeeded him as its chairman until March of 1865, and he again was followed by Alexander Sim —all three of them men of outstanding commercial ability and experience. The manager of the branch, Henry Thomson, had shown his shrewdness in the difficult negotiations over the London Mercantile Tariff and, after he resigned in 1865, his successor, Cozens Smith, gained sufficient prestige in fire insurance circles to be offered, and to accept, the managership of the Imperial Fire Office in 1873.

The fault lay not so much in men as in circumstances—the unreliability of works and warehouses rapidly and haphazardly constructed to cope with the continuous spread of industry, the advent of gas for lighting purposes, and the increasing use of petroleum and other oil products over the inflammability of which the inhabitants of our island kingdom showed a sublime and frequently disastrous innocence until legislation in the seventies curtailed the growing incidence of domestic and industrial accidents. And it was not only at home, but also abroad, especially in the United States, that all these risks and dangers were encountered after the company started to extend its fire business overseas.

At first all seemed well on the surface with policies increasing yearly. The first policy to be taken out was one on the premises of Thomas and Francis Hicks, the sugar refiners, which was another example of a member of the Board insuring his interests with the Commercial Union. In 1865, however, operations showed an unfavourable result. Fire losses in that year were very heavy, especially in the London docks and waterside premises. To counter these dangers and to secure a wider field of profitable work the directors established local boards "with the co-operation of influential gentlemen extensively engaged in commercial and manufacturing pursuits" at Liverpool, Manchester, Glasgow, Dublin and Belfast. But worse was to follow, for in the next year the Fire Fund was depleted by extensive losses and had to be restored by a sum of £25,000 appropriated from the Reserve Fund, and the company for the first and only time in its history failed to declare a dividend.

After this a drastic revision of risks was undertaken and the Fire Fund made a steady recovery though it sustained fairly serious losses in the Boston (U.S.A.) Fire of 1872 and in another at St. John, New Brunswick, in 1877, accounts of which appear in later pages.

Despite its recovery in the seventies the Fire Fund began to show an unsatisfactory rate of progress during the first part of the eighties. In this period bad management was as much to blame as circumstances and events. There was too much underwriting of uncertain risks, especially in overseas countries, with the result that percentage of losses to premium income rose rapidly until they reached the alarming figure of 78 per cent in 1882 and 71 per cent in 1884. The latter year was one of unusually widespread fires both at home and abroad, but even so the Board decided to supersede the then Fire Manager and eventually, in 1885, appointed E. Roger Owen as head of the branch. Owen immediately proceeded to reduce liabilities. Although this policy entailed cutting down premium income in its first stages, the cumulative results were successful, and within a few years income was mounting again and the percentage of losses had been brought down into the fifties. The appointment of Roger Owen was the start of a career that in due course was to have far-reaching effects on the fortunes of the Commercial Union.

4

How the early growth of the Company was nurtured can in some measure be summarised by an analysis in round figures of the funds of its three branches as they stood after five quinquennial intervals commencing from 1865:

|        | *1865* £ | *1870* £ | *1875* £ | *1880* £ | *1885* £ | *1890* £ |
|--------|-------|-------|-------|-------|-------|-------|
| LIFE-  | 32,500 | 44,500 | 216,000 | 480,000 | 548,000 | 772,500 |
| FIRE-  | 53,000 | 190,000 | 402,000 | 610,000 | 867,600 | 1,183,000 |
| MARINE- | 85,000 | 169,000 | 171,000 | 222,000 | 221,000 | 250,000 |

Its development during this period was also reflected in the early extension of activities outside the Metropolis. Within five years it had appointed agents in many parts of the country. In 1865, as we have seen, it established local boards of directors at Belfast, Dublin, Glasgow, Liverpool and Manchester, and at the same time opened branches in those cities. An Edinburgh branch was started in 1869 and four years later branches were established in Birmingham and Newcastle-on-Tyne. By the eighties the company's interests were similarly represented in Aberdeen, Warwick, Bristol and Southampton. In 1887 it widened its London business by establishing a West End branch in Pall Mall.

# CHAPTER III

# *A Spreading of Wings—1861-1889*

I

TAKING into account the vast contemporary expansion of British trade overseas and the wide array of commercial interests represented on the Board, it is scarcely surprising that the Commercial Union's activities were extended outwards to the four corners of the world almost as rapidly as they were pushed forward at home.

As early as December 1861, the company entered the German market with the appointment of Herr Brauer of Hamburg as its agent. Rangoon was the next place where an agency was established and there the firm of Halliday, Bulloch & Co. was chosen in September, 1862. This business, under a later title of Bulloch Brothers & Co., was also to continue to act for the company for many years.

Other agencies appointed in 1862 were at places so far apart as Colombo, Cape Town, Kingston and Bridgetown. Before the end of 1863 the Commercial Union was likewise represented in Montreal, Lima, Valparaiso, Shanghai, Manila, Natal, Port Elizabeth, Bombay, Madras, Karachi, Batavia, Smyrna and Trinidad. In the next few years the network of agencies continued to be extended. Most of them operated for fire business only. The establishment of such a network was necessarily a process of trial and error, and in some places a succession of new agencies came into being as the years went by until firm and solid roots took shape.

28

2

By far the most important, the most difficult, but ultimately the most rewarding overseas venture of the Commercial Union in the nineteenth century was its penetration of the United States market. Its initial operations there were to be confined almost exclusively to fire insurance business and it only entered that field at the end of the sixties. Its reluctance to do so earlier was understandable. A Board minute of November 1st, 1864, mentions that "after careful examination of statistics of America for the previous five years, and having considered the state of affairs it was unanimously agreed that it was advisable to postpone the consideration of commencing business there". The "state of affairs" alluded to was nothing less than the American Civil War which lasted on to May of the following year.

The immediate aftermath of the war was intense, and especially in the conquered Southern States. Dislocation of the nation's political and commercial life was general, but the Northern States were the first to recover, followed in slower degrees by the Southern, where the freeing of the negro slaves and the white owners' loss of property produced their own particular social and economic problems. But recovery, once it started, went apace—and to such an extent that even before the seventies the United States started to enter an era of enterprise and prosperity that was to lay her foundations as a world power. After 1865 the nation's population increased more rapidly than ever and, swollen by millions of immigrants from Europe, was to reach the 50 million mark by 1880.

"Within five years," a government report stated in 1869, "more cotton spindles have been put in motion, more iron furnaces erected, more iron smelted, more steel made, more coal and copper mined, more lumber sawn and hewn, more houses and shops constructed, more manufactures of different kinds started and more petroleum collected, refined and exported than during any equal period in the history of the country."

The most spectacular development was the opening up of virgin territories in which the construction of new railroads played their part, 25,000 miles of new tracks being laid between 1868 and 1872 alone. And the completion of the Union Pacific in 1869—the first railroad to span the American continent—brought the Pacific Coast and all the far west beyond the Rockies into closer union with the older states. Two segments of civilisation in the Western Hemisphere had suddenly clicked together in a grand pattern started from two separate ends.

It was on the Pacific Coast at San Francisco that the Commercial Union first made contact with this vital new America, when, in that eventful year of 1869, it appointed John Rae Hamilton as its agent there for the conduct of fire insurance. But in the following year, impelled by the opportunities of wider development, it decided to launch itself into the commercial heart of the United States by establishing its foundations in New York. From what has been said its timing of such an important step was well judged, but it was to share the experiences of other British insurance companies in the set-backs and disadvantages which, like tares amongst the wheat, accompanied successful harvesting in new territory. There were, for instance, the unusual risks of conflagration in the comparatively new towns and villages, while windstorms and hurricanes on a scale beyond anything known in the British Isles were devastating in their effects. Then, too, there were problems and difficulties encountered through the legal framework in which insurance activities had to be conducted in the United States.

It was this legal framework, to which the British companies were unaccustomed, that occupied much of the time of the Commercial Union's representatives when they visited New York in September, 1870. They were A. J. Mundella, a newcomer to the Board, and Cozens Smith, the company's Fire Manager.

The then New York State legislation covering insurance, which set the pattern for most of the other states, was founded on acts passed in 1851, 1859 and 1866. Briefly, the position which Mundella and Cozens Smith discovered was that to establish and operate an insurance business it was necessary to secure a certificate from the State's Insurance Superintendent for which various particulars, including amount of capital, had to be filed; that each distinct branch of insurance work had to be conducted by a single and separate company; that it was necessary for a company to deposit $100,000 and to be established on a paid-up capital, invested in approved securities, of not less than $100,000. In addition, a company was obliged to submit annual returns covering new issues of policies, revenue account and balance sheet, and a statement of business in force set out in a prescribed form.

Other matters attended to by this two-man deputation were the selection of a firm of managing agents, their investment with a power of attorney, and the establishment of a local board of directors. Cozens Smith returned to London in October, bringing Mundella's and his report and recommendations, while Mundella remained in New York to complete formalities as the representative of the Board.

Alliger Brothers were chosen as the company's managing agents. The men appointed to the local board, eleven in number, were eminent business personalities and included Henry Buckman, President of the Union Square National Bank, George Bliss, member of the banking firm of Morton, Bliss & Co., J. C. Henderson, President of the Matteswan Manufacturing Co., William Orton, President of the Western Union Telegraph Co., and J. W. Harper, partner in the well-known publishers of that name.

With this influential support the Commercial Union started to operate fire insurance in New York and the adjoining states on January 1st, 1871.

3

Without any doubt Mundella was the prime mover in this event and the reasons for this become apparent if one considers his extraordinary character and career.

Mundella made a particular impression on his colleague, Falconer Larkworthy, who had much to say of him in his reminiscences published years later. From these it appears that he was in the middle forties, and had been representing Sheffield as a Liberal in the House of Commons for some twelve months, when he was invited on to the Board of the Commercial Union. The son of an Italian refugee, who had settled in Leicester and married a local girl, Mundella was at the start of what may be called the second stage of his career when his associations with the company began. With little education to help him on his way, he had already built up a successful hosiery factory in Nottingham and been elected the city's Sheriff. Selling his business when it was making an annual turnover of half a million, he had recently come to live in London, where he was now energetically engaged in the dual activities of a political careerist and a "guinea-pig" director.

This was the point in his life when he went out to New York for the Commercial Union in 1870. But the tale must be completed. He continued to keep his hold on Sheffield voters, representing the Brightside Division, after it was formed as a separate constituency, up to his death in 1897. This was a considerable feat for it was a chequered constituency containing all shades of political opinion. The secret of his success in Sheffield was his capacity for securing government contracts for its leading manufacturers and thwarting proposals for the creation of state-owned arsenals.

In his business life Mundella continued to secure as many director-ships as possible with a lack of discrimination that eventually landed him into trouble at the height of his political career. In 1893 he was President of the Board of Trade. The New Zealand Loan and Agency Co.—subsequently reconstituted and today a most reputable institution in the financial world—was suddenly suspended in that year and an enquiry into its affairs instituted. Mundella's initial mistake was to use his official position to try and quash the proceedings. This he was prevented from doing by the perseverance of the Official Receiver supported by the Judge, Justice Vaughan Williams. By then Mundella had ceased his connections with the New Zealand Loan and Agency Co. and was in no way involved in its issue of false balance sheets and unearned dividends which was the subject of the enquiry, and his attempt to stop the cause of justice was entirely due to a typically well-meant, but nevertheless false sense of loyalty to his late colleagues.

His second mistake was made under examination, during the enquiry, on the point of having sold his shares when he knew the company was in difficulties. He replied that he had sold them because he considered that in his position as President of the Board of Trade it was undesirable that he should hold shares in any public company. If he had added the qualification "with which I have ceased my connection as a director", all would have been well, for he still held one directorship and that was with the Commercial Union, a fact which opposing Counsel used to the best advantage.

After this not even the readiness of Lord Rosebery to retain him in his administration could prevail against the pressure of public opinion and, to avoid embarrassing his chief, Mundella resigned from office.

Known among his friends as "Anthony John" and called by his enemies the "Wind-bag", Mundella was an imposing figure with a robust, impulsive temperament and over-optimistic views delivered in a loud and rather pompous manner. But he had brilliance and many admirable qualities, and the fact that he remained on the Board of the Commercial Union up to his death was a token of the esteem in which he was held by his colleagues there.

This digression has taken us some distance in time and space from the American scene, but it will help to explain subsequent events. It has been said that the decision to enter the United States market was well-timed. On the other hand it seems to have been put into effect with an almost too exuberant rapidity. Mundella's gift for penetrating into business circles at high level probably accounted for the distinction of the New York directors chosen to form the local board. Equally, however, his over-sanguine temperament was almost certainly responsible for the recommendation of Alliger Brothers as the New York managing agents—a serious lack of judgment which was to reveal itself in due course.

## 4

Typical of insurance risks in America's swiftly expanding cities during the seventies were the great fires of Chicago and Boston. Of the two the Chicago fire, which occurred on October 9th, 1871, was the graver; it was, in fact, one of the most disastrous conflagrations of the nineteenth century. The Commercial Union was fortunate in suffering only small losses, but this was due to its position as a newcomer. The cause of the fire was never discovered. One theory was that it resulted from a kerosene lamp being knocked over by a cow. Wilder rumours attributed it to incendiarism on the part of malicious persons from the Southern States or of the Ku-Klux Klan.

Whatever the origin, the rapid spread of the conflagration was due to a stiff gale blowing from the south-west. Twelve thousand buildings, covering an area of nearly five square miles and valued at £33,000,000, were destroyed. The adjusted losses under the insurances of this vast amount of property totalled nearly £20,000,000, of which some £1,200,000 was paid up by the British offices involved.

In the Boston fire of November 9th, 1872, the company's losses were around £56,000, most of which were incurred over retail stores and warehouses. This fire started in the engine-room of a dry-goods establishment and might have been prevented from spreading if the horses belonging to the fire department had not been suffering from an epidemic illness, with the result that the firemen themselves had to haul their engines into action. Another unfortunate factor was that, though Boston was one of the most substantially constructed American cities, her streets were narrow and her high buildings were surmounted by mansard roofs. It was these roofs, out of reach of water from the engines, that conveyed the fire from house to house. In its final stages the fire, which had been partially quelled, broke out again when the city's gas mains caught alight. Some 750 buildings, including many of the largest business blocks and covering about sixty acres, were reduced to ruins. From the figures given by the Government of Massachusetts the value of the property destroyed was around £15,000,000 and the covering insurance some £13,000,000, of which foreign companies, mostly British, were responsible for nearly £1,000,000.

Many American insurance offices were bankrupted by these two fires. The Commercial Union, in common with the British companies, paid up promptly and in full. It was a testing time for them all, but promoted a confidence in British underwriters which was to grow and strengthen with the ensuing years.

During this period of its operations in the United States the Commercial Union was ably represented by a number of agencies, three of which have continuously served its interests to the present day. Of these the Nelson & Ward Co. of Jersey City received its appointment on May 1st, 1871, while Drew and Miller, soon afterwards to amalgamate with the firm of R. S. Critchell—founded in 1868—under the title of the Critchell-Miller Insurance Agency, was appointed direct by the Board in London in 1872 to represent the company's interests in Chicago. These distinguished agencies have made important contributions to the company's success in the United States.

The development of the Middle-West was reflected in the Commercial Union's appointment of Alex E. Case of Marion, Kansas, in October, 1879. He was then a public official with a colourful, pioneering career going back to the days of the Civil War. Arriving in Kansas in 1866, he had started to look for a " soldier's homestead " which he found at the settlement of Marion Centre at the junction of Cottonwood River with smaller tributaries—a well-watered countryside with a fertile soil. He had covered the last seventy-five miles there on foot. With a good background of education in Pennsylvania, Case became a popular and important member of this community, served in the Kansas legislature in 1869 and later became county actuary and county surveyor. When he first went into the insurance business, his office was in his home—a log cabin which he had moved from a ranch and trading post on the old Santa Fé trail. The association of the Case family business, now known as the Case & Son Agency, with the Commercial Union has since developed on the closest terms during a period of more than eighty years.

5

On September 10th, 1877, private information reached the management in London that there were serious irregularities in the accounts of Alliger Brothers. The Board met the next day to consider this unpleasant revelation. It acted with understandable speed. A telegram in cypher was despatched to Morton, Bliss & Co. to take preventive measures on the firm's behalf. It also arranged for W. Middleton Campbell, a recently appointed director of the Commercial Union, to sail for the United States on the 13th, accompanied by the Secretary, Stanley Brown.

While these representatives were still on the high seas, Elijah Alliger arrived in London and appeared before the chairman, Henry Trower, and four other directors on the 19th. He admitted a deficiency of about £25,000 to £30,000, accounting for this by excessive and personal losses on investments and promising to give security for the deficit and gradually liquidate it, if his firm was continued in the service of the company.

Middleton Campbell and Stanley Brown reached New York on the 22nd, and a few days later cabled home a report of their investigation which, in the words of the Board Minutes, " revealed a gross deficiency of $162,509 being $89,465 overdrawn for personal account and $73,044 for expenses: that there had been great irregularity in the recording of money and stating of accounts, that Alliger Brothers had never been solvent since they undertook the Company's Agency and that severance of the connexion seemed advisable ".

This news created serious discussion among the directors about the instigation of proceedings against Alliger Brothers, but eventually it was agreed to accept a recommendation from Campbell and Brown, who wrote from New York to say that " while maintaining their strong opinion that such a breach of faith has been committed as necessitates the severance, they think that in Mr. Alliger's mind there has been no criminal intention to defraud the Company, and feeling that he has been sufficiently punished for his delinquency by loss of position, and the necessity of starting in the world afresh, they recommend . . . that a letter should be sent to the firm in that spirit ".

It was also decided to make immediate payment of all the Alliger liabilities.

So ended an unfortunate episode in the company's early career in North America, but it brought about the establishment towards the end of that year, 1877, of a fully constituted branch in New York with powers to conduct business throughout those portions of the United States east of the Rocky Mountains extending from the Canadian border in the north to the Gulf of Mexico in the south. A new board with powers to direct and supervise these operations was appointed. It consisted of the Hon. David Wells, at one time Comptroller of the United States Currency, William Allen Butler, the company's American solicitor, George Bowdoin, a partner in Morton, Bliss & Company, Eugene Dutilh, President of the Orient Mutual Insurance, William Orton, a member of the first board, John Terry, a partner in E. D. Morgan & Company, and S. van

Ransselear Cruger. The manager selected was Alfred Pell, a well connected New York citizen in his early forties, who had for some years been the Liverpool and London and Globe's New York manager.

A few months later, in July, 1878, a parallel reorganisation was carried out on the other side of the continent when a Pacific Coast Branch supplanted the agency in San Francisco and was placed under the management of John Rae Hamilton, hitherto the agent. The area covered by this branch in its early years extended through the States of California, Nevada, Utah, Arizona, Oregon, and the territory of Washington.

With this reorganisation the Commercial Union entered into a period of wider and greater fire insurance activities in the United States. Heavy competition, with a tendency to accept uncertain risks, resulted in vicissitudes during the early eighties, and in 1884 an overall deficit, even though small, was incurred. These experiences were similar to those of other companies, American and British. They were eventually solved by a policy of careful pruning of portfolios.

By the late eighties the company's activities had spread to almost every corner of the great domain, following in the wake of pioneers, settlers, new industries, extended railroads, and highways built into the heart of virgin regions. This comprehensive growth was recorded by Roger Owen in reports which he submitted to the Board after a visit to America in 1887. At that time the New York office directly controlled business in the Middle States of New York, New Jersey, Pennsylvania, Maryland and Delaware, and the District of Columbia; in the New England States of Maine, Vermont, Rhode Island, Massachusetts and Connecticut; and in the Southern States of Virginia, North and South Carolina, Georgia, Florida, Alabama, Louisiana and Texas. In Boston and Philadelphia there were general agencies appointed on special terms with some degree of independence.

At Chicago there was by then an office which directly managed, under general control from New York, business in the Western States of Illinois, Michigan, Wisconsin, Minnesota, Nebraska, Colorado, Iowa, Kansas, Dakota, Wyoming, New Mexico, Indian Territory and Montana. Another office, established at Cincinnati, was responsible to New York for operations in the Central States of Ohio, Indiana, Kentucky, Tennessee, Arkansas and West Virginia.

Beyond the Rockies the branch at San Francisco still remained independent of New York and embraced, in addition to the Pacific Coast territory of the United States, British Columbia and Honolulu. As the result of Roger Owen's recommendations, Alaska, which America had purchased from Russia in 1867, and the Hawaiian Islands, were shortly afterwards opened up from San Francisco.

6

North of the Border, in the vast area of what was called British North America until the creation of the Dominion of Canada in 1867, the Commercial Union had established its first footing at Montreal in 1863. Its general agents there were a firm called Morland Watson & Co., the principal in which was Frederick Cole. Under Cole's management both fire and life operations were extended in due course through various parts of the Province of Quebec by means of sub-agencies. In Quebec itself fire insurance activities were in 1865 put into the hands of a firm named Forsyth & Pemberton who seem to have functioned independently of control from Montreal.

During the sixties progress was slow and uncertain. In 1864 there was a loss on the fire side of £1,480 and, indeed, the total surplus of that account from 1863 to 1865 was only £1,497. However, in 1874, Canadian operations were put on a sounder and wider basis, Frederick Cole being appointed general Fire and Life agent for Eastern Canada and two residents of Toronto, Westmacote and Wickens, receiving a similar appointment to cover Western Canada.

Means of transport and communications in this far-flung northern part of the North American continent being what they were at that time, it was felt desirable to appoint independent agents in the eastern maritime provinces. Accordingly, two other agencies were also established in 1874, one at Halifax, Nova Scotia, under B. W. Salter, operating fire insurance only, and another at St. John, New Brunswick, conducting life as well as fire, which was put into the hands of A. C. Fairweather, an influential and highly respected barrister in that province. Five years later the Commercial Union entered the province of Manitoba and also started to work outwards into the North West Territory from Winnipeg where an independent agency was established under the Hon. G. McMicken, a well-known resident.

The conditions governing insurance in Canada during the years around and after its creation as a self-governing Dominion of the British Empire arose, naturally enough, out of the political, social and economic developments in what even by that time was still largely a virgin mass of land.

The Dominion of 1867 consisted of the two eastern sea-board provinces of New Brunswick and Nova Scotia and the two inland provinces of Quebec and Ontario. There were no connections by rail between the sea-board provinces and the rest of Canada. Quebec and Ontario, isolated from the sea except through the St. Lawrence, were themselves fairly well knit together by rail and by navigation on the Great Lakes. In fact, the Commercial Union played some part in the seventies in the railroad system of this area, becoming responsible through its Toronto agency, George Hargraft and Son, for insuring the properties of the Detroit Grand Haven and Milwaukee Railroad—an American company—and those of the Great Western of Canada Railway. The Hargraft connection with Toronto has been maintained to the present day.

Westwards from Ontario lay a wilderness of swamp and rivers and, when Manitoba was created a province of Canada in 1870, 1,300 miles of this desolate country separated the Dominion's capital, Ottawa, from the provincial capital at Winnipeg. Westwards again from Winnipeg stretched 1,000 miles of prairie and beyond the prairie rose the serrated ridges, five hundred miles in width, of the Rocky Mountains, across which no suitable pass was known. Thus British Columbia, which became a province in 1871, lay isolated along the Pacific Coast. The rest of British North America, after it was conveyed to Canada by the British government in 1878, remained for years scarcely populated, especially in the far north.

The completion of the Canadian Pacific Railway in 1885 linked east with west and from then onwards a steady growth of rail and road communications began to unify the Dominion into a nation. Between the end of the sixties and the end of the eighties, the population, reinforced by a flow of immigrants, rose from some three million to some five million. Three-quarters of the increasing population was absorbed by the towns, Montreal, for instance, becoming a city of a quarter of a million inhabitants and Toronto's population reaching 180,000.

This was, however, no easy period for the growing nation or for business conducted in its midst. In fact, the Commercial Union's growth in Canada reflected the Dominion's own growing pains. The development of exports, which were the new nation's life blood, did little more than keep abreast of the rise of population, but despite many fluctuations they increased from 48 million dollars in 1868 to 88 million in 1891.

The contemporary pattern of legislation in the Dominion bore similarities to that of the United States. An Act of 1860 required companies not incorporated in a specific province to submit their returns to the Minister of Finance. This Act was superseded by another in 1865 which was itself amended in 1869. Under this new legislation no company could transact insurance business in Canada, other than ocean marine, without a licence from the Minister of Finance. This was only obtainable by a deposit of $50,000 for each branch of insurance with a provision that, if a company practised both life and accident, or fire and marine, it only had to deposit this amount for each combination of two branches. Companies with head offices outside Canada were obliged to file a copy of their constitution together with the power of attorney of their agent; they had to have $100,000 of unimpaired paid up capital, any deposit being treated as part of this. Their annual statements in a prescribed form had to be printed and laid before Parliament.

The regulations over life assurance were even more complicated and troublesome to carry out than those applied to the underwriting of fire risks, and this fact explains why the Commercial Union, like other British offices, gradually tended to concentrate its Canadian activities on the latter. The problem in this field was how to strike a happy balance between zeal and caution in acceptances, especially in the new towns and cities which outside "Main Street" largely consisted of timber buildings. Even the cautious Fairweather agency ran into trouble over the great conflagration at St. John in 1877, when a large part of the city was reduced to ruins, inadequate

extinguishing appliances and water supplies adding their contribution to the disaster. In this the Commercial Union became involved
to the extent of nearly £72,000. The risks in the outlying prairie
towns and villages of the North West Territory, which were completely timber built except for a few stores, were particularly serious,
as was instanced by the partial destruction in 1886 of Calgary where,
however, the company's share in losses was fortunately slight.

Prompt and generous settlement of claims over these and other
losses enhanced the company's reputation. At the end of the
eighties it was doing the best business of any office in St. John—a
fact largely due to its treatment of claims in 1877—while in the city
of Winnipeg its reputation and success were unrivalled.

More than any other man, Frederick Cole blazed the trail for
the Commercial Union during its early years in Canada. But on his
death in 1887, the Board decided that the time had come to make
a further reorganisation of its activities there and Roger Owen was
deputed to go over and investigate the position of the company's
affairs and their future possibilities.

Owen's report gave a picture of fairly general progress in most
parts of the Dominion. By far the largest volume of business related
by then to fire insurance. Life assurance came next in importance
and, what is interesting, is that marine underwriting had recently
been started at Toronto in regard, almost certainly, to shipping on
the Great Lakes.

Owen's recommendations led to the centralisation of control of
the company's operations in the provinces of Quebec and Ontario
at Montreal and the institution of a branch there for that purpose.
The agencies of Winnipeg, St. John and Halifax were, however,
left to function independently as their districts were too remote and
scattered at that time.

7

The Commercial Union made its first contact with the business
life of Australia in January, 1877, when it appointed as its agency
for fire and marine operations in the province of Victoria the
Melbourne branch of the New Zealand Loan and Mercantile

Agency Company Ltd. This company's business relations with Australia were by then almost as much advanced there as with New Zealand. Its selection for the appointment was, no doubt, made on the recommendation of Falconer Larkworthy who had been associated with the company's development and was still interested in it through his position as Managing Director of the Bank of New Zealand.

It seems to have been a stop-gap arrangement, however, for in January, 1880, the Board of Directors, deciding that "Australia and Tasmania be constituted a Branch District of the Company having offices at Melbourne with the title of the Australian Branch", appointed W. H. Jarrett as Resident Manager and Underwriter. For some short time before this appointment Jarrett had been acting as local Melbourne agent for the Fire Department and he also brought experience of marine business to his new position, having been underwriter for the New South Wales Marine Insurance Company.

All the Commercial Union's existing agencies in Australia and Tasmania were now brought under control from Melbourne, but this system of centralisation was not to last for long. At the end of 1880 the Commercial Union purchased outright for £13,750 the Sydney Fire Insurance Company and for £4,000 the New South Wales Marine Insurance Company. This brought their activities into New South Wales where a branch and local board of directors were constituted in 1881. At around the same time another branch and local board were established for South Australia at Adelaide. And six years later the company entered Queensland with the launching of a branch at Brisbane.

From then onwards each branch functioned as a distinct organisation, corresponding direct with the head office in London. Centralisation of Australian activities in the nineteenth century was not really a practical proposition for the simple reason that each colony was very much a law unto itself until the creation of the Commonwealth of Australia in 1901.

In the colony of Victoria marine business came up against increasingly heavy competition, but by the end of 1889 had brought in a net profit of some £20,000. Fire insurance activities met with even fiercer and frequently unscrupulous competition. In its very early years it was decided that the branch should retire from the tariff agreement in the colony. This led to the breaking up of the tariff organisation and a great reduction in rates. By the end of the eighties the net loss on the branch's fire activities totalled about £27,000.

This was not surprising. None of the companies had fared well. In 1889, however, the branch probably had a larger share of the business than any other company, and certainly than any other English company in Victoria. Moreover, it was starting to reap the benefits of new events and developments. One of these was the Melbourne building boom of 1887 to 1890; another was the establishment of a new Tariff Association with a raising of rates and enforcement of more systematic regulations over the storage of goods. Although still far from perfect, Melbourne's fire brigade and municipal water supply were being rapidly improved.

In New South Wales progress was altogether more satisfactory and over fire insurance alone in the eighties a net profit of some £50,000 was secured. Here the results sprang not only from first-class management and an influential board of directors, but primarily from the acquisition in 1880 of the two local companies out of which the branch was formed. This experience was not lost on the Board, as future developments both at home and overseas were in due course to show.

In Queensland something like two-thirds of the net profit on fire insurance—about £12,000—accrued from districts outside the capital, where certain heavy losses were incurred on a number of fires. Transactions in marine underwriting were disappointing, a fact attributed to the employment of mercantile firms in the colony to represent marine companies as agents.

The branch in South Australia showed unsatisfactory results during the eighties and over fire insurance incurred a net loss of nearly £1,700. A good part of this was due to the conflagration of 1888 in the mining town of Broken Hill which, though situated over the border in New South Wales, was covered from Adelaide owing to its direct railway communications with the South Australian capital. Unlike the solid construction of Adelaide and other Australian towns Broken Hill was then mainly built of timber. Efforts to rebuild the place on more modern lines were only put in hand after the fire. In 1889 prospects for the future were made much brighter by the company's acquisition of the Mercantile Marine and Fire Insurance Company of South Australia, a business of high standing in the colony.

The Commercial Union's progress during its first twelve years in Australia was not spectacular. But if one takes into account the conditions of life and business there at that time, this could scarcely be surprising. At the end of the seventies the sub-continent had only been settled for just over seventy years. The far interior had scarcely been penetrated and the colonies were settlements, of British emigrants, lightly populated and existing on the maritime fringe and the immediate hinterlands slowly being advanced inwards. Rail development in the seventies had helped this shallow advance into the interior and had also brought the separate colonies into somewhat closer touch with each other. The wool and mining activities of the eighties added their further impetus to trade and population, the growth of the latter being largely due to emigration.

The full effects of the opening up of Australia, with its influence on her exports and imports, and the consequent shape and size of fire and marine insurance practised there, were not to be felt till years later, when at the start of a new century she achieved the status of a self-governing Commonwealth.

8

Europe provided the Commercial Union with a considerable proportion of its revenue from fire business during these years. But in no single country, with two exceptions, was the amount of business transacted sufficiently important to warrant a branch organisation. The two exceptions were Spain and Germany.

The Spanish branch was established at Barcelona in 1884 and an ambitious organisation was rapidly built up. Unfortunately, it proved too ambitious. The management at Barcelona, partly through inefficiency, partly through geography, failed to control the great variety of industrial and agricultural risks, accepted at rates dangerously below those of the local offices. And it was not until the middle nineties, when the company disbanded its Spanish organisation and reverted to the use of direct agencies, that it reaped satisfactory rewards from that country.

The German branch, established at Berlin in 1885, got off to a flying start through a treaty arranged with the German Officers' Association (Deutsche Offizier Verein)—an arrangement not only valuable in itself, but also in the other influential connections which it opened up. For many years the company's fire insurance activities in Germany, which became well spread through most of the German Empire, yielded larger results than those in any other European country, and the German organisation was to continue in existence up to the First World War.

The Commercial Union established itself during its first thirty years in many other parts of the world through agencies, but until the nineties it was mostly in those countries which have figured in this chapter, that its volume of business became so substantial as to require branch organisations. The underwriting of fire risks was infinitely the largest factor in its overseas activities and revenue, and some rough measurement of its progress can be conveyed by the record of premiums during the late eighties. Taking the years 1884 and 1889, the round figures were as follows:

|  | 1884 £ | 1889 £ |
|---|---|---|
| U.S.A. | 310,000 | 455,000 |
| Europe | 132,000 | 119,500 |
| Canada | 59,000 | 70,000 |
| Australia | 46,000 | 70,000 |
| Asia | 33,000 | 38,000 |
| South America & West Indies | 10,000 | 35,000 |
| Africa (principally South Africa) | 1,700 | 2,000 |

# CHAPTER IV

---

# *New Events in the Nineties—1890-1899*

I

F ROM the early years of the company's existence great importance had been attached by the Board and management of
the Commercial Union to the establishment of roots throughout the British Isles. Well before the end of the eighties they had
regionalised activities in the United Kingdom through branches
covering large areas of the country. Fire and life operations in the
North of England were controlled through a branch at Newcastle-
on-Tyne; in Yorkshire through a branch at Leeds. Similar operations
were conducted in the North Midlands through Nottingham, in the
Midlands through Birmingham, in the Eastern Counties through
Norwich, and in the West of England through Bristol. In Ireland
the district branch was at Dublin, while Scottish activities were
covered through Edinburgh and Glasgow, the Clydeside city also
having a separate office and agency for the Marine Department.

Lancashire was accorded a particularly important place in this
scheme of things. There was a large branch at Liverpool, and at
Manchester the company operated its most important provincial
office, supported by a local board of directors and dealing with
marine as well as fire and life underwriting.

A new development of these provincial interests had taken place
in 1889 when the Commercial Union bought up a small business,
the Nottinghamshire and Midland Fire Insurance Company, and
reorganised its North Midland branch at Nottingham, creating a

local board of directors. This development was carried a stage
further in 1894. In that year the company made the first really considerable acquisition in its history up to that date with the purchase
of the West of England Fire and Life Insurance Company.

The circumstances, in which this acquisition took place, caused
much public interest and in insurance and financial circles were
watched with keenest attention. The West of England during an
existence of nearly ninety years had made its own particular mark
in British insurance. It possessed a very strong board of directors, its
activities were well spread throughout the country, it had built up
connections with the Continent through an office in Paris, and for
some period in its career was the sixth largest British insurance office
despite the difficulties inherent in its rather remote location at
Exeter. At the time when it passed into the hands of the Commercial Union it was by no means a moribund concern. It was, however, in difficulties, the first indication of which had appeared in a
press announcement that it caused to be made in the autumn of
1879. This stated that investigations had shown that the branch of
the business " covering loans on personal security coupled with life
assurance " had not been profitable. Bad debts were written off and
in order to meet the deficiency and close this account £25,000 had
been transferred from the Fire Fund.

Despite this winding up of the Personal Loan Department the life
underwriting experience over the following decade continued to
cause public uneasiness and the company encountered some editorial
criticism in London newspapers early in 1889, both for its unsatisfactory method of valuation and the small margin by which its
assets exceeded its liabilities. Its Fire Department on the other
hand was showing an average profit of 10 per cent over the five years
from 1888 to 1892. In fact, the highest rate of profit during that
period was 21 per cent and it was only in 1892 that a small underwriting loss occurred. This experience was actually better than that
of many of the leading offices at that time even though Exeter itself
had earned the unhappy title of the " Fiery City ".

However, the position was now far from satisfactory, and some
dissension on the board was reflected in counsels offered from quarters outside the company, which suggested that the life business
should be run off and its assets converted into a closed fund, the

company concentrating its activities on fire insurance only. At first this viewpoint gained its adherents, but on reflection the Board decided that it offered a very uncertain solution of their problem because it would have had unfortunate repercussions on future agency development.

This was the dilemma confronting the West of England when the Commercial Union approached it in January, 1894. The negotiations that followed were carried out between the enterprising Roger Owen and Edward Smithett, the West of England's Secretary. The two men reached a provisional agreement by the end of the month and on February 9th, John Trotter, then the Commercial Union's Chairman, went down to Exeter and formally signed a memorandum of agreement with the West of England's President, John H. Ley.

The acquired company's capital was £600,000, of which £210,000 had been paid up—that is to say £35 out of every £100 share. Briefly summarised, the terms of the acquisition were:

1. The Commercial Union allotted for each share of £35 paid up, £50 of 4 per cent Debenture Stock redeemable at its own option —110 per cent at the end of ten years, 105 at the end of twenty and at the end of thirty years absolutely 100 per cent.
2. The Life Funds were to be vested in trustees and worked out as a separate series by the Commercial Union at the same expense rates as incurred by them in their own business.
3. The staff were taken over on their existing agreements and the directors were continued as a local board.

The agreement was confirmed at an extraordinary general meeting of the proprietors of the West of England in March and sanctioned in the High Court before Justice Chitty in June. A pleasant sequel was John Ley's election to the Board of the Commercial Union, while Edward Smithett, after serving for some years as "Secretary to the Local Board", was later transferred to the head office of the Commercial Union as manager of its Town Fire Department.

This amicably arranged and successful negotiation secured to the Commercial Union a subsidiary company with fine traditions and

PLATE III

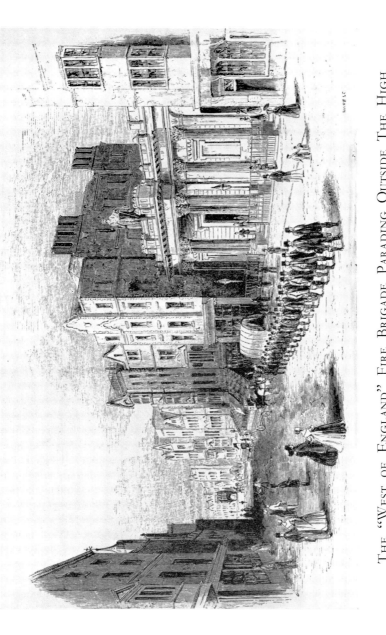

THE "WEST OF ENGLAND" FIRE BRIGADE PARADING OUTSIDE THE HIGH STREET OFFICE IN EXETER, 1835. THIS FINE BUILDING WAS ALMOST TOTALLY DESTROYED IN AN AIR RAID ON 4TH MAY, 1942.

assets of nearly £1,500,000. It was another feather in Roger Owen's cap, but it also redounded in a special way to the credit of Jeremiah Colman, who had been elected to the Board in 1886 after the death of his father and was the company's Chairman in 1892 and 1893 at a time when the affairs of the West of England had begun to attract the attention of the Commercial Union. In their early discussions about a take-over bid most of the directors favoured a course of payment in shares. Colman, however, disagreed with this proposal and pressed his view that, if it was a good purchase, it would be very much to the company's advantage to pay in debentures.

"I believe the shareholders of the West of England," he also told his colleagues, "would be quite as pleased, or perhaps more pleased, to have the dividends, which they have been receiving, assured to them as interest from debentures instead of as dividends from speculative shares."

There was a great deal of opposition to Colman's proposal and in the end he only got it agreed by a small majority. But in the event it carried the day with the West of England's shareholders and, what was ultimately much more important, it inaugurated a policy that was to be pursued most successfully by the company over subsequent amalgamations and acquisitions.

2

On grounds of sentiment, if not of business, it seems regrettable that the West of England was soon merged completely into the Commercial Union and became known as its Exeter Branch. In this respect its treatment differed from that of certain other companies that were subsequently to become subsidiaries of the group.

Like its new proprietor the West of England had originated through a fire, this event occurring in the small town of Chudleigh about ten miles from Exeter on Friday, May 22nd, 1807. It was afterwards to become known locally as the Great Fire. This title was well earned for, breaking out at noon, it swept through the heavily thatched township and destroyed 180 out of its 407 houses. No lives were lost, but the damage was estimated at £60,000 and a large part of the population was rendered homeless.

Such were the distress and dismay caused by this disaster that at the next Devon Assize the Grand Jury took a course, quite outside its normal proceedings, of recommending the formation of a "Proprietary Fire Insurance Society" and this led through various informal and formal meetings to the establishment in 1807 of the West of England Fire Insurance Company, in which Lord Clifford of Chudleigh and Samuel Frederick Milford, a Deputy Lieutenant of Devonshire, played the leading part. Milford became the company's first Chairman—an excellent appointment as he was not only an able economist, but also a warmhearted philanthropist, beloved and revered throughout the county.

Under Milford's chairmanship a large and influential board of directors—at one time it reached the remarkable number of seventy members—superintended the company's affairs which at first consisted entirely of underwriting fire risks. Their rates were based on the London companies' tables. These were for common risks up to £10,000 at two shillings per cent, hazardous up to £6,000 at three shillings per cent, and doubly hazardous up to £3,000 at five shillings per cent.

"Abundant provision having been made for all purposes," the prospectus ran, "the responsibility of the proprietors will be limited to the amount of the capital, namely £600,000 and it will be a stipulation in every engagement entered into by the company that the proprietors shall under no circumstances be answerable for more than the amount of their respective subscriptions." The proprietors were entitled first to five per cent per annum on the amount of paid up capital, and out of the profits every fifth year three-fourths was to be set aside as a reserve till such reached £20,000; thereafter three-fourths was to be divisible among the proprietors. The remaining one-fourth was to be divided quinquennially among the policy holders in proportion to the aggregate amount of their respective payments.

A year after its establishment the company's title was changed to the West of England Fire and Life Insurance Company and it started to practise life assurance based on the profitable Northampton Tables. This side of its business was so remunerative from the outset that in 1818 it was able to announce that its rates would be reduced to "10 per cent less than London Rates".

The relations between the Board and its first Secretary, John Gliddon, came to an untimely end in 1810 when he was "indited for defrauding the Company of divers large sums of money". It was his successor, Charles Lewis, who built the fortunes of the West of England, lived to see it surpass the Imperial, in which he had started his career, and at his death in 1854 left it as the sixth largest life and fire business in the country.

In view of its origins it is not surprising that the West of England always had a great sense of duty to the community in the matter of fires. The "West of England Fire Brigade" was for many years an institution in the life of Exeter and in the thirties of the last century, when it was not usual for the brigade of one office to extinguish fires on the properties insured by other offices, it came to an arrangement with other companies to co-operate in the fullest measure. In the course of time "West of England" fire engines made their appearance in the streets of all the principal towns in the West Country and the company also maintained its own fire brigade in London up to the formation of the London Fire Brigade, established jointly by the fire insurance offices in 1832.

For more than a century the West of England office was a familiar building in Exeter's High Street. It was erected in 1820, but thirteen years later a somewhat striking frontal façade was added to it. This consisted of Corinthian columns supporting a plinth surmounted by a figure of Alfred the Great which had been adopted from the company's early fire mark. Destroyed during the Baedeker raids of 1942, this former office has since been replaced by a modern building.

Though merged into the Commercial Union, the West of England was wisely left to maintain its directors as a local board and the Exeter branch has ever since possessed this association with the West Country through a group of men distinguished in their social and commercial connections with its life. Furthermore, the association of the Exeter branch with the region in which it works has been strengthened and widened in recent years by the appointment of Committees of Reference for Cornwall, Dorset, Plymouth, Sidmouth and Somerset.

3

One of the results of the acquisition of the West of England in 1894 was an addition to the Commercial Union's premises in London, for it converted the former company's office at New Bridge Street into its City office. In the same year it purchased part of the business of the Economic Fire Office which was in the process of liquidation—a purchase that widened its activities in the Newcastle-on-Tyne and Gloucester areas. Both at home and abroad enlargement of the company's scope of work was rapidly taking place and the completion of a new head office in Cornhill, the need for which had been decided some time earlier, became more than ever essential.

The only extension which had been made to the Cornhill premises since 1863 was through a purchase of property in Change Alley at the back of the building for £40,000 in 1876. However, in February, 1893, further premises in Change Alley were advertised for sale. The buildings were very old and consisted of offices, one or two shops and the King's Arms Tavern. The company was able to buy this rambling property for £71,000 and its first intention was to convert the cellars running between its offices acquired in 1876 and this newly acquired accommodation into a subterranean passageway. But before this contract was completed three properties—25, 26 and 27, Cornhill—divided by the Alley from these other buildings, were offered for sale by auction. Against high competition the company managed to secure them for £90,000, and 23 and 24, Cornhill were also subsequently acquired at the cost of £52,976.

Both of these blocks were then demolished and the Commercial Union's new head office, erected by Cubitt & Co. on this large site, was completed and occupied in May, 1896. To mark this occasion the company's London staff were subsequently entertained at dinner by the Board.

Board and management alike had reason to be proud of their new quarters which greatly improved the appearance of that part of Cornhill facing the Royal Exchange across the street and were a token, if this indeed was needed, of the Commercial Union's growth towards maturity in just over thirty years. However, the total costs involved were very considerable and presented quite a problem despite the company's increasing prosperity. This problem was partly solved through negotiations with Lloyds Bank which were concluded by the Bank's purchase of 19-20, Cornhill and part of the premises in Change Alley, which the company no longer required.

This transaction had a strange sequel. A claim was made on the company by a bank manager at Margate on the ground that he had introduced the Bank as the purchaser. Having regard to the close relations existing between the two institutions and the fact that years before the Bank had told the Commercial Union that it would be a willing purchaser, the company repudiated the claim. The claimant went so far as to take action in the High Court, but was defeated.

Another problem presented in the construction of the building was solved by a curious piece of luck. To build it as a comprehensive structure from ground level upwards it was necessary to obtain permission from the Court of Aldermen to close a small section of Change Alley and this depended on showing proof that it was private property. It so happened that during these negotiations the Commissioner of Police came to see Henry Mann, the company's Secretary at that time. The purpose of his visit was to seek permission to control the alley owing to objectionable happenings there. It was private property, he said, and so the police had no authority over it. Mann shrewdly asked him for a written application and this was duly laid before the Court as evidence of the company's rights. This certainly helped to secure the necessary consent. And so the passage between the two blocks of properties was closed, the company making a new alley on the east side of its new building and selling small portions of land to the Scottish Widows Life Company and Glyn's Bank.

When in due course the accountants worked out all the figures over the new building—the expenditure on acquisitions and construction, the law suit and the various incidental expenses less the profits on their sales to Lloyds Bank and other purchasers—it was found that the new head office had cost the company £248,000. As the area on the ground floor was 6,499 square feet, the book value of the land including the building, was just over £38 per square foot. This was, to say the least, a substantial new asset.

The King's Arms Tavern disappeared from the City scene with this event and a passing reference must be made to its memory. Built in 1748, it became a well-known centre for meetings and conferences. Of these the most far reaching in its effects was one convened in 1756 by a traveller and philanthropist, Jonas Hanway. Presided over by the Lord Mayor, the Right Hon. Slingsby Bethel, it adopted a scheme for forming the Marine Society. The "Seven Years' War" had started in the previous year, the Navy badly needed recruits and the objects of the society were to hold out inducements to landsmen, or men who had never been to sea, to volunteer their services. Such was the society's success that from 1756 up to the end of the Napoleonic Wars in 1815 it fitted out nearly 40,000 landsmen for the Navy. Extending its operations later to another activity, it has since been responsible for the training of upwards of 70,000 boys for the Royal Navy and Merchant Service.

Well before the end of the eighteenth century the King's Arms was no longer a tavern and was used entirely as a place suitable for meetings. It passed eventually into the hands of the Hankey family of Fetcham Park, and it was a member of that family, John Barnard Hankey, who sold the freehold to the Commercial Union in 1893.

4

The completion of the new head office was not before time since the company continued to develop its activities overseas as well as at home, with all the consequent supervision which this entailed. By the early nineties it was transacting fire, life and marine business in India, Canada and South Africa, and fire and marine business in Australia, New Zealand and on the Pacific Coast of the United States. Elsewhere abroad it was concentrating almost entirely on fire insurance and, generally speaking, it was in this field of underwriting that it extended itself throughout the world during the last decade of the nineteenth century—to such a degree, in fact, that by 1899 its foreign net premium income in this sphere more than trebled that obtained in the United Kingdom.

This advance was made in the teeth of adversity and growing difficulties though the contrasts in experience between one part of the world and another were exceedingly wide, unexpected reversals in some countries being offset by surprising successes elsewhere.

It was in the United States that the Commercial Union continued to secure its largest income from any one nation through fire transactions overseas. But the vicissitudes of its business there were baffling in the extreme. During the early nineties there was a succession of fires in those states which came under the control of the New York branch. 1891 was the worst year experienced by all fire offices, British and American alike, since the years of the Chicago and Boston conflagrations. The branch was fortunate in sustaining a loss not exceeding £36,000. Many of the smaller local companies went to the wall or were taken over by larger concerns. The Commercial Union came to the rescue of two of them and also took over the business in the western states of the Union of California. Throughout 1892 and 1893 numerous heavy fires continued to occur and in the latter year the branch incurred a trading loss of £60,000 as well as a small loss on its tornado business.

Matters were made no easier by a financial crisis which now hit the country. By the end of 1893 158 national banks, 172 state banks and 177 private banks were in liquidation. Vast railway schemes virtually came to a standstill and nearly 40,000 miles of track, including the Erie Road, the Union Pacific and the Northern Pacific, fell into the hands of receivers. Only a small amount of British capital was lost in the bank crashes, but a great deal disappeared in the half-bankrupt railways.

By the middle of the decade drastic pruning of risks restored the fortunes of the New York branch to a healthier state, but no sooner had it started to feel the benefits of this than it had to face a whole series of restrictive legislation introduced in a number of states against tariff associations formed to fix new and more reasonable rates. So serious did the situation become that as early as 1895 the board decided to form the Commercial Union Fire Insurance Company of New York to take over part of its American activities and to protect the name "Commercial Union", if legislation compelled British companies to withdraw altogether from the United States. Constant attempts to introduce further restrictive legislation followed and these included differential taxation for foreign companies. Competition and reduction of rates increased and in the last years of the century an abnormal number of small fires added to the general difficulties.

The New York branch struggled manfully through all these adversities, though its trading profits in 1899 were some £20,000 less than those in 1890. Fortunately, the affairs of the Pacific Coast branch fared better and its trading profits in 1899 were about £12,000 up on those in the first year of the decade.

The tale of events in Canada was much the same as in the eastern half of the United States. This was particularly disappointing because by 1890 the Commercial Union had established itself so well in the Dominion that it had outstripped almost every other fire office. And in 1891 ambitious schemes were being planned to press business forward in Manitoba and those districts of the North West which were by then being rapidly developed by plough and axe, the Winnipeg branch being placed under Montreal so as to secure direct supervision of this effort.

But the years that followed were chequered by fires in many parts of British North America. Of these the most serious was that which occurred on July 9th, 1892, at St. John's, Newfoundland, which, being outside Canada, was dealt with direct from London through an agency started as far back as 1864. This disaster, which destroyed half the city, caused a total loss to the various underwriters of a million pounds, the Commercial Union's share in which was nearly £52,000.

Three years later there was a series of losses at Toronto, and business in the maritime provinces was to fare even worse with a conflagration at the town of Windsor, Nova Scotia, in 1897, and numerous fires elsewhere during 1899. In Manitoba and the West, where prospects had seemed so fair, prairie fires and wind-storms became so frequent that the company abandoned the underwriting of agricultural risks in 1897.

Whereas the decade in British North America opened with trading profits of some £26,000, it closed in its last year with trading profits only just exceeding £15,000.

5

This picture of a temporary decline in the company's affairs on the North American continent is in marked contrast with the march of events in Asia during the same period. In India especially the progress achieved was more than considerable. This was a reflection of developments that had been taking place in two previous decades. The economic importance of the sub-continent had been growing rapidly. During the eighties India had become one of the largest of Britain's overseas markets. In fact India and the United States accounted between them for over a quarter of British exports in that period. The Commercial Union's organisation in India had moreover undergone a transition since the days of the agencies established during the sixties.

A branch with a local board of directors and a manager had been opened at Calcutta in 1870. This transacted life assurance in addition to fire underwriting, and for some period at least the life side of affairs was sufficiently important as to require the services of two medical officers. About the same time an agency for marine underwriting had also been appointed. After some diminution of business in the early nineties the Calcutta branch began to show excellent results. In the final years of the century it forged ahead despite the outbreak of plague in India during 1896 and 1897.

At Bombay the earlier agency of 1863 had been succeeded in 1877 by a more influential one dealing in fire, life and marine. In 1893 a branch was established in the city for the first time. Though it got off to a slow start in its fire underwriting, it later made rapid progress, gaining a continuous increase of business, as in the case of Calcutta, despite the plague.

In Southern India the company's experience had been less satisfactory. The Madras organisation had been brought up to branch status at the same time as Calcutta's and almost identically on the same lines. For an area less economically developed the experiment had proved too ambitious and the branch was given up after only one year. Resurrected in 1897, the branch now started to make headway over fire underwriting in Mysore and the South. In Ceylon the company benefited from its acquisition at home of interests in the

Economic Fire Office which had built up valuable associations with the underwriting of tea estates on the island.

An outstandingly interesting development of the Commercial Union's operations in the Far East at this period took shape in the summer of 1894. This was the acquisition of the Straits Fire Insurance Company of Singapore. Up to this time the Commercial Union's business in the Far East had been undertaken through numerous agencies scattered across Malaya, the Straits Settlements, the islands of the Indonesian archipelago, and along the coast of China. No adequate co-ordination of the company's interests in this far-flung area of land and sea had been possible under these arrangements and, though business had not been unremunerative, the fuller potentialities of the area had remained untapped.

In 1890 the Commercial Union had entered into a reinsurance contract with the Straits Insurance Company. Established only four years earlier, this concern had shown considerable enterprise in extending its connections. However, it soon became obvious to the management of the Commercial Union that serious personal differences of opinion were developing among the directors of the Singapore business regarding the relative importance of their marine and fire activities and that these in turn were causing a good deal of uneasiness and agitation among their policy holders in the Straits Settlements and elsewhere. At a point where a final split in the company's affairs arrived the Commercial Union stepped into the opening and made an outright purchase for £12,872 of the Straits fire business which by then had been registered as a separate company under the title of the Straits Fire Insurance Company of Singapore. It then converted the company, with its various assets, connections and agencies, into an Eastern Branch.

All the liabilities of the acquired company were run off in 1895 at the cost of this new branch and, moreover, £10,000 of new premiums were obtained against losses just exceeding £2,600, which included claims under the "Straits" policies. Thus in one year some two-thirds of the purchase price was defrayed out of net income. This was quite an achievement—more especially so as the Australian and New Zealand sides of the "Straits" business had fared badly that year. "All these outside liabilities have, however, been run off," a record of the Commercial Union's fire transactions for 1895 commented, "and the Company has upon its books the nucleus of a business in the Far East which could not have been obtained by any other means."

It is not difficult to detect the shrewd and sure hand of Roger Owen in this event. At a minimum cost, rapidly paid off, the company had enhanced and consolidated its position in the Far East. In the place of an agency it now had a branch with an office on the water-front at Singapore—that once small settlement of fisherfolk which Sir Stamford Raffles had persuaded the Sultan of Johore to cede to him in 1819 and which had since become the most important halting place on the trade route between India, the Far East and Australia, as well as the seat of British administration in the Straits Settlements, the Federated Malay States and our possessions and protectorates in the Indonesian archipelago.

### 6

The manner in which the "Straits" after its acquisition was converted into the Commercial Union's Eastern Branch is a story in itself. It was essential that a senior officer should be sent out from London to deal with the constitution of local boards at Singapore and Hong Kong, to select personnel from the existing staff, and to correlate the numerous agencies, especially in places where both the Commercial Union and the "Straits" were represented. Roger Owen was too occupied with the affairs of the West of England and other matters at home to go abroad in 1894 and G. C. Morant, then Assistant Fire Manager, was deputed to undertake this mission. Next to his chief, Morant had been the most assiduous traveller to foreign parts on the company's business since his appointment in 1887. He was a perceptive observer, a good negotiator and an intelligent judge of men.

Morant left London early in October and was back again in February of the following year, busy on his long report. This was a document with intriguing undertones. Its descriptions of Penang, Singapore, Hong Kong, Shanghai and the principal cities of Japan, rapidly changing under the impact of Western civilisation, were detailed and colourful. Its accounts of personalities met, of suspicions, jealousies and even malicious gossip, couched though they were in the formal language of an official record, were recorded with a pleasantly dry humour. It is easy to read between the lines and appreciate the difficult situations and characters with which Morant had to contend and the finesse he brought to these encounters. Social and commercial life among the European communities of the eastern tropics, at the time when Morant saw it, had obviously not changed at all since a decade earlier when Joseph Conrad, now engaged in translating his experiences into vivid fiction, had plied from one port to another as a master mariner.

Morant's first problem was the reconstruction of the former board into a local organisation. In this he was greatly helped by the advice of its late chairman. But, to quote from his report, he also called several times on each of the former members of the board, " as the singularly strained relations which appeared to exist among the Directors themselves and between the Directors and the Secretary, made it particularly necessary that I should, in the interests of the Company's future business, avoid any act of omission which might have been misconstrued ". He found, on visiting the office of one director, that he had resigned his seat and left for Europe, and had to use all his diplomacy to dissuade his late business partner from applying to take his place. His second interview was with a gentleman who took up " a somewhat singular and aggressive attitude and assumed that we should not require his services ". Discovering that, since the transfer of the business, he had been taking away insurances as they matured to another office by cutting rates, Morant took him at his word. Then there was the late Secretary to interview, who " did not give me a very cordial reception, possibly because at the time he was too much engrossed in racing matters, having a few days previously carried off several prizes at the local race meeting, and being then engaged in arranging the sale by auction of his stud ".

The question of appointing a manager immediately presented difficulties as, Morant's choice having fallen on a certain individual, information reached him that the person concerned was unpopular and had been blackballed at the club—allegations which after " careful and exhaustive enquiry " he found to be absolutely unfounded.

At last, however, the local board was established out of past members and new additions, the manager was appointed, and Morant pursued his way onwards to disentangle the claims and conflicting interests of the widely spread agencies.

Morant's recommendations in the light of his tour led to the Shanghai and certain other distant agencies being hived off from control by Singapore for reasons of local pride and geography, and these then came under direct control from London. Of particular interest was the creation of a sub-branch at Hong Kong and a decision to operate the underwriting of typhoon risks in that colony. This decision was made after much investigation into the history of typhoons there, the most serious of which had been in 1841, when a typhoon swept everything before it, again in 1862 when Hong Kong, Macao, Whampoa and Canton received a visitation which caused severe loss of life, and in 1874 when what became known as the "Great Typhoon" created considerable damage on land, wrecked twenty vessels and killed a large number of people. However, having regard to the considerable lapse of time between these events and the experience which the Commercial Union had gained of tornado insurance in the United States, the company went ahead with this class of underwriting. It was to prove popular among property owners in the colony and to become a by no means negligible sideline to the company's fire insurance activities there which increased to such an extent that the establishment was promoted to a branch in 1899.

By and large these were years of good progress for the company in Asia. Its net trading profits from fire insurance during 1890 in that area were slightly under £16,000. In the last year of the century they totalled over £26,000—a figure that seems negligible today, but which at that time and in that continent was quite considerable.

## 7

The company's progress in Australasia was even more impressive and the set-backs during this period were few and far between. This was partly due to the accelerating growth of Australia's population and cities. Census returns at the beginning of the decade in Victoria revealed that the colony's residents numbered by then over

1,137,000. In New South Wales the population exceeded 1,147,000. Sydney, its capital, accounted for over 387,000 of this figure. The number of houses in the colony had reached nearly a quarter of a million—no negligible figure to fire insurance underwriters, and the more remarkable considering that a very serious fire had swept through Sydney in 1890. The Commercial Union escaped well out of this conflagration, though many companies were involved in heavy losses.

Other causes that contributed to the company's progress in the sub-continent were extensions of its establishment there. In 1891 it purchased the Marine Insurance Company of Western Australia, which was in the process of liquidation, and established a branch at Perth, the capital of the rapidly developing youngest colony on the mainland. This branch did well from the start, and another acquisition in 1898, that of the Cornwall Insurance Company of Launceston, gave it a profitable foothold in Tasmania, where previously it had been working through an agency.

The Commercial Union's worst experience in Australia during the nineties was at Melbourne where it incurred a considerable loss in the fire of 1897. But two excellent years of business followed this event and the trading profits on fire insurance alone in 1899 exceeded £42,000—a figure nearly £25,000 higher than that of 1890.

Meanwhile, there had been an extension of activities to New Zealand. This was in 1890, when the colony was fifty years old and the white population had grown from 50,000 to over 600,000. In that year the Commercial Union purchased the Colonial Insurance Company of New Zealand, a fire and marine business with headquarters at Wellington. Though its gross revenue at the time of the purchase exceeded £67,000, it was in difficulties and the Commercial Union was able to take it over for the small sum of £8,134. The business was then converted into a branch and this prospered so well during its first year of underwriting that it defrayed the purchase costs out of net premium income and, moreover, showed a profit of £5,697. No attempt was made to break into the life assurance market where existing offices were too firmly entrenched and the government itself had operated an increasingly powerful state assurance organisation since 1869. Even in fire and marine underwriting the competition was soon found to be exceptionally strong, but the Wellington branch more than held its own and returned satisfactory profits, except for one year, throughout the nineties.


8


Until 1890 the Commercial Union had transacted some small amount of business in South Africa through agents in Durban and Cape Town, appointed respectively in 1862 and 1863. By 1890, however, South Africa was very much in the news and the City was actively interested in developments there. Since the day in 1884 when a party of prospectors had stumbled on gold in a pebble reef near a Witwatersrand farm, the Rand had risen to fame and increasing prosperity as a gold bearing area. In 1889 it produced £1,300,000 worth of the precious metal, and the prospects of much higher yields were great. Yields were, in fact, to reach over £5,000,000 in 1893 and £15,000,000 by 1898.

This and other developments were vitalising trade and commerce throughout the colonies, as they were then called, and were having their effect also on the maritime activities of the larger ports such as Cape Town, Durban and Port Elizabeth. The Commercial Union decided that the time had come to establish itself more firmly in the southern part of the African continent and in 1890 opened a branch for South Africa at Cape Town, appointing a local board a few months later. Results were rather variable and disappointing in all three spheres of insurance until 1894 when the Company purchased the Provident Assurance and Trust Company of Port Elizabeth.

This business covered an unusual array of interests, including land and estate management in addition to fire, marine and "land transit" insurance. Its subscribed capital was £200,000, but its reserve fund was a mere £17,000 fortified by a still smaller item in the accounts—a "dividend protection fund" of £1,000. It was obviously in no shape to carry on an independent existence and had already been approached with a take-over bid by the Imperial Insurance. The Commercial Union now arrived on the scene with an outright offer of £44,000. This was £1,500 more than the Imperial's, and included a guarantee to absorb management and staff.

At this point dissension arose between the Provident's board and its shareholders, and an extraordinary general meeting was called. In addressing the meeting the Chairman argued that they could not as "honourable men" discontinue negotiations with the Imperial which were in their final stage. The "honourable men" were not, however, impressed by this call to their moral feelings and one of them rose to say,

> "I want shareholders to look after their own interests. Why should they lose two shillings per share? If they have 500 shares, they will lose £50 by accepting the Imperial offer, and I do not think there is a Scotchman who would throw away £50."

Amid laughter he added:

> "I speak as a Welshman, and no Welshman would throw away £50."

As the shareholders at the meeting ran into several hundred, this statement could scarcely have appealed to their pockets. On the other hand it was symptomatic of their general mood. The Chairman and Board were outvoted and the Provident passed into the hands of the Commercial Union.

One result of this event was the removal of the South African branch from Cape Town to Port Elizabeth. This arrangement did not meet with the approval of Morant when he visited South Africa in 1896. While he was favourably impressed by the purchase, which had brought with it good marine connections and some fair amount of life business, he regarded Port Elizabeth as being too much off the beaten path as a headquarters and not comparable in appearance and importance with Cape Town. Port Elizabeth's rail connections with other cities were very bad at that time. From Cape Town, however, there were express train services weekly to the other principal centres—an interesting commentary on the contemporary railway facilities in the colony.

Even in Cape Town he was not altogether pleased with the state of affairs which he found when he arrived there. Life business was poor as the local offices were too strongly established in that field, and both fire and marine underwriting needed new connections. In Durban, too, he was disappointed with the amount of life and marine work transacted.

The highlight of Morant's tour was Johannesburg—centre of the

Rand gold mining developments—which, incidentally, had figured in the Jameson Raid only a few months earlier. He was moved to excitement by its extraordinary and rapid development. "Those who have not visited it," he wrote in his subsequent report, "can scarcely realise the extent of this town, the substantial character of the numerous buildings recently erected, the animation of the streets, the displays of its shops, and the importance of the trade carried on."

Kimberley, which he visited next, was a rather gloomy contrast at that time. He found the town still one of considerable importance and business activity, "although its days of development and expansion are past". Alas, poor Kimberley! The diamond rushes that had made its grandeur in the seventies were by then a memory and four years hence it was to suffer a protracted siege. But better days were eventually to come.

On the whole Morant's impressions of the company's prospects in South Africa seem to have been unduly pessimistic. Undoubtedly Cape Town merited the senior place in the administration of the Commercial Union there, and this was to be restored to it in 1907. But the shift of importance to Port Elizabeth in the nineties was by no means unwise as a temporary measure, for it enabled maximum advantage to be taken of the acquisition of the Provident. In the years that followed a good rate of progress was maintained, especially in fire underwriting, and this was continued even during the South African War. The accounts of the branch showed a trading profit of nearly £14,000 in 1899, whereas a small loss had been incurred in its first year's workings.

## 9

Europe came next to the United States in the volume of overseas fire insurance transactions conducted by or for the Commercial Union during the nineties. Results were, however, disappointing on the whole.

France was among the more profitable of the continental countries. A branch office was opened in Paris in 1890 under the management of Moreau, a partner in the firm of Haine, Morant and Moreau, but

F

it was later closed and succeeded by a general agency in the name of Haine and Morant.

In Greece, where the company had been active earlier in the century, nothing now was in its favour. There was a disastrous fire at Salonika in 1890, through which it sustained a considerable loss and subsequent relations with reinsurance companies became so unsatisfactory that it suspended its Greek activities in 1894.

The principal countries where the company had direct agencies working for it were Scandinavia, Holland, Portugal and Turkey. Despite some vicissitudes these on the whole returned useful results. In Spain, too, the company's fortunes showed an upward turn after a branch at Madrid, which had proved a failure, was disbanded in 1893 and management of affairs was transferred back to Barcelona, being put into the hands of a general agent.

It was in Germany that the Commercial Union continued to make outstanding progress. In 1891 it purchased the direct business of the "Lubecker" and at the same time considerably expanded its agencies, with the result that its net revenue rose by nearly £19,000 in one year. In 1893 it promoted a Hanseatic Tariff Union in which German as well as British companies doing business in the Hansa towns became members—a quite remarkable achievement for a foreign concern and, as a Fire Department report on that year described, "a circumstance hitherto unparalleled in Germany". In the last year of the decade, when continental business was almost everywhere in disarray, the German side of the company's business was forging ahead. The company's net trading profits on its European transactions that year were some £20,000—only £2,000 more than in 1899—though it should be added that this comparison does not altogether do justice to its work on the continent during the nineties, for in several years these figures exceeded £50,000.

10

Elsewhere in the world the Commercial Union was continuing to extend itself, especially in South America—where in 1891 it established its first branch at Buenos Aires—in Central America, and in the West Indies.

The wars that flared up in the final years of the nineteenth century were too localised to have any serious effect on British or international trade. As we have seen, the South African War did not retard the general progress of the Commercial Union even in that area itself. The only effect of the Spanish-American War on the company's fortunes was to raise the loss ratio of the Marine Department in 1898, but as that was a good premium year, the losses were brushed aside. As a sidelight on the war, however, they have some interest. All the losses were Spanish. After the Battle of Manila Bay the American Fleet virtually controlled the waters round the Phillipine Islands. The *Isla de Mindanao* was burnt and sunk during that battle. The *Panama*, on her way from New York to Cuba a few days before, was intercepted and captured by the Americans. The *Antonio Lopez* was reported to have been run ashore at Solinos near San Juan, Porto Rico, at the end of June, to prevent capture, but was entirely destroyed by the warship, *New Orleans*, a month later.

With the close of the century the Commercial Union could look back on thirty-eight years of solid progress achieved in the face of steadily increasing competition and of all the incidental problems which this brought with it. At the end of 1863—the first year in which its three departments were functioning—its Fire Fund amounted to some £43,000, its Life to £24,000 and its Marine to £73,000. Its assets neared £394,000. Its nominal capital was £2,500,000, of which only £250,000 had been paid up. It paid its shareholders a dividend of 5 per cent free of income tax on that year. By the end of 1899 the company's Fire Fund amounted to nearly £1,266,000, the Life to over £2,100,000, the Marine to £361,000. Its assets, including those of the Life Department, had grown to nearly £7,400,000. An important feature of these was its very substantial holdings in colonial and overseas government securities, especially in India, and its holdings in railway stocks and shares, particularly in the United States and Britain. Altogether its investments exceeded £2,000,000. It had, indeed, already become something of an investment institution which ranked it on a plane with the large insurance companies of the time. Also included in its assets were mortgages on property at home and abroad which totalled £1,675,000, while its own freehold premises, mostly occupied as offices in the United Kingdom and overseas, accounted for some £572,000 of the general figure.

The shareholders had every reason to be grateful to their board and management. The paid up capital remained at £250,000 and was profusely covered. The annual dividend, free of income tax, had risen to 25 per cent in the early nineties, and in 1899 it reached 32½ per cent. When William Dawes, then Chairman, presided over the thirty-eighth meeting of shareholders, he must have enjoyed an easy and amiable task.

The Commercial Union had passed successfully through its years of growth. With the turn of the century it was about to enter its years of active expansion.

# PART TWO

# *Years of Expansion*

## *1900-1914*

# CHAPTER V

## Strength Through Union—1900-1914

I

U NTIL the turn of the century the practice of accident insurance had been mostly confined to "personal accident" risks, and even this type of service to the community was scarcely known before the middle of the nineteenth century when it was in the main brought about by railway travel and its attendant risks. "Whether you are thinking of the safety of your life by land, or by railway, or by sea, or of the unbroken condition of your arms and legs, or of the maintenance of general health, or of the interests of wife or children when you may be no more—BE ASSURED," was a fairly comprehensive layman's description of "personal accident" coverage in the fifties. Thus wrote Charles Dickens in his magazine, *Household Words*.

The larger insurance offices, in which rank the Commercial Union had come to stand, did not concern themselves with the accident field until the turn of the century. But they then began to realise that its range was becoming so considerable that it merited serious attention.

This enlargement of range was brought about by a number of developments, nearly all of which sprang from the new scientific discoveries and engineering inventions of the later years of the nineteenth century, when electricity and the distillation of petroleum began to offer additional sources of power and lighting to those of steam and gas and, simultaneously, remarkable changes were taking

71

place in the heavy chemical and other industries. The cumulative effect of these developments was a vast increase in the scope and variety of industrial output and all which this entailed in the shape of new plant and in the recruitment of labour for works and factories. New forms of accident underwriting, embracing employers' liabilities, workmen's compensation, and protection of the public against industrial risks, had their origins in all this surge of manufacturing activity and the legislation introduced to cope with its problems. The Workmen's Compensation Act of 1897 extended safeguards to employees in industry provided by the Employers' Liability Act of 1880, and a second Workmen's Compensation Act, to be passed in 1906, was still further to enlarge these safeguards. The Factory and Workshop Act of 1901 increased the precautions against explosions in factories and workshops introduced by the Boiler Explosions Acts of 1882 and 1890.

Meanwhile, the Locomotives on Highways Act of 1896, repealing the old "Red Flag" Act of 1865, had opened British roads to the petrol-driven motor car. By 1900 there were 2,000 of these vehicles in use. By 1907 their number had risen to some 120,000, while in London alone over 800 motor omnibuses were plying the streets for passenger traffic. Road accidents inevitably took an upward turn and promoted the first excursions into car insurance. Moreover, the general growth of business was largely responsible for the extension of earlier forms of accident insurance such as fidelity guarantee, burglary, third party, plate glass and so forth, normally comprised under the terms "general accident".

It is hardly necessary to emphasise the possibilities opened up by these new trends in insurance, but on the other hand it was obvious that accident insurance had become so variegated and specialised by the beginning of the century that it could not be safely entered on any scale without expert knowledge; and it was, therefore, necessary to find experienced staff. The most satisfactory and suitable way of securing such equipment was to take over a well established accident office. There were only twenty-four of these, of sufficient calibre, in existence. The Commercial Union was among the first of the large offices to negotiate the purchase of one of them and its choice fell upon the Palatine Insurance Company. Whether, in actual fact, the motive was a direct implementation of such a policy or not, seeing that the Palatine was even stronger on its fire than its accident side, the result itself was definite enough.

The Palatine was a Lancashire business, as its name implies, based on Manchester, with branches and wide connections in the United Kingdom and overseas. It had been founded in 1886, but its associations went back to 1870 when the Mutual Fire Assurance Corporation, merged into it in 1890, had been established. It was from this absorption that it derived its special character in fire operations, for the Mutual had been started by a powerful group of Lancashire and Yorkshire manufacturers, who were dissatisfied with the then existing tariff rates for cotton and woollen mills, and it subsequently built a particular name for itself as a pioneer in the encouragement of the use of fire extinguishing appliances. It was probably more responsible than any other fire office for the introduction of sprinklers into factories and warehouses, offering and maintaining low rates for companies that installed them. On the accident side the Palatine was also well-known as a pioneering concern and had been the first office to introduce personal accident policies free of all normal restrictions except over injuries resulting from war, rebellion or self-infliction.

Negotiations with the Palatine board were successfully concluded in May, 1900, the purchase price agreed to being £272,000 of 4 per cent debenture stock redeemable not later than the end of 1929. The business was then reconstituted as a subsidiary company. At the same time it was decided that an Accident Department should be established by the Commercial Union and, to quote from a Board minute, "that at the outset the business should be conducted on the lines upon which the 'Palatine' is now working".

Modifications of the considerable home and overseas organisation of the Palatine were subsequently carried through, but the majority of the staff was very wisely retained and the business was left with a reasonable measure of independence, though its accident transactions came within the direction of the Accident Department and, indeed, formed the nucleus of this new unit. Moreover, Sir Thomas Brooke, former chairman of the Palatine, and another director, W. J. Thompson, accepted invitations to join the Board of the Commercial Union, and Brooke was also appointed a member of its new Accident Committee, the chairman of which was William Dawes.

It had been a brilliant achievement which considerably augmented the Commercial Union's fire insurance interests besides bringing it into the field of accident underwriting. At one move the company had become the only completely composite British insurance office —handling, as it did, all four branches of insurance, a unique position which it was to hold for several years. Nor did it rest on its laurels, for in the following year it purchased for £40,000 the assets and goodwill of the Globe Accident Insurance Company, a small office established in 1890, which gave it an entrée into plate-glass insurance. It followed this up by acquiring another small business, the Vehicular and General, a few months later.

2

These external successes produced their internal problems. For some time the relations between Board and management had been strained and these had been reflected in relations between the departments. The establishment of yet another department now brought matters to a head.

The company's administrative system had not substantially changed since 1861. The Board continued to keep a very tight hold over executive matters, even at times dealing with decisions of quite minor importance. Control of departments was managed through committees of directors appointed yearly by the Board and it was the chairman of each committee who reported to the Board on his department's work. The managers of the departments attended the meetings of these committees and made their recommendations to them, but they were not admitted to the sanctity of the board-room.

There had at least been one advantage in this procedure—the committee chairman had to carry full responsibility on the Board for his department's activities. If the manager had been admitted, his responsibility would have been diluted. This, however, postulated the assumption that the board was an executive as well as a policy-making body—a conception which worked well in 1861, but not so well in 1901, since the whole practice of insurance by then had become too complex for any but highly experienced professional men to deal with it. A further disadvantage was lack of co-ordination of the departments. When difficulties arose between the departmental managers, their only recourse was to the Secretary, but as he himself attended the meetings of the board solely as a recorder, his powers to represent their respective view-points were almost negligible, and he was in no position of responsibility to adjudicate between them.

This was the dilemma that confronted the Board in 1901 when it was faced with a growing number of altercations and the possible loss to the company of the services of Roger Owen. It was a somewhat different type of board from the one which had founded the business forty years earlier, for it no longer consisted almost entirely of the City's merchant princes. Banking interests, for instance, were strongly represented on it. Middleton Campbell, who will be remembered as a newly joined director deputed to visit New York in 1877 to clear up the Alliger liabilities, had become a director of the Bank of England in 1886 and was to be elected Governor a few years hence. Another and younger member of the Board was Walter Murray Guthrie, Conservative Member of Parliament for Bow and Bromley, a director of the London Joint Stock Bank and later to become Vice-Chairman of the National Discount Company. For a number of years, too, Robert Barclay had been an important influence in the company's affairs.

Then there were men who brought to the Board the lustre of successful careers overseas in the service of their country. Of these the most eminent was General, later Field-Marshal, Sir Henry Norman who, after a brilliant and courageous period of soldiering during the Indian Mutiny, had been successively Governor of Jamaica and Governor of Queensland, and in 1893 had withdrawn his acceptance of the Governor-Generalship of India on grounds of age. Another director who had built a name for himself in India was the Rt. Hon. Sir Andrew Richard Scoble. Taking silk in 1876, he had later occupied various important positions in the Indian Legislature and before returning to England had for several years been a member of the Council of the Governor-General. After eight years as Conservative member for Hackney he had retired from politics and become a member of the Privy Council. Another successful barrister on the Board was the Hon. Sir James Francis Garrick, who had been successively Attorney-General and Post-Master General of Queensland and in recent years its Agent General in London.

Perhaps the most versatile of these men of affairs was the Rt. Hon. Leonard Courtney, later to become Lord Courtney of Penrith. A Cambridge wrangler, he had subsequently studied at the bar and later held the Professorship of Political Economy at University College, London. He had then proceeded into politics, becoming Under Secretary successively at the Colonial Office and Home Office, Financial Secretary to the Treasury, and Deputy-Speaker of the House of Commons.

From what has been said it will be seen that the Board of 1901 was an amalgam of businessmen, bankers and "elder statesmen". In the face of a crisis it might have been expected that these three elements would have pulled against each other, but in actual fact some strange cross-currents of ideas and feelings showed themselves when the Board received a communication from Roger Owen intimating that he was about to transfer his services to the Phoenix Fire Office.

Owen's services to the company as its Fire Manager have been frequently referred to. But his personality and his views require some further mention. By 1901 he was regarded as the most able fire manager in British insurance, in addition to which he had gained an over-all knowledge of the other fields of insurance business, partly owing to his overseas missions, in which he had been made responsible for investigating every side of the Commercial Union's activities, and partly through the various acquisitions of other companies, in the negotiation of which he had conducted the principal executive work. Of Welsh origin he was an ambitious man with an extremely clear perception of the future problems and possibilities that lay before the world of insurance and the part which his own company could play in that world. He had particularly strong ideas about company acquisitions. Speaking about Owen years later Sir Jeremiah Colman was to remark:

"My partners and friends had been buying businesses when they were derelict, but Mr. Owen took the view that it was no good doing this if you wanted to increase your premium income; the only way was to buy a business with a good clientèle and a good connection."

Altogether, it will be appreciated that Owen had begun to feel increasingly frustrated in the midst of the rapid growth and transformation of the company. He had no direct access to the Board and his own position was becoming every day more full of anomalies. It was obvious to him that the state of internal confusion could not continue without severe damage to his own career, the work of his colleagues and the interests of the business as a whole. The offer of the Secretaryship of the Phoenix Fire Office gave him the opportunity to press his claims as General Manager with full control under the Board of the Commercial Union's Fire, Life and Accident Departments.

Owen's intimation produced sharp divisions of opinion in the board-room. Sir Andrew Scoble, for one, did not subscribe to Owen's opinions about company acquisitions. Furthermore, he took the view that "you must not allow your managers to be your masters". In this he was strongly supported by Middleton Campbell and by most of the old guard who believed that management ought to be kept in its place. On the other hand John Trotter, a go-getting man of affairs who had himself brought a considerable amount of business to the company, came down strongly in favour of retaining Owen and giving him the powers that he requested. Sir Jeremiah Colman took up a similar attitude and so, too, did Sir James Garrick, who added weight to Owen's protagonists as he was then the company's Chairman. Discussion of the matter was protracted and acrimonious, but resulted in a decision by a very small majority to retain Owen's services.

The way was now clear for urgently needed reorganisation. Owen was appointed General Manager of all departments except the Marine which was left in the control of Richard Jones. Morant succeeded Owen as Fire Manager, and Lane, late General Manager of the Palatine, was put in charge of the Accident Department. T. A. Young, the Actuary, decided to retire and his place was taken by his assistant, A. D. L. Turnbull. Henry Mann continued to be the Secretary.

All this had been no minor storm. It had been a very real crisis, and its solution was a victory not just for the management, but for commonsense and a change of outlook on business administration in a rapidly changing world. It consolidated the relations between Board and management and, in providing the Board with the counsels of a General Manager, gave it a more knowledgeable control over the company's operations. It enabled the managers to present their views to the Board through a representative who fully understood them and their problems and it led to a seriously needed co-ordination of departments and of subsidiary companies. Most important of all, it so fortified the whole administrative fabric of the Commercial Union that it was able to go forward on an even keel into the great period of expansion that now lay before it.

3

The accident side of activities grew rapidly and its scope was further widened by two interesting acquisitions. In 1903 the company purchased that part of the Vulcan Boiler and General Insurance Company's business which related to workmen's compensation and general accident and fidelity. This Lancashire concern, founded in 1858, was among the earliest pioneers of steam-boiler insurance—the part which it continued to retain and conduct, as it still does, after being taken over by the London Assurance in 1920.

In 1906 the company absorbed the second oldest accident office in existence—the Accident Insurance Company. This had been established in 1849 and had itself, in 1867, taken over the Accidental Death Company. This latter concern, founded in 1850, was one of the first businesses to undertake railway accident insurances and, incidentally, in its early days covered death from all accidental causes at a premium of £1 per annum for £1,000 at death.

Throughout its existence the Accident Insurance had specialised in personal accident work, but within that sphere had covered an extraordinary variety of risks. A prospectus that it issued in 1883 details claims paid in the preceding year relating to "Riding, Driving and Walking", 546 in all; "Business and Professional Casualties", 361; "Home and Domestic Casualties", 249; "Travelling", 46; "Animals", 19; "Sport and Pastimes", 173. These categories are further divided under numerous headings which make curious and frequently amusing reading. One wonders, for instance, what really happened to an unfortunate "organist and piano tuner of Kent" who was involved in a "Church Accident". How did a "general dealer of Wiltshire" damage himself seriously enough while playing billiards as to be paid £18? What could a "gentleman of Essex" have done to have hurt himself while playing croquet? More understandable perhaps is the case of a "licensed victualler of Middlesex" hurt in a skittle accident. But what kind of a party could it have been in which a "farmer of Norfolk" was so seriously damaged while dancing that he was paid £42 17s. 2d.? Tennis must have been a faster and fiercer game in those days than we of a later generation would have expected. Casualties under this heading were quite considerable and, irony of ironies, one third of them were surgeons and doctors.

The Accident Insurance must not be allowed to fade out of these pages without special reference to one particular policy that it bequeathed to the Commercial Union. It is now the oldest personal accident policy on the company's books and was issued on January 21st, 1896, to a youthful subaltern in the 4th Queen's Own Hussars. It covers accidental death in the sum of £1,000, with subsidiary benefits, including weekly payments in the event of total or partial disablement caused by accident, at an annual premium of £6 14/-, which includes an element of extra premium to cover hazards arising from steeplechasing and other forms of racing, as well as travel or temporary residence outside Europe. The name of this policy holder is Winston L. S. Churchill. Recently the Chairman and Directors of the Commercial Union wrote to him that they "would deem it an honour if Sir Winston Churchill would agree to accept this policy as fully paid up and in force for the future, free of further premium payments". They received a reply thanking them "for their most courteous action".

4

The extension of the Commercial Union into the accident field was part of a still wider trend of development. In the first quarter of the present century the British insurance system was transformed by a process of amalgamations—and to such an extent that, though by 1925 there were about as many companies transacting insurance business under their own specific names as in 1900, the majority of them had in actual fact lost their independence and become members or associates of a few groups. Almost certainly the most spectacular expansion through acquisition in the insurance sphere during this period was that of the Commercial Union, and it was in the decade preceding the First World War that most of this expansion took place.

The first of the important large-scale fusions was undertaken in 1905 and involved the transfer of no less a business than the Hand-in-Hand. Founded in 1696 during the reign of William III, this Society practised fire and life underwriting and was the oldest existing insurance office in the world. Criticism of the project both inside and outside this venerable and highly respected institution became vehement during the negotiations, but a speech by Andrew Johnston, one of its more experienced directors, at an extraordinary general meeting of shareholders convened in January 1905, put the matter in fair and convincing perspective.

"Our constitution," declared Johnston, "is archaic and inconvenient. Although we have been in existence 207 years, no office has ever copied it. This is a pretty good proof that insurance experts do not think it a very good constitution. Tested by the results in life business we have undoubtedly gone ahead in recent years, but in fire our progress has been extremely slow. At the present time the fire premiums are about £130,000, which is a mere trifle, and even the advance which that represents has only been attained at the cost of a considerable amount of friction with other offices. In the face of the small figures of the fire business, it is a perfect farce to speak of the Society as a beneficent public institution whose disappearance is to be compared to that of Westminster Abbey or the Tower of London, and such talk seems to me childish. There is no doubt a great deal in the sentimental view, in the fact that this is the oldest office, and so forth. But sentiment may be deferred to at too high a cost."

Criticism apart, and this faded out after Johnston's speech, the real problem was how to fuse a mutual society with a proprietary office. This entailed a Petition to Parliament and a special act which received the Royal Assent on June 30th. In brief, this enabled the Commercial Union to take over the whole of the assets and liabilities

PLATE IV

Hand-in-Hand. Original Seventeenth Century
Treasure Chest, the Mace, and Silver Armlets
dated 1696.

of the Hand-in-Hand Fire and Life Insurance Society on a guarantor basis. The Society was then merged into the Commercial Union. It is perhaps idle to speculate in 1961 as to whether the merger could have been carried out in such a way as to preserve as fully as possible the identity of the Hand-in-Hand, but it is more than likely that the legal and practical difficulties would have been insuperable.

Further changes in the Commercial Union's capital and constitution now became necessary in connection with transfer and merger schemes that were being put into effect or in contemplation. In 1907 the company's capital was increased to £2,950,000 and in 1908 it secured an Act of Parliament whereby its original deed of settlement was exchanged for a memorandum and articles of association.

Early in 1907 the company purchased for some £31,000 a small fire business, the Scottish and Mercantile Insurance Co. Ltd., founded in 1894. This was a mere curtain-raiser to a far greater event in that year—the acquisition of the Union Assurance Society. This distinguished, world-wide and historic office, established in 1714, had become a composite concern handling life and accident in addition to its original fire business. With a subscribed capital of £450,000, of which £180,000 was paid up, its accounts for 1905 had shown a fire premium income of over £690,000 with a general reserve of over £278,000, and a profit and loss balance of nearly £130,000. Its Life Department had secured a premium income exceeding £351,000, and its funds totalled over £3,492,000. Only a major disaster could have forced a ship in such good trim to seek another's help. The major disaster was the San Francisco earthquake and fire of 1906, the effects of which are described in later pages. In this acquisition the Commercial Union paid the Society's members £10 for each paid up share and also £13 in 4 per cent redeemable debentures. The Union's identity was preserved, a new company styled the Union Assurance Society Ltd. being formed to continue its fire and accident business, and the Life Assurance Fund was maintained intact as security for the existing policy-holders. The home and overseas staff of the organisation was taken over, and Joseph Powell, the General Manager, was appointed Deputy General Manager of the Commercial Union.

By 1910 the Group's accident insurance business, started only nine years earlier, had become the second largest department of its

G

activities, ranking next to fire insurance, and was bringing in a premium income exceeding half a million sterling. On June 1st of that year, however, it vastly extended its operations in this field by purchasing the largest and most successful British accident office, the Ocean Accident and Guarantee Corporation Ltd., established in 1871. This was a company at the very height of its prosperity, with a premium income of nearly £1½ million and reserves of over £1,270,000. The purchase price was inevitably high, the shareholders receiving for each £1 of paid-up share capital £7 in cash and, in addition, £5 in 4 per cent redeemable debenture stock of the Commercial Union, the second part alone of this transaction involving the creation of over £860,000 of stock. The total purchase price was, in fact, twelve times the Ocean's paid-up capital. With this transaction the Commercial Union leapt at one bound into a leading position in this branch of British insurance, and moreover without saddling itself with an increased share of capital.

Other and smaller additions during this period were subsequently made to the Group by the purchase of the Plate Glass Insurance Company of the City of London in 1910, the Imperial Accident Insurance in 1912, the Midland Plate Glass Insurance, and a small fire business, the King Insurance Company, in 1914.

An association, rather unusual in character, yet highly successful in outcome, was started by the Commercial Union in 1911. An agreement was entered into that year with the Liverpool Victoria Corporation, whereby all its workmen's compensation policies were issued by the Company. Here it should be explained that the Liverpool Victoria Corporation had been formed three years earlier to undertake general business through connections of the Liverpool Victoria Friendly Society—activities previously transacted for the most part by the London and Lancashire and by the Royal.

The Corporation's interest was not confined to workmen's compensation. Indeed, it embraced accident business generally and, moreover, fire and life. A further agreement was come to in 1912 whereby the whole of this business in the United Kingdom would be conducted under the guarantee of the Commercial Union. Two years later the Corporation went into voluntary liquidation and the business was purchased by the Commercial Union.

Following on this purchase a Liverpool Victoria Branch Board of the Commercial Union was established. Composed of the Liverpool Victoria Friendly Society Committee of Management, including the Secretary and Treasurer, and the Agency Manager of the Commercial Union, this body has continued to supervise the work of the branch up to the present day.

The build-up of revenue from this association has proceeded with cumulative rapidity. The combined fire and accident revenue has grown from some £10,000 in 1914 to some £1,310,000 in 1959, while the life sums assured have risen from some £374,000 to over £3,600,000 during the same period. In fact, this association represents today one of the major connections of the Commercial Union in the United Kingdom.

# CHAPTER VI

## Three Outstanding Accessions

### I

TIME and experience have brought co-ordination into the practice of insurance and a certain degree of uniformity in the services rendered—developments as much in the interests of the public as of the underwriter. But even the great composite companies continue to display their own intrinsic individualities, and their own particular conduct of business today is largely the result of the associations and traditions that have gone to their making.

This is certainly true of the Commercial Union which has gained not only strength and influence through the absorption of other companies, but what is equally important, certain unique traditions and a wide professional expertise that could not otherwise have been secured. Brief accounts of most of the companies that joined the group in the first decade of this century have been given in the preceding chapter, but histories of three of them—the Hand-in-Hand, the Union and the Ocean—deserve a place of their own since their contributions to the whole character of the group have been outstandingly important.

Though merged into the group after being taken over, the identity of the Hand-in-Hand has never been completely lost. Its office in New Bridge Street has been retained and activities there are attended to by a local board and branch. Thus there remain some

84

vestiges at least of insurance traditions so venerable as to date back to within thirty years of the Great Fire of London.

When founded, the Society was given the unwieldy title of "The Contributors for Insuring Houses, Chambers or Rooms from Loss by Fire by Amicable Contribution". This name was soon shortened into "The Amicable Contributors for Insuring from Loss by Fire", and later to "The Amicable Contributionship". Even the last of these titles was such a mouthful that the Society became familiarly known as the "Hand-in-Hand" owing to its use of clasped hands on its fire marks and its firemen's badges. William Cowper so referred to it in his poem on "Friendship", written in 1772:

> "A Friendship that in frequent fits
> Of controversial rage emits
>    The sparks of disputation,
> Like 'Hand-in-Hand' Insurance Plates
> Most unavoidably creates
>    The thoughts of conflagration."

Daniel Defoe's name has been coupled with the formation of the Hand-in-Hand, but it seems unlikely that he had anything to do with it as his views on insurance were far from favourable and his name does not appear among the directors in the original deed of settlement. Incidentally, they included a woman, Mary Biddle—an unusual membership of a board in the seventeenth century.

The original "Proposals" for founding the Society were drawn up at "Tom's Coffee House, in St. Martin's Lane, near Charing Cross, where attendance is daily given". They clearly show that it was a mutual business from the start and that the members paid in advance 12 shillings per cent for septennial policies on brick buildings and double that amount on timber, 10 shillings being returnable at the end of the period on brick and £1 on timber respectively. The reason for the adoption of these septennial policies was to avoid the yearly stamp tax. In addition, as the subsequent Deed stipulated, members were liable to contribute to any loss exceeding the amount of the Society's funds in proportion to their interest, "provided that no person be charged for any one loss above 10 shillings for each £100 secured on brick houses and double the rate on timber houses".

The great rival of the Hand-in-Hand in its early years was the Friendly Society, which conducted an advertisement campaign against it in the press that started counter advertisements by the Hand-in-Hand. Two of these advertisements are worth reprinting here; in those days *"fortiter in re"* was not complemented by *"suaviter in modo"* among business competitors.

"The Amicable Insurers (or Hand in Hand Office) having lately in an advertisement given out that they insure cheaper than the Friendly Society; This is therefore to undeceive the Town, who may take Notice, That the Premium in both Offices being much the same; and their contribution to make good one and the same Loss being 5 times as much as in the Friendly Society, anyone may easily see that the Society insure cheaper by Four Fifths of the Contribution or 4s in 5 (Witness the Loss in Newport Court) and as for the Profits which the Amicable Office pretend to divide, I do not find that those who have insured there near 5 Years ever received a Farthing; besides let any-one consider how they can make good a Loss of £1500, since they oblige themselves by their Settlement to contribute but 10s per Cent., and the Loss they had of but £520 was of 5s per Cent. But the main thing to be enquired into by those that have Houses to insure is, What Office has the best security for Payment of Losses, and for the Money deposited; for both which purposes there are good Land Securities settled by the Undertakers of the Friendly Society; neither of which the Amicable Society can pretend they have."

*Post Boy*, July 10, 1701.

"Whereas the Undertakers of the Friendly Society have lately in the Post-Boy published divers Reflections on the Amicable Contribu-tors, this is to satisfie all impartial people, that the Amicable Con-tributors do insure 9s in 21s cheaper than the Friendly Society, besides other advantages; they allow that the Contribution in their Office to £520 loss in April 1700, was 5s *per* Cent., there being then but about one third of the Houses Insured that are now; as to the Dividends of profits they have been faithfully allowed to every man's account, and within the year last past have arisen to 3s 4d per Cent. as by their Books more particularly does appear; the like Mistakes the Contribu-tors are ready to prove as to the other allegations of the Society, to anyone who will call at their Office at *Tom's* Coffee House in St. Martin's-lane near Charing Cross, or apply themselves to any of the Directors."

*Post Man*, July 17, 1701.

Many of the journals and periodicals of that period rejoiced in appearing with a subsidiary or explanatory second title. That of the

*Post Boy* was simple enough—*Foreign and Domestic*. The *Post Man* described itself much more grandiloquently as *The Historical Account of the Public Transactions in Christendom*.

This press campaign continued, reaching its highest level of vituperation when the Friendly Society referred to "the false Mountebank-like Pretensions of the Hand-in-Hand Insurers". However, the "Mountebank" went from success to success. By 1731 it had extended its activities to within about ten miles of London and Westminster. The premium was then 4 shillings per cent on brick and double on timber up to a limit of £2,000. But a few years later much higher acceptances were being undertaken—one of £16,000 on Bedford House and another of £33,000 on Woburn Abbey. In 1766 there was a warning against insuring such heavy amounts; the Society lost £25,758 by a single fire in Cornhill while other fires in that year brought its total losses to £53,538. Surviving these, it was transacting business in most of the Home Counties by 1780 and in most parts of the United Kingdom by 1805.

It was in that year that a second deed of settlement enabled it to insure goods, merchandise and stock-in-trade. Four years later it was involved in losses over the fire which destroyed the original Drury Lane Theatre—an event commemorated by James and Horace Smith in their *Rejected Addresses:*

> The Engines thundered through the street,
> Fire-hook, pipe, bucket all complete;
> And torches glared, and clattering feet
> Along the pavement paced. . . .

> The *Hand-in-Hand* the race begun,
> Then came the *Phoenix* and the *Sun*,
> The *Exchange*, where old insurers run,
> The *Eagle*, where the new . . .

Incidentally, the Society had formed its own fire brigade as early as 1699, when it consisted of eight "watermen" provided with "Coates, Caps and Breeches of blew lined with red, a red edging being put in upon ye same". By 1707 it had its own fire engine, and a policy of 1769 bears an engraving of a rather primitive manually-worked engine of that period.

In 1836 the office's operations were extended by yet another deed of settlement to the life assurance field and its name was altered to the Hand-in-Hand Fire and Life Insurance Society. It was under this title that it eventually became merged into the Commercial Union.

2

The San Francisco Earthquake in 1906 has already been referred to as the major disaster which brought the Union Assurance Society into the Group. Through the disaster the Union was involved in payments amounting to £829,446. These so seriously depleted its reserves that it was left with an insufficient margin of safety to accept the large-scale risks expected of an organisation of its status. But such indeed was its status that the Commercial Union wisely decided to leave it to operate with a large measure of independence, according it a board of directors and retaining its head office in London as well as its far flung organisation and staff at home and abroad.

Interestingly enough, the Union's associations during its early years had been closely linked with the Hand-in-Hand. Fires in London were increasing so rapidly in the reign of Queen Anne that a number of merchants and traders in the City convened a meeting in 1714 at the Amsterdam Coffee House in Threadneedle Street and "agreed to join in a Society for insuring goods and merchandise from loss by fire" on terms "purely calculated for the publick good and not for the private advantage of any particular person". For the first eighty-three years of its existence the Union confined its activities to goods, merchandise and household effects. Its connection with the Hand-in-Hand was extremely amicable. It adopted as its "Marke" a double hand-in-hand reversed and for many years was familiarly known as the "Double Hand-in-Hand" Office, one of its provisions stating that any dispute over the right or amount of indemnity was to be decided by the directors of the Hand-in-Hand Office who, being "indifferent and disinterested persons, may well be presumed to be proper judges". The disinterestedness is a little doubtful, but what is very certain is that the co-operation of the two offices promoted a most profitable habit on the part of their clients of insuring their warehouses or dwelling-places with the Hand-in-Hand and their possessions inside them with its counterpart.

In its first year of trading the Union underwrote goods and merchandise amounting in value to £492,165 at premiums totalling £666/17/6d. This did not satisfy the directors and to stimulate interest in their enterprise they decided that on the day of the next general meeting of the Society "the Foreman and Porters do walk through the Principall streets of London and Westminster and attend the General Meeting—one thousand proposals to be delivered by the Porters the day they walk the streets—and agreed that two trumpets be allowed the Porters in their march, and that the Porters march be from Blacksmiths' Hall into Fryday Street down Watling Street through the south side of St. Paul's Churchyard, Fleet Street, Strand and the Hay Markett up Monmouth Street, Holborne, Newgate Street, Cheapside, Cornhill, Leaden-hall Street through Aldgate, the Minories, over Tower Hill into Thames Street, thence the nearest way to St. Margarett's Hill, from thence to Thames Street, and so to the Hall again to be there by three o'clock".

The event duly took place, but its planners had overestimated the men's staying powers and underestimated their thirst. Not altogether surprising, therefore, is a note in a subsequent board minute recording that "the Foreman of the Porters appeared at this Board and received a reprimand by the Chairman with the consent of the Board for his and the rest of the porters being in drink on the day of the last General Meeting".

Despite this the practice was continued for nearly a century. Perhaps the length of the march was reduced or porters with remarkably temperate habits engaged? History, however, offers no information on these matters. At any rate the Society's affairs quickly prospered and in 1716 it secured an office of its own in Gutter Street, hiring a house there from a city alderman, Sir Edward Clarke. Four years later it escaped reasonably well from the South Sea Bubble, selling its investments in South Sea Stock at 338 per cent before the bubble completely burst. It was less fortunate over a fire in the same year at a brewery in Wapping, due to the act of an incendiary, which involved it in a payment of £20,000.

An especially unusual feature of its early career was the Union's appointment of agents in distant parts of the United Kingdom. It started insurance in Ireland, with the appointment of Messrs. Exham of Cork, in 1717. This firm still acts as its agents, and there is little doubt that it is not only the Union's oldest agents, but also the oldest existing insurance agency in the world.

A sign of the Society's progress was its considerable investments during these years, among which was a purchase of bonds in 1737 of the "United Company of Merchants of England Trading to the East Indies"—forerunner of the famous East India Company. Another sign of growing strength was the Board's decision in 1750 to raise to £5,000 the sum to be covered by a single policy on property. Four years later it transferred its head office to Maiden Lane. Well before that date it had established a branch office for the West End in the Haymarket, this being subsequently transferred to Tom's Coffee House in St. Martin's Lane.

Though the Society continued to concentrate on insuring goods, and not buildings, throughout the eighteenth century, it had its own body of "firemen", distinguished by their brown uniforms and silver badges worn on their arms, whose duty it was to remove goods from places on fire to safe accommodation. By 1762 they appear to have been formed into a fire brigade equipped with an engine. This engine figures prominently in a Hogarth engraving issued in September of that year and dealing with the last notable event in his life. In it that supreme artist of irony in black and white throws his brilliant powers of satire into a campaign in support of Lord Bute, then Prime Minister. This was a deviation from the strict line of political neutrality, which he had observed throughout his career, and was probably caused by his connection with the Court, as he had been appointed Sergeant Painter to the King in 1761.

The satire is quite definitely directed against Pitt as well as John Wilkes and his friends. Europe is depicted as on fire; France, Germany, Spain are in flames, which are extending to Great Britain. This destruction is being assisted by Pitt, who is fanning the flames with a pair of bellows. He is mounted on stilts and a Cheshire cheese hangs from his neck with £3,000 on it—an allusion to his remark in a parliamentary debate that he "would sooner live on a Cheshire cheese and a shoulder of mutton than submit to the enemies of Great Britain". An alternative interpretation is that the suspended article is a millstone, intimating that so ponderous a load must in time sink

PLATE V

"The Times" Engraving by Hogarth, 1762.

This Political Cartoon Shows the Union's Fire Engine in Action.

his popularity. Bute, attended by English soldiers, sailors and High-landers, is operating a Union Office engine for extinguishing the flames, but is impeded by the Duke of Newcastle with a wheel-barrow full of copies of the *Monitor* and *North Briton* (the latter being Wilkes' paper), intended for feeding the blaze. The respectable group underneath Pitt are the Aldermen of the City worshipping the idol they had set up, while in the foreground the musical King of Prussia, Frederick the Great, who alone is sure to gain by the war, is amusing himself with a violin among his unhappy country-women. The picture of the Indian alludes to the West Indian conquests which, it was said, "would only increase excess and debauchery". The breaking down of the Newcastle Arms and the drawing up of the patriotic ones refer to the resignation of Newcastle and the appointment of his successor. The Dutchman, smoking his pipe and sitting on a bale of goods, is supposed to indicate the preferable neutrality of the Netherlands. The wagon labelled " Her-mione " contains treasure taken from a Spanish ship captured off Cape St. Vincent, while the dove with an olive branch flying above the flames needs no explanation.

Despite severe losses in the Gordon Riots of 1780, when Newgate and Holborn Bridge were destroyed by fire, the chapels of various embassies sacked, and a vast amount of damage done to property in various parts of London, the Union continued to proceed from strength to strength. In 1798 its volume of business necessitated a move to a new head office at 81 Cornhill. Seven years later it increased its capital and extended its operations to insurance of buildings. In 1813 it started to undertake life assurance and in the same year opened a branch in Bond Street and an agency in Dublin. In 1814 it established a Scottish agency in Edinburgh. All this, be it noted, during the Napoleonic Wars.

After the Battle of Waterloo the Directors turned their eyes towards Europe and in 1816 established a German branch at Hamburg. Twelve years later they started a German Life Company and opened sub-agencies at Berlin, Leipzig, Hanover, Mecklenburg, Breslau, and later at Koenigsberg. This was followed up by the formation of branches in other continental countries including Switzerland, Holland and Spain.

On its life assurance side the Society's policies in the nineteenth century covered many notable people. One of the earliest proposals was that of the Duke of Argyll. At the time of the advent of steam an entry in the board minutes of 1816 resolved that "R. Trevethick . . . be insured for £2,500, seven years at five guineas extra on account of the dangers of his projected voyage to Peru where he is going to work mines by steam". The Cornish inventor reached his destination safely and was received with great ovation. During the Crimean War the Union granted special rates to officers proceeding on active service. In 1855 it received the distinction of insuring the lives of "Her Gracious Majesty Queen Victoria" and "H.R.H. The Prince of Wales".

Extension of the business in the United Kingdom marked the decade from 1878 to 1888, during which branches were opened in Liverpool, Manchester, Newcastle, Birmingham, Glasgow, Edinburgh, Bristol and Leeds, replacing the earlier agencies in those cities. Important development of the Society's overseas activities followed between 1888 and 1890, when branches were established in New York and Montreal. And in 1904, with its acquisition of the Scottish Alliance Insurance Company, the Union broke into the accident market, in which it was to extend itself into every class of insurance included in that section.

Such was the all-round expansion of the Society's activities that in 1905 it acquired the lease of 1 and 2, Royal Exchange Buildings and erected a new head office on that site. It was, indeed, something of a tragedy in the insurance world that this successful and honourable business should have been so badly damaged a year later at the height of its career by a disaster so far distant and unpredictable that it was compelled to yield its independence. But this at least may be said, in regard to the results of that event, that the Union has since continued to achieve a progressive career within a wider orbit and to enhance a name commanding world-wide respect.

3

The largest British accident office in 1910 was the Ocean Accident and Guarantee Corporation Ltd. For that reason alone its amalgamation with the Commercial Union Group of companies in that year caused intense interest in financial and commercial circles both at home and abroad. It also brought a considerable accession of strength to the Group's position in the fire field.

Incorporated as the Ocean Railway and General Travellers Assurance Company Ltd. at the end of 1871, the business started its career in a modest way, but became a great pioneer of certain aspects of assurance against accidental death or personal injury incurred by railway passengers, persons undertaking sea voyages and "professional mariners".

Its early operations were conducted on the first floor of a building at the corner of Queen Victoria Street and Poultry, over the premises of the well-known jewellers, Mappin and Webb. It specialised in what was at that time a novelty to the public and underwriters alike —the sale of tickets insuring against the type of travel risks already mentioned. A problem over the issue of tickets to railway travellers was that of stamp duty. To overcome this the company had to secure a special act of parliament in 1872 providing that, instead of such policies issued by it being subject to stamp duty, five per cent of the premiums it received should be payable to the Inland Revenue authorities. This was a valuable privilege because it would have been impracticable to arrange the sale of tickets to passengers at railway booking offices or newspaper stalls if each ticket had had to be separately stamped.

This act was passed too late in 1872 to benefit the company's premium income for that year, which amounted to less than £2,500. As claims and expenses represented 135 per cent of this sum, the Board had to meet current outgoings from capital. However, the company's fortunes took a turn for the better during 1873 and by the end of that year it was showing signs of developing into a profitable concern. This improvement was due partly to a reduction in working expenses, partly to the fact that the privilege over the issue of insurance tickets at railway stations was now making its effect felt, and partly to a small but useful amalgamation in the preceding year with the Commercial Accident Company.

In 1875 the Board decided that the company's title did not sufficiently indicate the nature of its business and it was changed to that of the Ocean Railway and General Accident Assurance Company Ltd. Two years later it formed an additional business, called the

Ocean and General Guarantee Company Ltd., to undertake fidelity guarantee work. To all intents and purposes this functioned as a new department and was managed in the same offices and by the same directorate and staff.

During 1878 three other small companies—the "Star Accident", "Railway and General Accident" and "Commercial Guarantee"—were taken over. The next few years were a period of steady expansion both on the casualty and fidelity sides, the former receiving a big stimulus in 1881 from the Employers' Liability Act which first imposed on employers in the United Kingdom obligations towards their employees beyond those which already existed at Common Law. The Accident and Guarantee Companies ran side by side until 1890, when they were amalgamated by act of parliament under the title "Ocean Accident and Guarantee Company Ltd.", the word "Corporation" being substituted for "Company" by special resolution in November of the same year.

Meanwhile, there had been an interesting sequel to the concession granted by Parliament to the Ocean in 1872. The weekly newspaper, *Tit-Bits*, had conceived the idea in 1887 of offering payment of £100 to the next-of-kin of any person found killed in a railway accident while carrying a copy of the newspaper. The idea had been prompted by a letter sent to their publishing office from a woman who wrote that she had been left penniless, when her husband had been killed in a railway accident, and that a copy of *Tit-Bits* had been found on his person. When, however, the paper announced its scheme, the Inland Revenue authorities declared that it was illegal for lack of payment of the stamp duties. This placed the proprietors in a most embarrassing position that was fortunately solved by an arrangement under which the Ocean started to underwrite their scheme from their first issue of 1888 and onwards. The privilege of compounding stamp duty was subsequently extended to other publications offering similar coupon schemes to their readers, but by then the Ocean had established a leading position in that field.

By 1893 the growth of the corporation's activities necessitated a new head office and it moved to the site of its present building in Moorgate. Its premium income in the year following this move reached £124,000—more than double that of three years earlier. It now began to extend its policy of expansion through acquisition and it is of some interest to note that in this respect it was already a good deal earlier on the scene in the home country than the Commercial Union, particularly in the accident field. In 1894 it absorbed the Imperial Union and Accident, in 1898 the General Accident and Guarantee and Indemnity, in 1899 the Security, and in 1901 the Employers' Indemnity. The accident and fidelity portfolios of various other offices were also acquired during this period.

These acquisitions greatly strengthened its experience of industrial insurance and enabled it to take the fullest advantage of the results of the first Workmen's Compensation Act after it came into force in 1898 and the vast majority of employers insured themselves against their new liabilities. In that year the Ocean's total premium income reached £718,000, and three years later, in 1901, it passed the £1,000,000 mark. This was at that time a record in the history of British insurance, being the first occasion when an accident business had issued accounts showing a premium income of seven figures.

In 1906 the corporation entered the fire insurance field and in 1907 its premium income from all sources amounted to nearly £1,500,000. When its merger with the Commercial Union was announced in 1910, the *Post Magazine*'s comment on the event was that it " makes it once more evident that in the sphere of insurance amalgamations all things are possible. That our largest Accident Office should be thus prepared to terminate independent existence is only to be explained by the liberality of the terms secured. Far from having fallen on evil days, it is at the height of prosperity— in a position, as its recent report reminded us, to absorb rather than be absorbed ".

Since 1910 the Ocean has retained much of its individuality and, indeed, in the development of casualty business overseas, especially in the United States and Commonwealth countries, has set the pace for the whole Group.

# CHAPTER VII

---

# *Eventful Years Overseas—1900-1914*

I

EXPANSION of the United States economy in the early years of the present century was phenomenal. In industrial output she came to outstrip every other country in the world including the United Kingdom and also Germany, whose growth as an industrial nation was likewise proceeding apace. Disasters and financial panics, including the serious economic crisis of 1907 and 1908, did little more than temporarily impede the river of progress which, like the Mississippi, "just kept on rolling along".

In such conditions insurance business rapidly increased, but the risks encountered on the American continent continued to be great and only a powerful group of companies, such as the Commercial Union was building up in those years, could safely undertake them.

"To go into America and do a large fire business is a very dangerous thing for anybody who has not got a long purse", was the comment of John Trotter when he presented the Group's accounts to the shareholders in 1905.

An early example of these risks had occurred on a day in May of 1901 at the fashionable holiday resort of Jacksonville, Florida. This town was basking in warm sunshine when it was suddenly attacked by fire. Its exact origin was never known, though one theory put forward afterwards was that it started in the works of a fibre company. The fire burnt itself out within four hours, but very little of Jacksonville was left standing by then. All the public buildings, except the offices of the United States Government, were destroyed; the chief shopping quarter of the town and a number of hotels were in ruins. Some 148 blocks of property went up in the flames and the damage amounted to over £1,500,000. About a tenth of this sum was paid up by British underwriters, the share in this of the Commercial Union and its Palatine associate being some £36,000.

Less than two years later the parent company and its associate were involved to the extent of £120,000 in the great "Baltimore Conflagration" over which British offices paid up some £1,150,000 out of total losses exceeding £15,000,000. There was no doubt about the origin of this disaster which broke out on a Sunday morning in February, 1904, in the basement of a wholesale dry goods store in Hanover Street, the centre of the great maritime city's dry goods trade. Within a few minutes the flames in the basement reached a gasoline tank which exploded and set the whole building alight. Huge showers of sparks were hurled into the air and, fanned by a strong westerly wind, descended on two neighbouring chemical works which burst into flames. In about an hour, thirty more buildings in this densely constructed area became involved and the brigades were nearly powerless to stem the fire's advance. Skyscrapers, some of them reaching twenty storeys in height, collapsed, as one report expressed it, "like birdcages in a furnace", and this despite the fact that they were granite constructions built over steel frames.

The high wind continued, driving the fire eastward and causing it to ravage most of the business quarters. Among the buildings totally destroyed were the Calvert Building, the offices of the Equitable Life Assurance Society, the skyscraper of the Continental Trust, the Baltimore and Ohio Railway's station and offices, the Customs' House, the Stock Exchange, the Corn and Flour Exchange, the offices of the Maryland and Southern Chesapeake Railway and of the Pennsylvania Railway, the Postal Telegraph Company's building, and that of the Western Union Telegraph. In addition, almost all of Baltimore's banking offices were destroyed.

Towards the afternoon the flames began to reach the docks and wharfs, but the Harbour Master and his staff managed to remove

H

over a hundred vessels into Chesapeake Bay. The fire brigades of Washington, Philadelphia and New York now began to arrive on the scene, but the heart of the city had already become engulfed and they could not save its leading hotels and the electric light works. On the Monday morning the wind died down, but the fire continued to spread slowly and, refanned by a returning wind later in the day, reached the city's eastern outskirts where it burned through timber yards and factories before it was finally checked.

Seventy blocks, comprising nearly 2,500 buildings, were totally destroyed in this catastrophe, and the only consolation for the citizens of Baltimore was that human casualties were amazingly small.

It was the density of the buildings, and not their individual construction, that was largely responsible for this holocaust, and the lesson learned at Baltimore was the importance of having plenty of wide streets in a large city.

2

This event caused consternation throughout the United States, but it was to fade into insignificance with a disaster two years later which sent a shudder of horror throughout the world. No human forethought could have prevented the fate which overtook San Francisco on April 18th, 1906, when an earthquake, stupendous in its effect, rocked the city to its foundations and was followed almost immediately by a vast conflagration. The San Francisco tragedy has been so frequently retold in print, as well as in radio and film documentaries, that it needs only brief description here. The first of the shocks occurred just after five o'clock in the morning and caused the buildings throughout the business area to collapse. The gas pipes were ripped open in many places and a great volume of gas, escaping into the air, caught fire. Simultaneously, the city's water mains were opened up, depriving the brigades of their requirements to quench the rapidly spreading fires. Other shocks followed, buildings and whole streets crashed downwards into the flames and by the early evening the heart of the city, including almost all its important buildings, lay in a confusion of ruin. It was commonly regarded at the time as the greatest devastation that had visited a city since the burning of Rome in the reign of Nero.

"Nothing, apparently, except Divinity itself, to prevent the conflagration from finally burning to the ocean," wrote George Brooks, who survived the event and was the secretary of the California Insurance Company, later to become a member of the Commercial Union group. "A most sublime tragedy! It meant the impoverishment and lack of homes to thousands; it meant the sweeping away of years of endeavour; it meant beginning again to climb the uphill trail to success; and last but worst, it meant the tremendous death toll either from immediate causes or from after effects. Even today, years after the conflagration, many men and women live in San Francisco in a greater or less degree of ill-health, the seeds of which were planted by the terror and strain which they endured on the morning of that day."

Brooks must have been an extremely able, courageous and high-principled personality. *The Spirit of 1906*, a booklet that he published fifteen years later, is a vivid account of his experiences during the disaster and its aftermath. Of particular interest is his description of the subsequent meeting of representatives of the fire insurance companies, interested in the conflagration, that took place in Reed's Hall, Oakland. The losses involved were so great and in many cases so incalculable that some of the companies advocated an agreement to pay out not more than seventy-five per cent of the claims. Brooks and representatives of other offices, however, pressed their view that "in the last analysis there was no logical, honest argument for the discounting of payments unless it were a case of absolute insolvency with individual companies". Their view prevailed and it was to the credit of many of the companies involved that they decided to pay their clients' claims in full.

"As the days passed and the tumult and shouting died," Brooks goes on to record, "it gave a certain amount of satisfaction to find that amongst the jeerers and sneerers at the memorable Reed's Hall meeting, those who had battled most vigorously for the horizontal cut of twenty-five cents were those who afterwards developed into the worst welshers and shavers in the entire history of the loss settlements of the San Francisco or any other conflagration. The 'sparkling' Rhine, the 'still' Moselle, the far-famed 'Dutchess', the German of Freeport, the Traders of Chicago, the Austrian Phoenix, the Calumet, the American of Boston and others soon after sought the seclusion which a receiver or cessation of business in California grants, and like the Arab, they folded their tents and silently stole away."

The Commercial Union and its associates, the Palatine and Commercial Union of New York, were very heavily involved in the San Francisco losses. Unlike most of the other companies, however, their policies contained conditions excluding liability for losses by fire resulting from earthquake. The Board in London decided to take legal opinion about its position and was advised that the wording of these conditions did not entirely protect their companies. Influenced also by the dictates of humanity and prestige, the directors resolved that generous compromises would have to be made and Roger Owen immediately proceeded to San Francisco to disentangle the mass of claims in that spirit. When all was settled, the Group paid out over £800,000, a sum equal to 34 per cent of the fire premium income for the year, but despite this heavy loss the dividend was maintained at £3 per original share.

The settlements were commendable and prompt, and so, too, were the actions of the Commercial Union's treaty re-insurers—the "Badische" in association with the "King", the "First Bohemian", and the "Nye Danske", who paid in full the large sums which had to be collected from them. In this respect the Group may have been more fortunate than other businesses.

3

In the whole history of fire insurance nothing had hitherto occurred comparable with this catastrophe of 1906. It was estimated that it cost the world's underwriters at least £45,000,000. The repercussions were inevitable; many small companies went to the wall, while others of quite considerable size and standing were so badly hit that they were forced out of independent existence.

On both sides of the Atlantic the Commercial Union Group came to the rescue of the distressed, but reputable, businesses so hit. Before San Francisco the Group in the United States, it will have been noticed, already consisted of the parent company, its English associate, the Palatine, which was already operating in North America before its acquisition, and the Commercial Union of New York which, it may be remembered, had been established in 1895. A small business, the Greenwich of New York, so called from its foundation in Greenwich Village in 1834, had also been purchased after the Baltimore conflagration, which had involved it in losses amounting to some 200,000 dollars. After San Francisco the Group's American operations were still further widened by the acquisition in 1906 of the American of Philadelphia, an old established fire office affected by the disaster and, as we have already seen earlier, the notable acquisition of 1907 in the United Kingdom of the Union which had been involved in losses over the disaster to the extent of over £800,000. The Union had built up wide and substantial fire insurance interests in the United States since 1881 and its reputation and activities there added greatly to the Group's influence and importance.

Six years later, in 1913, came the accession of the California Insurance Company, already referred to. The Commercial Union's associations with the Pacific Coast were of long standing and well established at that time, but the California's were even older and went back to within a decade of the great gold rush, which between 1848 and 1854 had transformed an almost virgin territory, inhabited by only two thousand white men, into a state with a population of 300,000. Founded in 1864, it limited its early activities to marine insurance, but soon launched out into fire underwriting. This second venture was embarked upon with extreme prudence in view of several fires already experienced by San Francisco. An old record of 1866, listing suggestions for local agents, speaks for itself:

"Avoid all unreliable, speculative, careless, shiftless property owners, all litigious and embarrassed applicants; turn a deaf ear also to applications on property vacant or badly managed, or which by the nature of its use becomes a nuisance to the neighbourhood; avoid livery stables where open lights are permitted; refuse all risks not subject to inspection, and special hazards using earth oils for lubricating purposes."

As time went on and the construction of towns in California and elsewhere in the far west improved, the company extended its operations and by 1879 was represented by a hundred and fifty agencies scattered over seven states and territories. In 1905 it was reorganised, George Brooks playing the principal part in this reconstitution and becoming its Secretary and Managing Underwriter. It passed with flying colours through the critical period following the earthquake of 1906. Under the leadership of two of the directors, W. E. Dean and Mark Gerstle, as well as that of Brooks, the stockholders covered the total losses of 1,800,000 dollars by paying in 305 dollars for each share they held in the company. This action created such confidence in the business that it subsequently had no difficulty in raising more capital and resuming progress. When the Commercial Union acquired the California, it was a thriving concern and the Board in London wisely retained the services of its chief executive, George Brooks.

4

The Commercial Union Group was by 1910 one of the most powerful British combinations in the American fire insurance market. Until that year, however, its operations remained confined to this field except on the Pacific Coast where it also dealt in marine underwriting, and at Milwaukee where it dealt with shipping on the Great Lakes through an agency. In that year it extended its marine underwriting operations to New York and other states.

For some time the Board had contemplated the idea of entering the accident field in the United States and in 1908 the Accident Committee had proposed doing so through the purchase of the Casualty Company of America. Nothing seems to have come of this. Entering into the field had its particular problems. Business of this nature had grown to large proportions, more or less contemporaneously with its development in the United Kingdom and covering roughly the same range of transactions. On the other hand American legislation permitted only such companies to practise casualty business—the name under which most accident business was conducted—as those which confined themselves entirely to such work. No fire office, for instance, could under these legal conditions simply add a new department to its organisation to operate in the casualty sphere. For this reason no member of the Commercial Union Group could offer this coverage to its clients except over such items as valuables in transit which fire companies were entitled to insure under what in American underwriting parlance bore, and still bears, the name, strange to British ears, of "dry marine".

Eventually, however, the Group came indirectly into American casualty business through the purchase of the Ocean in 1910. The Ocean, as we have seen, was by that year a British accident business of world-wide reputation and it had also made a particular name for itself in the United States since its arrival in New York in the nineties. Its early operations there were confined to the writing of credit insurance. This was not considered by American underwriters at that time as a promising or profitable field, but the Ocean made an unqualified success of it. Encouraged by this initial effort, the company started to expand into other activities, and by 1898 was transacting all lines of casualty insurance. From then onwards its operations spread to many parts of the country and it was a power in the land, with a large office in the heart of the downtown insurance district of New York, when it became associated with the Commercial Union in 1910.

By 1914 the Group's interests in the United States had, through the developments described in this chapter, come to comprise fire, accident and marine underwriting. And the size of its business there can be measured by its net premium income from its two largest lines in that year—4,563,068 dollars in casualty business through the Ocean and 1,107,000 dollars in fire insurance.

5

When Roger Owen returned from a visit to North America in 1903, he reported that the prospects of business in Canada "appear to be more hopeful and the conditions more favourable than they have been for many years". Some serious fire losses in 1900 and 1901 had brought about a satisfactory co-operation among the various larger offices in regard to raising rates, which for many years had been dangerously low. In Montreal the Commercial Union was transacting a fair share of business and in Toronto its activities were increasing. Of Winnipeg, Owen wrote that "the conflagration hazard in the business portions has largely disappeared through the erection of first class massive buildings in place of timber buildings. Winnipeg has undergone great changes and the surrounding country has been largely developed in recent years ". Manitoba and the west were emerging from the days of pioneering and the progress of insurance business in that area is revealed by the fact that the Winnipeg branch had established forty agencies within two years.

The Group's activities in Canada had also become augmented through its acquisition at home of the Palatine. This acquisition, moreover, had brought the Group into accident business in the Dominion since the Palatine owned the Canada Accident and Fire Assurance Company established in 1887. Though a small business at the time, the Canadian subsidiary had good connections and was to make gradual, but steady progress in the years before the First World War.

Only a few of the fires referred to by Owen had been individually serious and even the worst, that at Ottawa in 1900, had scarcely been a major disaster. This fire started in Hull, a French Canadian town consisting almost entirely of wooden buildings on the opposite side of the Ottawa River. A high wind drove the burning embers of the buildings across the river's narrowest stretch and did some considerable damage to the Canadian capital. The British offices were involved to the extent of over £400,000, of which the Commercial Union's share was only some £13,000. Rumour had it that the fire was started by a Fenian organisation, but Lord Strathcona, the Governor-General, stated that in his opinion it was due to some private incendiaries actuated merely by mercenary designs against insurance companies.

The only other fire of comparable size was one that occurred in Montreal the next year. This burned the Board of Trade Office to the ground and cost the Commercial Union £10,000. However, a few months after Owen's visit, Canada was treated to a really spectacular conflagration when the heart of the business quarter of Toronto was attacked at eight o'clock on the evening of April 19th, 1904. Believed to have started in a large soap factory through some defect in its electrical installation, it raged throughout the night. There was, as so frequently happens in North American conflagrations, a strong wind blowing, while a further misfortune was a shortage of water to feed the fire engines. The flames thus became unmanageable and made their way among the warehouses. Here dynamite was used to block the fire's progress, but it continued to spread, engulfing an ammunition and small arms factory which blew up. Not till seven o'clock the next morning, when the wind changed direction, was its path arrested, by which time three and a half blocks, comprising about 120 buildings, were completely destroyed. The surprising feature of this event was that no lives were lost despite damage amounting to about £1,500,000. The Commercial Union's losses, estimated at £40,000, were slight as compared with those of some other companies.

In that year of 1904 the combined net premium income of the Commercial Union and Palatine in Canada amounted to just over £72,000. This was at least an improvement over results at the turn of the century, but greater progress was still to come. The Union added largely to the volume of the Group's Canadian fire business from 1907 upwards and also brought with it the North West Fire Insurance Company of Winnipeg. In 1911 the Palatine launched out into the fire market on a larger scale. In 1912 the Commercial Union established a branch for the first time on Canada's Pacific Coast at Vancouver and also accelerated its business in the Atlantic maritime provinces. In the same year the North West Fire Insurance Company's field of activity was extended.

These developments quickly showed their effects. A highly successful year in 1913 was succeeded by an even more successful one in 1914, as the Canadian results from the three principal companies showed. Within the ten years from 1904 to 1914 the group's turnover in its Canadian fire activities had almost quadrupled itself, while in the accident field the Canada Accident's net premium income had also risen considerably. Roger Owen's predictions in 1903 had been amply fulfilled.

6

With the creation of the Commonwealth of Australia in 1900, the separate colonies became states knit together under a federal government, but each maintaining a large degree of independence in the government of its own internal affairs. However, the Commercial

Union continued to control its Australian interests in the same way as hitherto, the branches in each state dealing direct with Cornhill. And when St. John Welch, manager for New South Wales, succeeded Jarrett on his retirement that year, he succeeded him nominally as manager for Victoria and not for Australia. Jarrett's position had, however, been that of "*primus inter pares*" among the Australian branch managers and his mantle seems to have fallen on Welch. But despite Federation no centralisation of the company's affairs in Australia was to be adopted until 1928, by which time the improvement of communications and transport in the sub-continent and the increasing complexity of the Group's affairs there was to bring about the establishment of a controlling office in Melbourne.

Meanwhile New South Wales, Victoria, South Australia and West Australia had their own local boards of directors as well as branches. Affairs in Queensland were run by a local secretary, and in Tasmania by agencies at Launceston and Hobart. This was the organisation that existed when Morant visited Australia in 1900. He was favourably impressed by the progress that he found everywhere—as well he might have been for the net premium results of that year in fire insurance alone were to total nearly £70,000, to which the Palatine added another several thousand. From then onwards the progress continued almost uninterruptedly and received a further impetus from the accession of the Union in 1907. By 1914 the net premium fire income resulting from the Australian activities of the Commercial Union, the Union and the Palatine exceeded £150,000.

There is an interesting reference in the minutes of the Accident Committee which shows that as early as 1903 the Commercial Union started workmen's compensation in Australia. This approves an annual arrangement being entered into by its branch in West Australia with the Amalgamated Workers Coast Association of Perth. Besides covering ordinary compensation for accidents to its members the arrangement made provision for payment of £10 to each member on death from natural causes. Another reference in the Accident Committee's minutes shows that in 1907 the income from the accident activities of the Commercial Union and Palatine in Australia exceeded £33,000. This may seem a very small sum today, but it represented some four-fifths of the entire overseas accident business of the two companies that year.

It was a different tale of events in New Zealand. Here competition was extremely strong, and especially so after the government invaded the fire and accident fields in 1905, establishing the New Zealand State Fire and Accident Insurance Office. The Commercial Union's progress was arrested after this; in fact its fire transactions were running at a slight loss between 1907 and 1912. And the Union which started to underwrite New Zealand fire risks in 1908, employing the New Zealand Loan and Mercantile agency for this purpose, did little better.

It has been mentioned earlier that the war in South Africa had no serious effect on the Commercial Union's income from the colony. What business it lost in those areas involved in the campaign was more than counter-balanced by an increase of activity in the Cape. This resulted from its purchase in 1899 of the Colonial Assurance of Cape Town and of the local interests of the "Transatlantic" of Hamburg. The Colonial Assurance was a small concern, but had a good reputation. Its acquisition also provided the company with a local board of directors, consisting of well-known business men, and with premises of its own; and Cape Town became once more the Commercial Union's headquarters for South Africa.

After the war, however, the prospects opened up in the Cape failed to materialise. In 1904 business there resulted in a loss and it was only in the years immediately preceding the First World War that the Commercial Union began to show some moderate success despite increasing competition from non-tariff companies. At Port Elizabeth, however, a steadier rate of progress was maintained. In Natal and the Transvaal, too, business soon started to improve after the end of hostilities; and branches were opened in Durban and Johannesburg in 1906.

It was in the Transvaal also that the affairs of the Union prospered. Since 1898 it had been operating there through an agency, but in 1911 it transferred its main branch for South Africa from Cape Town to Johannesburg. As the centre of the Rand gold mining industry Johannesburg was now a great cosmopolitan city and the second largest in the Union of South Africa, while its neighbouring city, Pretoria, had become the seat of executive government of the Union when this was brought into being the previous year. In 1914 the company further extended its activities in the Transvaal through signing an important reinsurance treaty with the African Guarantee and Indemnity Company. Meanwhile, the Commercial Union had for the first time entered Southern Rhodesia, establishing a branch at Bulawayo in 1912.

In India and the Far East the Commercial Union made good headway in fire insurance underwriting despite increasing competition both from local companies and from European offices which were now pressing forward in the wake of the British pioneers. The value of possessing branches in Asia was exemplified in this steady progress, a new branch covering Japan being opened in Yokohama in 1901 and a new branch being established at Shanghai in 1908.

Elsewhere—in Central and South America and the West Indies—the Group improved its position despite various setbacks including the temporary suspension of business in Brazil and Peru during 1902 and 1903 due to hostile legislation against European offices, the revolution in Mexico in 1913, and a number of fires and earthquakes. From most of the latter events the Commercial Union companies escaped with moderate losses, but the Palatine's Jamaican agency was involved in the earthquake and fire which destroyed nearly the whole of the business quarter of Kingston on January 4th, 1906. The earthquake shook nearly every part of the town and neighbourhood, but its worst damage was along the harbour front where it razed three streets to the ground. Fire immediately broke out in these ruins and spread inland, the brigade being unable to control it as the water mains had been disrupted. Wharfs, warehouses, the Military Hospital, the Myrtle Bank Hotel, the Colonial Bank and the Savings Bank, the Supreme Court, the Jamaica Club, the Customs House, the railway terminus, several churches and all but one of the newspaper offices, were gutted. Worse still, over one thousand persons perished in this disaster. The total damage was estimated at £1,500,000, and the Palatine's share was just over £30,000.

7

As in the nineties, Europe continued to be the Commercial Union's second most important customer after the United States. The concentration was on fire business, and only a negligible extension even into the accident business on the continent was made after the establishment of its accident department in 1900.

The trend of its policy over fire underwriting became more actively concerned with direct business wherever opportunities were available and could be profitably exploited. Germany, with its well established branch in Berlin, continued to lead the field in this direction and right up to the outbreak of war in 1914 provided by far the largest profits of all the European countries. In 1903 the Haine, Morant and Moreau office in Paris was reconstituted as a general agency for direct French business and various sub-agencies were opened in the leading French commercial centres. This French agency was so energetically managed that business in France rapidly came to take second place after Germany. Due very largely to developments in Germany and France the income of the Commercial Union and its Palatine subsidiary rose from just over £90,000 in 1904 to nearly £200,000 in 1906.

Meanwhile the Union, acting through its independent agencies after its acquisition, was also making rapid headway in the fire field on the continent. Its net premium income in 1913 from that quarter amounted to nearly £114,000. The Commercial Union's exceeded £230,000 and the Palatine's £53,000. Thus their total net fire income from Europe in the year before the war broke out approached £400,000—a figure twenty times that recorded by the Commercial Union at the turn of the century.

8

We have seen in this and earlier chapters how the Commercial Union and its growing number of subsidiary companies were spreading their wings overseas. The great volume of their business, as we have also seen, was obtained from fire underwriting, and to a smaller extent from marine and life. Accident insurance overseas remained negligible for a whole decade after the Commercial Union had started its Accident Department in the United Kingdom at the turn of the century. However, from 1910 onwards this gap in the Group's foreign transactions was amply filled as the result of the acquisition of the Ocean.

The Ocean's acquisition brought the Group into global accident business in a very big way indeed, as will have been already noticed from the account of its activities in the United States. Though the bulk of its overseas income came from there, it was also well established in all the English-speaking Dominions by 1910. In Canada it had opened a branch in 1902 after earlier associations through an agency. In Australia it had a branch at Sydney. In New Zealand it had started operations as far back as 1899 and shared with the New Zealand Accident the prestige of a pioneer in introducing accident insurance into the life of the colony at that time. In South Africa it had operated a branch since 1902. Its contacts with Europe were on a smaller scale except with Holland, where for two years it had been doing a profitable amount of accident business through a branch.

The Ocean's impact on the Group's overseas activities was far-reaching. It is quite evident that it was given its head by the Board of the Commercial Union and, in fact, encouraged to act as a spearhead in exploiting the world's accident markets. In this sphere its net premium income rose from a round £900,000 in 1910 to a round £1,200,000 in 1914. The rest of the Group in 1914 netted a mere £180,000 from foreign accident business, but on the other hand harvested nearly £2,800,000 from fire transactions as against some £20,000 earned by the Ocean. These figures show an interesting and significant realignment of the Group's influence and prestige in world insurance during the years that immediately preceded the First World War.

# CHAPTER VIII

## On Land and Water

### I

A COMPOSITE insurance business touches life at so many angles that some account of affairs and incidents not directly concerned with its development, but nevertheless important and interesting from a human point of view, merit a place in its history.

Not many insurance companies, for instance, have assumed the responsibilities of administering a charity or endowment trust. But in 1912 the Board of the Commercial Union accepted a request to do so and subsequently performed a notable work, in an honorary capacity, for education, medicine and other causes over a period of forty-five years.

It came about in this fashion. During a long and active life an enterprising Scotsman, Sir William Dunn, amassed a considerable fortune in the development of South Africa, founding and controlling as its senior partner the merchant banking firm of William Dunn & Company of London with subsidiary firms in the Union itself. He also became a director of the Royal Exchange Assurance and the Union Discount Company, while his interest in public affairs brought him into the House of Commons in 1891 where he sat as a Liberal, representing his native city of Paisley, until 1906. While a young man in South Africa he had met and married his wife. There were, however, no children of the marriage and, when he died at the age of eighty-nine in 1912, there were no direct heirs to the baronetcy, which had been conferred on him, nor to his fortune.

Under these circumstances it was not altogether surprising that disputes and difficulties, referred to later, arose over Dunn's will which was proved for £1,137,429. It was also not surprising that his partners, James and William McFarlane, whom he had appointed as his executors and trustees, faced with their invidious and disagreeable task, decided that discretion was the better part of valour and asked their late chief's solicitor, Sir John Hollams, if he could arrange to release them from it.

It so happened that Sir John Hollams had also for many years been legal adviser to the Commercial Union. He still held that appointment and was greatly respected and liked by its directors, so much so that when he suggested to them that their company should administer the Dunn estate not as a matter of business, but as a public responsibility, they agreed to do so.

To set about this task the directors appointed a committee consisting of Sir Jeremiah Colman as chairman, J. Carr Saunders, who will be remembered as the company's first marine underwriter until he joined the Board in 1897, and Charles Gurney Hoare, another director and a member of the well-known banking family. (Two further directors were added to the committee in 1916—C. D. Seligman and Sir Edward Hope.) The testator had left instructions in his will that the residue of his estate after payments to his family was to be used—" To advance the cause of Christianity, to benefit children and young people, to support hospitals, and alleviate human suffering, to encourage education, and promote emigration." But before they could reach this interesting stage of their work the committee had to clear up a number of specific legacies to charity enumerated in the will as well as the matter of the family legacies and, in particular, a claim for a very substantial sum by Lady Dunn. This was based on the suggestion that at the time of their marriage Sir William had said that he could look after her money better than she was able to do and that, as a consequence, she had put it in his care. For some years a ledger account of his transactions on her behalf was kept, but unfortunately subsequent records had ceased. The committee accepted her claim and the court ruled accordingly.

When this and other claims had been settled, Sir Jeremiah and his colleagues were left with a residue of £665,526 for distribution to the type of causes which Dunn had specified. But this was not the end of their troubles. An anonymous writer stated that under a clause of the will the trustees were prohibited from giving support to any cause to which Dunn had not contributed in his lifetime. The Charity Commissioners also received objections from the same source and referred them to the committee who took the matter to court for an interpretation which, to the satisfaction both of the committee and the commissioners, went against the objection.

The trustees were now free to consider and make their endowments, and some of them merit special mention here for their important effects on universities, medical schools and hospitals. Of these the first and most ambitious was the building and equipment of the School of Biology at Cambridge which cost £210,000. This project originated in a conference arranged by Lord Knutsford between the committee and representatives of the academic and medical professions including Sir Walter Morley Fletcher, then Secretary of the Medical Research Council. It was the committee's choice out of four schemes subsequently prepared by Fletcher and endorsed by his council, and it was a choice largely inspired by the personality at the head of the school as it then existed—Sir F. Gowland Hopkins.

To carry through the scheme, which included endowments of a Professorship and Readership and a new building equipped with the most modern apparatus and instruments, a special committee was set up under the chairmanship of Sir Jeremiah Colman. This was a rare combination of finance and learning. The Commercial Union's members were C. D. Seligman, the Hon. A. M. Holland-Hibbert and Sir James Leigh Wood. The university authorities were represented by Professor Hopkins, Sir Hugh Anderson, Master of Caius College, and McLeod Innes, the Bursar of Trinity College. Sir Walter Morley Fletcher represented the Medical Research Council and Sir William Hardy the Royal Society.

"A confiding friend told me that I did not know what I had let myself in for," Colman wrote in later years. "It was suggested that the outlooks of shrewd business men and of University Professors were in such wide contrast that they could not be brought into harmony and that discussions and arguments would be interminable. . . .

I

The result entirely falsified the prediction, as never in a long and varied experience have I presided over a committee which has given comparatively so little trouble, and where business has been conducted so easily, harmoniously and efficiently."

The handing over of the School was accomplished with appropriate ceremonial. A banquet was given to the trustees in the hall of Trinity College. Its Master, Sir Joseph Thomson, presided, and was supported by the University's Chancellor, Lord Balfour. The lights of the hall shone down on one of the most representative gatherings of professors of medical schools, bio-chemists and other eminent scientists ever gathered together under one roof.

This event was not lost on Oxford ears, but the authorities of the sister university were diffident and uncertain about the best way of approaching the Dunn Trustees. Colman first heard about this from his friend, H. D. G. Leveson-Gower, the famous cricketer. Sometime later, when he was breakfasting at the Reform Club, a friend of his remarked,

" The Oxford people want to know how they can 'get at' the Dunn Trustees. They have the names of the Committee, but find them such a horrid lot of Cambridge men that they doubt Oxford having a look in."

"Each case stands on its merits," Colman replied. "If Oxford have a case, they are likely to get help. The best way will be for the Chancellor to meet me for a preliminary talk."

This duly took place and was followed by a conference between Oxford's leading scientists and the trustees at the Commercial Union's Head Office. The eventual result of this was the foundation, at a cost of £105,000, of the present Schools of Pathology and Pharmacology at Oxford.

It so happened that in the twenties Lord Balfour was elected Chancellor of Edinburgh University and it was not long before the trustees received a letter from him intimating that "Dunn was a Scotsman and you should do something for Edinburgh". The Edinburgh Medical School was out-of-date and needed remodelling. At first the trustees were reluctant to help, as the various sections of the School were working in insufficient harmony. But they were persuaded to come together and present a comprehensive scheme entailing an outlay of £60,000. With this report before them in 1929 the trustees promised £20,000 as an initial grant. The Rockefeller Trustees followed with a grant of £35,000, and with another £5,000 in sight, the School was completely reorganised.

Other important endowments followed—a Lectureship of Pathology at Guy's Hospital, new laboratories at the London Hospital, St. Thomas's and St. Bartholomew's, and the provision of new science schools at Christ's Hospital, better known as the Blue Coat School. Before the trust was finally wound up in 1957 several hundreds of smaller charities had benefited from it.

In the administration of the Dunn Trust the Commercial Union's directors gave their services voluntarily and without fees, while the fees charged by the company were purely nominal, amounting to a minute fraction of the value of the estate. Perhaps it should also be mentioned that from its quite early years the company itself had been in the habit of supporting good causes of one kind or another. Its experience over disbursements from the Dunn Trust, however, was to prove extremely valuable in regard to its own and those of its Group's benefactions at home and abroad which across the years have amounted to many thousands of pounds.

2

Events at sea have so far not figured conspicuously in our narrative. Though brilliantly managed by Carr Saunders in the nineteenth century, the Marine Department's activities were much smaller than those of the Life and Fire Departments. Of all fields of insurance the underwriting of ships and their cargoes is much the riskiest and requires of its operators a kind of second sense only gained through years of experience. Water is a more unpredictable element even than fire, and the sea, as Joseph Conrad wrote, " plays with men till their hearts are broken, and wears stout ships to death. Nothing can touch the brooding bitterness of its soul. Open to all and faithful to none, it exercises its fascination for the undoing of the best."

To his own particular professional aptitude a marine underwriter must also add a long purse if he is to conduct anything in the nature of large scale operations. This explains the extreme care shown firstly by Carr Saunders and subsequently by his successor, Richard Jones, to avoid heavy risks and maintain their department's work on sound rather than spectacular lines until it was in a position to launch out in a larger way. Thus at the turn of the century it was doing no more business than it had conducted twenty-five years earlier. All this time, however, it had been building up its fund and by the end of 1900 this exceeded £600,000.

It was now possible to extend operations and, with the prestige of increasing financial strength, to take a lead in the underwriting of marine risks. Other factors, too, were exerting their influence. The days of the sailing ships were coming to a close and between 1900 and 1914 the size of steamers, and especially ocean-going passenger liners, was steadily growing. Moreover, the gradual increase of the world's mercantile fleets was to receive additional momentum from the great growth in international trade that took place between 1909 and the outbreak of the First World War.

All this entailed underwriting on a grander scale than anything known in the preceding century and the Commercial Union was ready to accept such responsibilities. The risks of underwriting these larger hulls and their larger cargoes emerge with vivid clarity from the casualty books of the period. The entries of losses are brief and laconic; the human story must be read between the lines. To illustrate this a few examples will serve our purpose.

There was, for instance, the loss of the *Tantallon Castle*, a Union Castle ship of some 3,000 tons, which on a voyage from Southampton to South Africa, ran ashore on May 9th, 1901, at Robben Island near Cape Town during a fog. She had on board some 160 passengers, including the new Governor of Natal. No lives were lost, but she became a total wreck, and the Commercial Union incurred a small loss on the hull and a much larger one on her general cargo.

Strandings and founderings continue to be recorded, none of them dramatic or sensational until March, 1907, when the *Suevic*, a White Star liner of 12,500 tons, on a voyage from Australia to London, ran aground off the Lizard on Stag Rock. She was a fine ship, built seven years earlier, and as she lay near the treacherous Cornish coast, beaten by heavy seas until she broke in two, she became front-page news in the press. But there was a happy ending to this event. The crew and the passengers were safely landed, and the stern portion of the ship was eventually refloated and towed into Southampton, where a new bow was added and whence the *Suevic* took to sea again. However, nearly the whole of her cargo—wool, wheat, butter and other produce—disappeared in the wreck and involved the Commercial Union in a considerable loss.

*Waratah,* "sighted on July 27th, since when not heard of", is a name that occurs in the company's casualty records of 1909. This was among the most insoluble sea disasters of the present century. Speculation about her fate went on for weeks, but by the autumn all hope was given up. A new Lund liner of some 6,000 tons, she had put into Port Natal on a voyage from Sydney to London. Thence she had sailed for her next port, Cape Town, on July 26th, carrying a crew of 119 and 92 passengers. Heading into the Indian Ocean, she disappeared without trace. The question mark about her fate was never answered. The company's net loss on the ship and her general cargo, however, came to only a few thousand pounds.

Twin-screw liners were now coming to the fore. Of these the *Pericles,* of 10,900 tons, was a notable example. Launched in 1908, she belonged to the Aberdeen Line, and *The Times* described her as the "finest vessel of a fine fleet" when disaster overtook her in 1910. She was on her way between Melbourne and Fremantle. The weather was fair as she rounded Cape Leeuwin at a respectful distance of three miles. But she suddenly struck a submerged rock, started to founder and finally sank head down. The Commercial Union insured her hull and her cargo, which included large consignments of apples, butter and carcases of mutton. Of the total sum involved the company met over half the loss after the reinsurance claims had been settled. The miracle of this disaster was that all the 296 passengers and the 164 members of the crew were rescued from the ship before she took her downward plunge.

Turning over the pages we come to a year to remember—1912. Outside the periods of war it was one of the most disastrous years in the annals of British shipping. On March 18th the *Oceana,* a Maclay and McIntyre ship of nearly 5,000 tons, collided with a German barque, the *Pisagua,* about four miles west of Beachy Head while going down channel, bound from London to Bombay. She became partially submerged, but so quickly that ten of her crew and seven passengers perished. The *Oceana* was carrying specie, both gold and silver, as well as ivory and cotton. Fortunately for the Commercial Union some very successful salvaging by divers recovered most of this valuable cargo and, when the wreck was finally abandoned, the company's loss on this was negligible. But as underwriter of the hull it had to pay out £45,000—almost certainly the highest figure it had hitherto incurred in its marine activities.

Within a month a far greater loss and a far greater human tragedy was to occur. On the night of April 15th the White Star *Titanic* hit an ice-berg on her first voyage to New York and sank with a loss of 825 passengers and 673 members of her crew. The details of this catastrophe have been so fully retold in recent years that they need no description here. But it staggered the British public, which had been led to believe that this, the largest vessel in the world, with her 46,382 tonnage, was virtually indestructible. The owners themselves had so much confidence in her design, with its latest type of water-tight bulk-heads, that they had not insured her for her full value which was estimated at £1,750,000. Even so the gloom at Lloyd's and among London insurers generally was profound, for a loss of some £1,000,000 was involved which, as *The Times* put it, was "the heaviest individual loss that has ever befallen underwriters".

The Commercial Union was as heavily hit as any. Its share of the claim amounted to £145,723, of which £60,723 was for losses on registered mail posted from London, Hamburg and Paris.

Further heavy losses followed quickly in the wake of the *Titanic* disaster. In June the Cunard liner, *Carmania*, foundered, with a net loss on hull and cargo to the company of £27,000, and the United States warship, the *Arkansas*, was destroyed by fire while still on her building stocks—a net loss of nearly £60,000. A number of minor casualties occurred in subsequent months, culminating in November with the stranding of the *Marienbad*, and the collision of two new ships, commissioned by the Canadian Pacific, the *Empress of Asia* and *Empress of Russia*, during a gale which struck the Fairfield Yard on the Clyde.

The Marine Committee and Richard Jones must frequently have spent anxious, if not despairing moments, during that year of 1912. And yet, when Charles Gurney Noble reviewed the Commercial Union's activities at the next meeting of the shareholders, he could inform them that "the Marine Department was able to show the substantial surplus of £91,000 upon the year's working, which under the circumstances must be considered quite satisfactory".

The astonishing fact remains that by and large 1912 turned out to be an excellent year for Lloyd's and the marine insurance market generally. And though this may be partly accounted for by the upward surge of international commerce, a good deal of credit should be accorded to sound judgment and some to sheer good luck. The Marine Department of the Commercial Union might well have regarded 1912 as an *annus mirabilis*.

We must now turn back the pages of the casualty books to 1904 and 1905 and glance for a moment at the effects of the Russo-Japanese War on the interests of international shipping. Nothing had hitherto compared with the sea battles of that war, in which mine-laying and torpedoes played a large part for the first time. Nor had neutral countries imagined for a moment that their ships, if carrying non-contraband cargoes, would be interfered with on the high seas.

The first casualty, with which the Commercial Union became concerned, was the *Knight Commander*, an American vessel on a voyage to China and Japan. She was sunk off the Japanese coast on July 24th, 1904, by Russia's Vladivostok Squadron "on the pretext that she was carrying contraband cargo". The pretext was invalid and the company made a settlement with her owners.

In the following August Russia's Port Arthur squadron was brought to action by Admiral Togo and defeated, its remnants retreating into the port, and a few days later Admiral Kaimura's squadrons disposed of the Vladivostok Squadron under Admiral Jessen. From then onwards the Russian flag disappeared from the Pacific and the Japanese took their turn at playing havoc with neutral shipping. In one month alone, January, 1905, they captured five ships of various nationalities bound for Vladivostok and insured by the Commercial Union, and there could be little doubt about the fate of another vessel, the *Claverdale*, which set sail the previous autumn from Hong Kong to Vladivostok and was never heard of again.

At this distance of time the fate of the *Princesse Marie*, a steamer bound from Europe to Japan, is something of a mystery. Insured for "ship and war risk only" she is reported in the Marine Department's casualty books as having been "sunk on June 22nd in the China Sea by the Russian auxiliary cruiser, *Tersk*". As Russia's Baltic Fleet (sailing round the world to take the place of her Pacific squadrons reduced to impotency by the Japanese the previous summer), had been almost entirely destroyed in the Straits of Tsushima on May 27th, one can only conclude that the *Tersk* was a lone wolf seeking what prey she could devour.

Even before the Russo-Japanese War there had been uneasiness at Lloyd's and in marine insurance circles about covering war risks at sea, and the British Government had appointed a committee, known as the Austen Chamberlain Committee, to consider whether merchants and shipowners had found it difficult to cover such risks in the past and whether such difficulties would occur in the future. The Committee had reported that private enterprise could be relied on to carry the burden without government help. But after their experiences in the Russo-Japanese War and with one eye on the rapidly growing German Navy, marine underwriters became strongly opposed to the ideas formed as a result of the Austen Chamberlain enquiry. The Agadir crisis brought these matters to a head and in 1913 the Government appointed the Huth Jackson Committee to reconsider the problem. This body reversed the decision of its predecessor and its findings, as will be seen later, were to have some astonishing results in the First World War.

3

One further aspect of the Commercial Union's marine activities during the early years of the present century deserves a brief reference here before we pass on to other affairs. This was the very considerable part which it was then playing in the underwriting of ships on the Great Lakes and also in the St. Lawrence River Canals system which was completed in 1901. These operations were conducted through an American agency, David Vance and Co., at Milwaukee. Casualties were frequent, but the rates were high. And activity was intense and rewarding for, though the great period of timber transport on the Lakes was now ended, coal, limestone, iron ore and grain were being carried in the holds of the numerous "lakers" and "canallers".

Typical of accidents on the Great Lakes are these random extracts from the casualty records of the Marine Department during these years—"The *Sagamore* (lake barge) run into and sunk off Point Iroquois, Lake Superior"; "*Mark Hopkins*, steamer, wrecked near Long Point, Lake Erie"; "*Waverley*, sunk by collision with the *Turret Crown* off Sand Rock, Lake Huron"; "*A. A. Parker*, foundered during gale in Lake Superior".

In the water-ways connecting the Lakes or leading into them from the St. Lawrence the principal risk was grounding in shallow water or collision in fog. On the Lakes themselves—a vast area of water covering 95,000 square miles and lying on an exposed plateau in the heart of the North American continent—the perils were infinitely greater and more varied. In those years the navigational aids, ice-breaking services, and meteorological forecasts of the present time were in their infancy, and even the larger and safer craft of a later age are not immune to the unusual risks encountered on these inland waters.

From the end of November to mid-April the Great Lakes become unnavigable owing to ice, but masters were apt to risk a last moment dash in late November and be marooned throughout the winter. Fogs often descended on the Lakes even in summertime and it was these that caused many collisions. But most to be feared were the storms—those violent, sudden tempests arising from the clash of cold polar air with the warmer and moister breezes from sub-tropical Florida and Texas. An effective system of weather reporting has since reduced these dangers, but in 1913 the Commercial Union was involved along with other underwriters in a disaster resulting from a storm which swept the Lakes for sixteen hours on end, its velocity, exceeding sixty miles an hour, lashing their surface into waves thirty-five feet high. Ten ships disappeared in that catastrophe without leaving a trace, many more were forced ashore, and 235 lives were lost in three days.

Despite events of this kind and the frequency of smaller accidents the establishment of the Milwaukee agency was a venture that justified itself over the years, and almost certainly laid the foundations of the prominent position which the Commercial Union has ever since occupied in the underwriting of ships on the Great Lakes.

4

This chapter brings to an end the story of the Commercial Union's experiences, and its first stage of expansion into a Group of companies, between the end of the Victorian era and the convulsion of 1914 which was to change the whole existing order of social and economic life. How it was to fare onward through the First World War and into the new era that succeeded it must be left to later pages. But here we may take leave of it in 1914 by recording that it already ranked with its associated interests as one of the largest British insurance businesses. A leading article in the *Post Magazine* of May, 1914, paid tribute to "the energy and ability characterising the fifty-odd years of marvellous activity which have placed the company upon the summit of the fame it now occupies. An annual premium income from all sources now rapidly approaching £7¾ millions, an interest income exceeding £¾ of a million, and assets of approximately 25 million sterling, marked the close of the fifty-second year of this gigantic undertaking".

PART THREE

# The First World War
# and its Aftermath

## 1914-1929

# CHAPTER IX

# Uncharted Passage to Success—1914-1918

I

THE mood in which the British nation went to war in the summer of 1914 was a strange blend of patriotism, self-assurance, romantic excitement and all-pervading naïvety never to be repeated. "Now, God be thanked Who has matched us with His hour", wrote Rupert Brooke, and in this one line alone captured the innocent ardour of those early months of war. Even after the retreat from Mons the spirit of optimism remained unquenched, and there was a general belief that the war would be over and won by Christmas. Meanwhile, the watch-word was "Business as usual".

This was the mood of the public. It was also shared by many leading manufacturers, even including that genius of industry, the first Lord Leverhulme, who remarked that "war was only a passing phase of business life". But the mood was not reflected in the City, where business was very far from usual and the problems of financial and commercial houses conducting world-wide activities grew relentlessly from the first day. Like other large-scale British insurance businesses, the Commercial Union and its Group immediately lost direct links with their branches and agencies in Germany, Austro-Hungary and the Ottoman Empire. As the war proceeded, the German invasions of Belgium, north-east France and, later, Rumania, deprived them of other links. Losses thereby incurred were considerable, though not disastrous, as we shall see. But the problems of "trading with the enemy", as we shall also see, became intricate and bewildering. Added to these problems were the difficulties of communication with Russia and the final eclipse of business there after the revolution in 1917. Then there were the losses on exchange rates resulting from the issue of paper currencies in allied and neutral countries.

Another unexpected complication was a form of economic warfare between enemy and British insurance offices in neutral countries. This was experienced more seriously than anywhere else in those countries whose populations included large elements of Germanic stock and, consequently, Germanic business elements, such as South America and the United States. In South America attempts to damage British insurance interests continued throughout the war. In the Argentine, for instance, the German Banks in 1915 created for this end a special insurance company. The Banco Germanico de la America del Sud, an affiliation of the Deutsche Bank, took a leading part in its formation, and with the support of the most influential members of the German colony raised a capital of $2,000,000. In the United States enemy attempts to damage our interests automatically ceased when America entered the war in 1917. The importance of this event to the Commercial Union and other British insurance companies can be gauged from evidence given by Roger Owen before a Board of Trade committee some months earlier. Supporting his evidence, Owen provided some interesting estimates of the relative amounts of business being transacted at that time by foreign insurance companies in the United States. Though the British companies, twenty-three in number, did 51 per cent of the total, the share taken by their enemy competitors was also considerable, Germany with ten companies absorbing 18 per cent, Bulgaria with two companies and Austria with one taking another 4 per cent between them. America's entry into the war removed this competition and left open this section of the field, in part of which the Commercial Union and other British companies then came to take their share.

We must now return to 1914 and the matter of "trading with the enemy". This presented anomalies which the British government did not appear to have anticipated. Direct trading with the enemy was forbidden by a series of Royal Proclamations, each making modifications to its predecessor, in the summer and autumn. But the door was left open through neutral Holland for communications between Britain and Germany and certain forms of indirect trading through that door were permitted under the sanction of the Board of Trade.

The interests of the Commercial Union Group in Germany were more considerable than in any other European country. The parent company was principally concerned with extensive fire insurance activities conducted through its branch in Berlin under the able and energetic management of Theodor Zahn. But this branch was also used for the control of various agencies in a number of large cities employed over the running off of policies of the Union Life Fund, the claims on which by German citizens through death, and through requests for loans and surrenders, were still frequent. How to honour these varied commitments in an enemy country was the ironically moral problem that confronted the Board and management at Cornhill when Zahn sent a telegram in August, through the Commercial Union's agents in Amsterdam, requesting a remittance of 500,000 marks to cover outstanding claims on the Commercial Union's fire policies and the Union Life Fund. After lengthy consultations with the Board of Trade the management secured agreement to pay these German debts, a proviso being that, so far as the Union Life Fund was concerned, the money was only to be spent on claims through death.

A further Royal Proclamation, issued in October, put an end to any more transactions of this kind. And when shortly afterwards the Dutch agents passed on a message from Zahn that, acting under the authority of the German government, he was preparing to arrange a provisional sale of the Commercial Union's Berlin business to the Frankfurter (the Frankfurt Insurance Company), the Board could do no more than authorise a vague reply to Amsterdam, saying that it could take no action in the matter. The take-over took place, but there was an interesting post-war sequel to it, as will be seen in a later chapter.

In contrast with this affair was the Union's relationship with its subsidiary, the Aachen-Leipziger. Unlike the Berlin branch the Aachen-Leipziger was a duly constituted Germany company, even though the Union owned 1,937 of its 2,000 shares. The German government interned its English manager, F. W. Penney, and appointed a supervisor to control its operations shortly after the declaration of war. But a most astonishing state of affairs ensued, for the parent company with the sanction of the Board of Trade continued to correspond with its German subsidiary on matters of business through its Dutch agents. This arrangement continued for nearly two years and the German government on its side took no steps to stop it. In 1916, however, other German companies, seeking to secure the agencies and business of the Aachen-Leipziger, made strong representations to the German authorities that an English-owned institution should no longer be allowed to transact business on German soil. Faced with these representations, the German government contemplated ordering the forced liquidation of the company.

At this juncture the German supervisor advised the Union's management in London that steps to this end would be delayed, if it was prepared to negotiate a sale to a German office, urging strongly that, if it did not agree to this course, the shares would soon have little or no value. The management reported the position to the Board of Trade and early in July that department authorised the sale on the understanding that it was satisfied with the purchase price and that the purchase money would be deposited in a neutral bank.

What followed may seem surpassing strange to a later generation that has since experienced a "total" war. Herbert Lewis, whose name will frequently recur in later pages, was then manager of the Union and, on instructions from his board, proceeded to Rotterdam. There he met the German representatives of the Frankfurter and on July 15th concluded an agreement with them. By this the Frankfurt business bought the Aachen-Leipziger's shares for 1,937,000 marks, an amount of 500,000 marks being deducted from this figure in regard to a balance due to the Aachen-Leipziger over certain reinsurance arrangements; this deduction from the purchase price was to be paid by the Frankfurter to the Aachen-Leipziger and a precise adjustment of the accounts between the Union and its one-time subsidiary was left to be made after the war.

It was, of course, a provisional agreement subject to the joint approval of the British and German governments, both of which signified their consent before the end of July. To this arrangement there was to be a less satisfactory sequel than over the sale of the

Berlin business, but the telling of this also must be reserved for a later chapter.

One other fact about the Union's interests in Germany during the war deserves a place here. Its agent in Strasburg was a certain Charles Draber. This highly esteemed and estimable character raised money from his friends and associates to enable him to deal with claims and losses on the Union's Life Fund throughout the period of hostilities. The Union repaid the amounts owing after the conclusion of peace, by which time Alsace-Lorraine had been restored to France.

Another aspect of "trading with the enemy" related to reinsurance arrangements entered into before the war with companies of German and Austrian nationality. These were suspended by law, but complications over them arose and were far from easy to resolve, especially in neutral countries. Taking advice, presumably from the Board of Trade, the management at Cornhill decided to continue allotments by book entries, but informed the overseas branches and agents that the Group's companies could not send bordereaux or other documents or claim proportions of loss payments, even though these might have been under cessions allotted before the declaration of war.

2

With every month and year the head office at Cornhill had to face a constant succession of new and bewildering problems at home and abroad which in themselves reflected the unpredictable developments and vicissitudes of a convulsion never hitherto known by mankind. Every section of the business was affected, though in widely diverse ways, and a clear picture of the Group's passage through those difficult years can best be formed by contrasting the experience of the four departments of its work.

At home the progress of the Group's fire underwriting was well maintained from the outset but, as we have seen, it suffered contraction on the continent of Europe. This, however, was more than counterbalanced by the temporary advance of its interests in the United States despite the hostility experienced up to 1917 of enemy businesses and propaganda there. In 1914 the branch at New York

K

was extending its activities, while the income derived from that area controlled through San Francisco was strongly augmented as the result of the purchase of the California. In the same year, too, the Union's agency at San Francisco was successfully converted into a branch. In 1915 the increase in fire income continued, a loss of some £140,000 on business in Europe being again more than made up in the United States. On this occasion, however, the American results masked the realities of a deteriorating situation. The war was beginning to have adverse effects on commerce there. The Palatine and the Union both experienced a falling off of business, and there would have been a serious all-round reduction of United States profits except for an opportune contract signed with the American Central Insurance Company of St. Louis—an arrangement which was to bring into the group the following year one of the most historically colourful insurance offices ever promoted on the American continent.

The realities of the business deterioration in the United States, and also in Canada, became more apparent in 1916, and in the insurance market losses were increased by a succession of conflagrations, hailstorms and tornadoes, while in Canada the northern forests of Ontario were swept by widespread fires. But at home, and in every part of the world from which it was not excluded by war, the Group's fire underwriting that year was so satisfactory that its premium income reached for the first time a figure of £4,000,000.

From then onwards the Fire Department made remarkable progress. In April, 1917, America's entry into the war caused, as we have seen, a cessation of enemy insurance activities there, and it also brought about a great increase in the value of buildings, plant and machinery employed on munition making and other war activity. The continued development of munition making in the United Kingdom bore similar results, and the year at home was also notable for the purchase of the National Insurance Company of Great Britain, which will be referred to in the next chapter.

In the uncertain months of 1914 neither Board nor management could have envisaged the possibility that such a market as fire insurance could have been operated on much more than a survival scale. And yet in 1918, the last year of the war, the record of fire underwriting and its profits was the highest in the Group's history up to that date. The net premium income from home sources exceeded

£1,000,000 (as against some £700,000 in 1914), and from abroad £4,000,000 (as against some £2,800,000 in 1914). An interesting commentary on this achievement is that the loss ratio on the Group's total fire underwriting never exceeded 48 per cent in any one year of the war.

3

Throughout the period the Life Department was more seriously affected than any other. The tragedy of the struggle is reflected in the annual speeches of the Commercial Union's successive Chairmen. In 1915 the Group paid out £80,000 on deaths directly due to the war. The Board's policy over these claims was dictated by considerations of patriotism, honour and humanity. The losses, as Charles Seligman pointed out in his review of activities during 1915, fell almost exclusively on young lives and recent policies.

"In this connection," Seligman went on to explain, "I would like to add that we felt that, by treating liberally those of our policy holders who desired to join H.M.'s Forces, we were contributing something to help the general situation and to make enlistment easier; consequently we did not claim, as we could have done in many cases, any war extras on those who held our policies before the outbreak of hostilities."

Let us recall that 1915 saw on the Western Front the British attack at Neuve Chapelle, the Second Battle of Ypres, and the Battle of Loos. Simultaneously, there was a widening of the whole scope of war with the attempt to force the Dardanelles at Gallipoli, with the establishment of the Salonika front, and with the Angolo-Indian advance into Mesopotamia from Basra. No wonder the claims were high, but in 1916 they mounted still higher, for this was the year in which appalling casualties were suffered in the Battle of the Somme, in which there was a costly attempt to enter Palestine at Gaza, and in which took place the surrender of Kut in Mesopotamia.

In 1917 the claims settled for deaths directly due to the war dropped substantially. This despite the heavy toll of life in the Passchendaele battles. But in other theatres the tide was beginning to turn slowly in our favour and by 1918, once the German offensive of the spring in France had been halted, the war was waged to a successful end through advances on every front and subsequent mobile fighting infinitely less costly in human life than that resulting from assaults on entrenched positions.

Other war-time factors prevented the Life Department from making a rate of progress proportionately equal to experiences in the group's other spheres of activity. For one thing the field for new proposals was seriously curtailed by the continuously increasing absorption of the male population into the military forces, especially after the introduction of conscription in 1916. For another, the strain of the war and shortage of food began to tell on the British civilian population and there was a perceptible increase in mortality, starting in 1917 and culminating in the epidemic of Spanish influenza in 1918. A third cause that made itself felt from 1916 onwards was the increase in the rate of income tax, which affected the net rates of interest earned by the Group's various life funds and which could only be partially met by higher nominal rates obtainable on new investments.

4

Most remarkable of all was the Group's progress in the accident field. Its overseas interests in this sphere were scarcely affected by the loss of business in enemy countries for the simple reason that this had been negligible. Almost throughout the war there was a satisfactory expansion, with the Ocean in the lead, in most parts of the world, more especially in Australia, South Africa and the British colonies, while in the final year a large growth of business developed in the United States.

But it was not such easy going in some sections as in others. In the United Kingdom, for instance, personal accident and sickness insurance suffered an increasingly difficult passage. Up to the war it was the professional and commercial classes which had cultivated the habit of taking out such policies, but when they joined the fighting services, they understandably enough discontinued them. By 1916 a similar slump set in throughout the world, and this was aggravated by the reduction of agencies' field staff through military recruitment.

In the first two years of the war the employers' liability account was considerably affected by the dislocation of those particular industries from which the Commercial Union, the Ocean and other members of the Group obtained much of their revenue.

"A very large number of workpeople," Carr Saunders informed the shareholders in 1915, "have been withdrawn from productive labour, with a consequent reduction of pay-rolls on which our premiums were based. Though there is great activity in the manufacture of war commodities, the industries affected thereby are not those from which insurance companies derive their business."

But this was to be only a temporary phase and from 1916 onwards the Group's activities over workmen's compensation took an upward turn. Seriously wounded and disabled men, discharged from the fighting forces, were offering their services again in factories and workshops, and the Board took a leading part in a policy of encouraging employers to engage them, offering to charge only the normal rates of premium. This policy was not only humane, but also a positive contribution to the war effort, since the early conditions of "business as usual" had vanished by 1916 and a general gearing up of industries by the government to provide war requirements of all kinds had diverted many manufacturing companies into new channels of production.

Petrol came into its own in this First World War and was a vitally important factor in the winning of it—in the air, on the lines of communication behind the various fronts, and in the "tanks" first introduced to the battle-field by the British in the late summer of 1916. Almost equally important was its employment in the rapid transport of war products and food in the United Kingdom and, though the use of private cars was largely curtailed by rationing in the later years, the volume of petrol-driven vans and lorries steadily increased, and the Group became engaged in a class of commercial vehicle insurance which was comparatively new to underwriters and was to grow even more rapidly after the Armistice.

As an example of the unpredictable in war, a reference to plate glass insurance deserves a place here before we move on to other matters. Had anyone expected, for instance, that the allied countries would suddenly experience a great shortage of this commodity within the first few months after August, 1914? Yet this is what happened when the Germans over-ran Belgium and north-eastern France where the bulk of Europe's plate glass production was centred. The cost of replacements immediately rose and made quite a dent in the Group's income from that section of underwriting. Throughout the war the replacement of broken windows remained an expensive problem, one instance alone of which was the explosion in January, 1918, of a munitions ship in the harbour of Halifax, Nova Scotia. This blew out many of the city's windows and involved the Palatine and the Canada Accident, let alone other offices, in meeting claims that ran into many thousands, instead of hundreds, of dollars.

5

No department felt the impact of the conflict more directly than the Marine. Richard Jones, still in charge of it, was a sick man in August, 1914, but by some feat of will-power he gained a temporary respite of health and threw himself into his new responsibilities with all his customary ability and initiative. In fact, he undertook coolly calculated risks that many other underwriters almost certainly went out of their way to avoid.

Jones's policy will be more fully understood if we take into account the extraordinary degree of the British government's participation in marine war risks during this first world conflict. References have been made in earlier pages to the Huth Jackson Committee. This committee, which became so called in marine circles after the name of its chairman, was in reality a sub-committee of the Committee of Imperial Defence. Specially appointed in 1913 to enquire into the "Insurance of British Shipping in Time of War", it issued its report three months before the event came to pass. The report's recommendations were adopted by the government and a War Risks Office was established as an official organisation to act as a medium between the government and the mutual clubs and marine underwriters. Briefly, the arrangement come to was that the government assumed eighty per cent of war risks on British hulls, leaving the mutual clubs to cover the remaining twenty, the fixing of rates and settlement of claims being controlled by government regulations. The insurance of cargoes presented a more complicated problem, and in this case the government charged standard rates to ship-owners for all voyages, whether more or less hazardous, these rates being changed from time to time in the course of the war. On the outbreak they were fixed at five guineas per cent, but were lowered to one guinea at the end of 1914. At the end of 1916 they were raised to two guineas; in March, 1917, to three guineas and a month later to five. In March, 1918, a system of differential rates was introduced.

The results of this arrangement were astonishing and have been succinctly described by D. E. W. Gibb in his recent history of *Lloyd's of London*:

"Between 1914 and 1918 the government lost on cargo insurance seven million five hundred thousand pounds. In hulls and other branches of its war insurance it made a gross profit of thirty-two million pounds. That profit may be thought unnecessarily high, but so was the loss on the cargo. And the loss might have been avoided if the government underwriting had been more elastic, if the principle of one standard rate had never been adopted, or if it had been given up directly the pre-war misconceptions were dissipated by experience."

Though the views of the British tax-payers about these results may have been mixed, the position of the marine underwriters throughout most of the war was clearly defined. In regard to the insurance of British hulls they were free to accept or pass over offers as they wished, the one stipulation being that they were not to exceed the government's rates. In regard to foreign hulls they could accept risks and fix their own charges. In regard to cargoes they could do likewise, though the disadvantage during certain periods over insuring cargoes in British ships was the lowness of the government's rates. Moreover, both in regard to hulls and cargoes, the underwriters enjoyed the advantage, if they so desired, of accepting risks over the less dangerous voyages, leaving the government to carry the burden over the more dangerous, for which its rates were the same.

Altogether, then, the temptation to the underwriter was to play for safety within the large margin of fairly profitable safety available to him. But this was not the course always followed by Richard Jones —a fact which becomes apparent if one follows the Marine Department's experience and results year by year.

In the early stages of the war Germany pursued the perfectly legitimate method of damaging our sea-borne commerce through the employment of raiders and privateers. The first war risk casualty over which the Commercial Union was involved was the *City of Westminster*, captured by one of these on a voyage from Calcutta to the United Kingdom, with a small cargo loss to the company. Soon afterwards, early in September, the *Bowes Castle*, her hull partially insured by the company, was sunk by the *Karlsruhe*. On October 21st the notorious *Emden*, then operating in the Indian Ocean, accounted for four ships underwritten by the company, while eight days later the *Karlsruhe*, lying in wait off the West Indies, sunk or captured another seven in which the company was interested. She followed up this exploit by capturing the *Vandyck*, a vessel whose cargo was underwritten by the company, on a voyage from the River Plate to the United States. The *Leipzig, Kronprinz Wilhelm and Prinz Eitel Friederich* now joined the campaign against our shipping and their names appear several times in the Marine Department's casualty books during the later period of 1914, bringing the total losses of the five months on war risks up to nearly £60,000.

Well before the end of that year, however, the German raiders had been reduced in number, the Australian cruiser, *Sydney*, having driven the *Emden* ashore and destroyed her in the Cocos Islands, and the only cruiser to escape from the Battle of the Falkland Islands being the *Dresden*. Unfortunately, before she met her end some time later, the *Dresden* sent a number of ships to the bottom in 1915, including the *Conway Castle*, in which the Commercial Union was interested, on a voyage from South Africa to the United Kingdom. The *Kronprinz Wilhelm* and the *Prinz Eitel Friederich* also remained at large early in that year, but they too soon disappeared from the scene and safety was restored to the ocean highways.

Only for a short time, however. For now Germany decided to throw aside international law and introduced her ruthless submarine blockade. The results were immediate, and the subsequent entries in the Marine Department's casualty books for 1915 record in laconic but tragic monotony a long succession of torpedoings off the Scilly Isles, the Fastnet Rock, Beachy Head and Folkestone—and on May 8th, off the Old Head of Kinsale, the sinking of the *Lusitania*. The company paid out over £15,000 as its share on the loss of the great Cunarder's cargo, and a few months later a sum almost as large when the White Star's *Arabic* was torpedoed off the Fastnet Rock. The sinking of the *Arabic* also involved the company in indemnities on lost bonds to the value of some 200,000 dollars in United States railroad stock.

In that year of 1915 the Commercial Union incurred war risk losses on some 110 ships, hulls, or cargoes, or both, totalling some £224,000 and representing over half the claims on its Marine Department. In 1916 these casualties included over 225 ships, with total losses of some £402,000, representing nearly two-thirds of the year's claims. The premium income for the year showed an increase of some £186,000, but most of this was accounted for by acceptance of war risks and the losses over these became exceedingly heavy with the stepping up of the submarine blockade during the year's later months. Even so, there was a surplus of £240,000 on that year's workings and, what seems to have been a daring, indeed a rather risky policy, justified itself.

But it also seems that Richard Jones and the Marine Committee had seen the writing on the wall just in time and very wisely reduced their war-risk commitments in 1917, leaving the government to take up the slack. It was in this year that the last round of Germany's struggle with maritime Britain was fought out. It took the form of unrestricted underwater blockade and in the first three months alone of its operation accounted for the staggering loss of some 470 ships— neutral as well as allied. The company's war-risk losses over some 205 ships in that year amounted to nearly £309,000—about half the total claims settled by the Marine Department. The surplus on the year's workings was down by over £40,000 on that of 1916, and a stricter policy over the writing of war risks was subsequently adopted.

Continuous strain and tension had by now begun to tell once more on Richard Jones's health. Only a strong sense of duty had impelled him to carry on his heavy and anxious work, but at last his doctors insisted that he should give it up and the Board reluctantly accepted their **verdict.**

"During the twenty years that Mr. Jones was underwriter," stated the company's Chairman, Warrington Laing, in 1918, "he not only established a splendid record in our business, but from his great ability and thorough knowledge of his profession, he attained a unique position among London underwriters."

Jones was succeeded by his assistant, A. L. Page. But by now the enemy's power at sea was ebbing even more quickly than his power on land, and Page had an easier passage in 1918 than that of his predecessor during the height of war. Only some forty of the ships, in which the Commercial Union was interested as war-risks, became casualties that year and though there was a decrease in premiums, brought about by the reduction of the government's rates from March onwards, the total claims, including war-risks, amounted to some £328,000 as against income exceeding £820,000. The loss ratio in 1917 was 66·7 per cent; in 1918 it was only 39·9 per cent—"a very splendid result," as Sir Jeremiah Colman described it. His remark might well have applied to the department's war-time achievement as a whole because, in face of the great risks involved and the government's policy of large-scale participation in them, the temptation to avoid the more dangerous and to concentrate on the safer journeys and sea-routes must have been difficult to resist. In those years of ardour and endurance at sea the Commercial Union played a courageous part and greatly enhanced in marine circles a name already of high repute.

6

There was nothing quite similar in the First World War to the American "Lend-lease" of the second. The British government's problem of financing its purchases of food and war material in the United States thus became increasingly difficult with each month after the outbreak of hostilities, and well before the end of 1915 became so acute that the Chancellor of the Exchequer asked the chairmen and principal officers of insurance companies to meet him at the Treasury. The outcome of this meeting was that the insurance companies, including the Commercial Union, acceded to the Chancellor's request for the loan of their American securities. At the annual meeting of the company's shareholders in the following spring, Charles Seligman, the Chairman, made an interesting reference to this matter:

"Long before the government appealed for American bonds we had been quietly selling large blocks in New York to improve the adverse exchange situation. But we were still able to meet the government's appeal with a very large amount of American bonds which the government accepted 'en bloc'. This operation was carried through after December 1st last. Most of this and most of the money accruing during the year was lent to the government in one form or another. Over £3 million, or twenty per cent of our investments, was invested in War Loans of our own and of colonial and allies' governments ".

This policy of selling the Group's American securities to assist the American exchange was continued, and by the end of 1916 the government had purchased or borrowed nearly all of them. Moreover, within the first few months of 1917, the Group subscribed sums exceeding £5 million to the new British War Loan issued early in that year. The full measure of this contribution to the war effort is recorded in the balance sheet for 1918. The Group's total investments at the end of that final war year stood at nearly £13 million, of which some £3½ million had been placed in government securities (as compared with some £290,000 in 1914) and a further £9½ million in round figures subscribed to British war loans and to war loans and investments in allied countries.

Over forty years ago these were very substantial sums and constituted a striking example of the powerful influence that, not only the Commercial Union Group, but other large insurance concerns also, had come to exert in national and international finance—an influence which was to spread with the years until today it has become an exceedingly important economic aspect of insurance activities.

So much for the financial contribution of the Group to victory in the First World War. Far more poignant in human and spiritual values was the contribution made by its staff from management level to young clerks through service in the fighting forces. Of the Group's staff in the United Kingdom alone—some 2,500—four in five had gone to the forces, a quarter of these had become casualties and one in twenty had gained distinctions by the end of the war.

# CHAPTER X

## Two Acquisitions and a Sale

### I

THERE were other events in those years between 1914 and 1918 which bore no relationship to the war, but were of considerable importance in the Commercial Union's history. Board and management continued to pursue a policy of expansion abroad and at home, and two notable acquisitions, already referred to briefly, extended the group's influence in the United States, the United Kingdom and elsewhere.

The first of these was the purchase of a controlling interest in the American Central Insurance Company of St. Louis in April, 1916. Negotiations had started earlier in the year. They were marked by some tough bargaining, in the course of which the Commercial Union reduced the American Central's figure from 142½ dollars per share of £50 each to 141 dollars. This final offer was proposed under an arrangement whereby the Commercial Union would pay forthwith in cash one quarter of the sum and the balance, carrying interest at 4½ per cent, within two years. The board of the American Central then circularised the offer to its shareholders, among whom was the Mississippi Valley Trust, which owned a substantial holding. This body and some of the individual shareholders held out against acceptance. However, 66 per cent of the shareholders eventually signified their agreement and the Board in Cornhill decided not to press for further shares, having already obtained a controlling interest. The American Central has since become a wholly owned subsidiary.

This was an extremely valuable addition to the Group's complex in the United States, because it intensified its associations with fire, tornado and marine business in the heart of that vast and fertile area —watered by the Missouri and Mississippi—that stretched from the Middle West to the Rockies and from the Great Lakes down to the Gulf of Mexico. It was also an extremely interesting association from an historic point of view, for the American Central went back to 1853, to a period of one of the most turbulent phases in American commercial and social development, to the years when St. Louis was the gateway to the Western wilderness and simultaneously a focal inland port for the steamboat trade that found its ocean outlet at New Orleans.

Indirectly, the American Central came into existence as the result of a disaster that had overtaken St. Louis in 1849, when the whole of the city's business area and its riverside wharfs, as well as twenty-three steamboats and many barges, were destroyed by a fire. The total loss in this conflagration amounted to six million dollars, a large part of which was incurred over the steamboats' cargoes. All the St. Louis fire insurance offices, with one exception, lost their entire capital and assets and could not pay their claims in full.

This was a stunning blow not only to the local insurance underwriters, but to the whole business community of St. Louis. Fortunately for the city, however, the discovery of gold in California replaced the temporary loss of its position as an inland port and gave it a central position in a railway system rapidly pushed westwards in the wake of the gold rush. Its activities as a port also revived quickly and in 1850 an estimated two billion dollars' worth of trade passed through its fourteen mile length of wharfs and warehouses.

All this resurgence of trade, however, created a serious problem— the need for insurance protection. This was a normal demand of an expanding economy, but insurance companies in the Eastern states had taken fright and refused to transact underwriting. So the business community of St. Louis was forced to create its own underwriting enterprise. At least seven new local companies were organised in the early fifties; some succeeded for a few years, others for longer, but the only one to survive them all was the American Central.

Incorporated in February, 1853, the American Central showed amazing vitality from the outset. This was largely due to its first

President, John F. Darby, a lawyer and banker, a former mayor of the city and a member of Congress. About the same time as he helped to found the insurance office he was also actively engaged in promoting a state railroad convention which was to establish St. Louis as a centre connecting the Eastern states with the Pacific Coast, the first concrete sign of which appeared in the autumn of 1858, when a semi-weekly overland mail arrived in the city over the Missouri Pacific Railroad.

The fifties were the golden age of the paddle-steamer packets on the Missouri and Mississippi. The underwriting of cargoes was something in the nature of a gamble. Seventy-three out of 360 steamboats were lost in forty years. One unscrupulous scheme was to pack up old bricks and rubble as merchandise, insure this specious cargo heavily, and then burn the craft on some wild stretch of river. Convictions were few, evidence hard to obtain. But what the underwriters, including the American Central, lost in cargo insurance, they more than made up through fire business in the rapidly growing towns and inland ports.

In 1859 the American Central became a joint stock company and thereafter played a big part in the commercial and industrial development of Missouri and its neighbouring states as the railroads gradually took the place of the river traffic. Four other St. Louis citizens succeeded Darby during the twenty-five years that followed his death. One of them was George Plant, a railroad pioneer and an organiser of the Bank of Commerce. Then came George Cram, President from 1874 to 1907 and the first President who was a professional insurance man. Born in New Hampshire, he had served as an officer in Sheridan's Cavalry during the American Civil War. After the war he entered the insurance field in New England, later became Secretary of the Western Insurance Company in St. Louis and Western Manager for the Mercantile Fire and Marine Insurance Company of Boston, and in 1868 had joined the American Central.

When the State of Missouri established an Insurance Department in 1869, several of the weaker offices went to the wall. But others were strengthened by its impact and these included the American Central, which took on fresh capital and, building up a strong agency network, expanded its activities in the West and South-West.

Northwards these activities ranged up to the Great Lakes and

PLATE VI

St. Louis Waterfront, 1853, the Year American Central Insurance Company Started Business.

there, in 1871, the company's ambitious programme was dealt a heavy blow. "American Central was speedily called upon by the great Chicago fire to prove its fitness for survival", an insurance historian was to record in later years.

"Nothing has contributed more to the present gratifying exhibit of abundant resources, and widespread business", this account of the event went on to state, "than the stand taken by its officers. . . . The Company was called upon to meet losses that more than swept away its entire capital of $275,000. The ringing words of one of the board simply gave voice to the sentiment that animates every one of the present officers.

"There is but one course to pursue; pay your losses dollar for dollar; replace your capital; extend your business, and get your money back."

That precisely was what was done and, though the next few years were the hardest in its history, the company greatly added to its prestige and won through to ultimate success.

It has been mentioned that the American Central wrote tornado as well as fire and marine insurance. In the afternoon of May 27th, 1896, a tornado suddenly struck St. Louis, inflicting the heaviest damage on its eastern suburb. In half an hour thousands of families lost their homes, while some 400 persons were killed and 1,200 injured. Whole blocks of residences were blown down. Trees were uprooted and hundreds of miles of electric wires were snapped. The violent wind cleared the harbour of steamboats, breaking them into pieces on the Illinois shore. And even the Eads Bridge, regarded as unnecessarily massive and heavy, which spanned the Missouri, was seriously damaged.

The loss of property and shipping exceeded 50 million dollars, but the American Central escaped lightly out of the disaster. "We have 185 claims," its Secretary said in an interview. "They amount to not over $10,000. George Ittner took out a $3,000 tornado policy on his residence in Ann Avenue Wednesday afternoon at 3 o'clock without paying the premium. Within less than three hours his home was wrecked. Early next morning he came in and paid the premium and reported his loss: the first we knew of it. We paid him before night."

Edward Campbell, a Kentuckian, succeeded Cram as President in 1907, and he in turn was succeeded by B. G. Chapman, Jnr., who signed the agreement with the Commercial Union in 1916. In that year the company's capital was $1,000,000, its assets exceeded $4,000,000 and its premium income $2,000,000. In the course of just over sixty years of independent existence it had spread outwards from Missouri into all the states of the Middle-West and South-West and had more than justified its name of American Central.

2

The next acquisition negotiated by the Commercial Union was that of the National Insurance Company of Great Britain with its headquarters in Glasgow. It was a moderate sized, but prosperous business, with a premium income of some £70,000, mostly derived from fire insurance, and reserves of about £160,000. Negotiations with the company started in 1917 and were concluded in September. It had paid a dividend of 17½ per cent to its shareholders that year, which accounts for the purchase price of £6/2/- per share. But this was money well spent, for it had the effect of increasing the Group's home income in 1917 by 6 per cent.

This Scottish company was only on the verge of coming of age at the time when it joined the Commercial Union, for it had been born in 1897 at a time when considerable concern existed in the minds of many Glasgow business men about the imminence of a heavy increase in the rates of premium for local fire insurance. Unsatisfactory results from fire underwriting in the city had determined the fire insurance offices to introduce a stiff tariff. At this juncture a number of Scottish business and professional men got together and, in much the same mood as the one that activated the founders of the Commercial Union in 1861, declared their intention to establish " a sound office, with a large capital which, not being combined with the Tariff Rate Syndicate, will be able, with the aid of an experienced Manager and expert Surveyors, *to place each risk independently and upon its own merits*".

The men who founded this "sound office", with a capital of some £200,000, were headed by the Earl of Kinnoul, who became its first Chairman and continued to preside over its affairs until his death in 1916. Baillie James Steel, later to become Lord Provost of Edinburgh and to receive a baronetcy, was among their number, and there was one solitary director who came from south of the Border. This was Henry Beaumont, a Yorkshire business man and politician, but eventually he resigned his appointment owing to the difficulty of travelling north to attend meetings.

Throughout its independent career the manager of the National Insurance Company of Great Britain was James Glen. His appointment was largely due to the Glasgow members of the board. In 1897 Glen was assistant manager in the United States of the Manchester Fire Office, but he was well remembered and admired in Clydeside business circles. Trained in the Glasgow branch of the Liverpool and London and Globe, he had made a reputation as a fire insurance surveyor. In 1890 the Manchester Fire Office secured his services as their branch manager for Glasgow, but so impressed was its board with his development of the branch that five years later they sent him to the United States to reorganise their business there.

Persuaded by their Glasgow colleagues that Glen was the ideal man for the job, the board of the newly formed company cabled him an offer of the managership. It was promptly accepted and Glen returned to Scotland.

"Mr. Glen is a well-trained insurance man," wrote the *Post Magazine* of this appointment, "with a reputation to maintain and a still higher one yet to make. The National of Great Britain therefore decidely 'scores one' in its first move."

Offers of business poured into the company's office from the outset, but were received with a right measure of Scottish caution, and an offer from an Irish gentleman to place £100,000 in Dublin, with a promise of larger premiums, if he were appointed manager for Ireland, was not accepted.

True to the title of their company, board and manager quickly extended their activities beyond Glasgow. In their first year they opened branches at Dundee and Aberdeen, in the following at Manchester, and in 1899 they appointed inspectors for London and Newcastle and also started an accident department, taking advantage of the growing tendencies in this field at the turn of the century which have been referred to in earlier pages. Two further branches —at Leeds and Birmingham—were established in 1905.

The company's development was slow and sure, but in no sense

L

spectacular until 1907. In that year, however, it began to spread its wings. It made its first appearance in Europe with the establishment of an agency at Antwerp. Simultaneously it opened up connections in the United States and Canada as the result of a personal survey of North America undertaken by Glen. In India agents were appointed at Bombay and Calcutta. At home the company entered into workmen's compensation insurance under the new act and derived a considerable premium income from this source.

From then onwards the company's progress continued and it was in a flourishing condition at the time of its accession to the Commercial Union in 1917. After its acquisition the existing directors were continued in office during their lifetime and the staff was retained. Very wisely, too, because more than anyone else Glen had built up the business, he was left to manage it until his retirement in 1919. He was then invited to a seat on the board and thus remained in association with his company until his death at the age of seventy-six in 1928.

3

The passing of the West of England into the possession of the Commercial Union in 1894 may be recalled from an earlier chapter. An interesting sequel to this purchase occurred in July, 1918, when the Haldon estate a few miles outside of Exeter was sold in lots by auction for some £110,000.

The West of England had always been closely connected with the business and personalities of the family that owned this estate. Much of the family's revenue was derived from a chain of mining ventures in Devon. Unfortunately, these began to fail during the sixties and seventies of the last century through lack of capital and rising costs. To meet this situation the family raised a very large mortgage with the West of England on their agricultural estate of some 10,000 acres. But this was not the end of the matter, for default in payment of the mortgage interest occurred in 1890, and the West of England had no alternative except to enter into possession of the estate. This then figured to the tune of about £100,000 in the assets of its life fund, constituting nearly a quarter of that fund.

The board's dismay and embarrassment at having to take this course of action were understandable. Instead of a comfortably large mortgage yielding a safe 5 per cent, they suddenly found themselves owners of an estate including a family mansion, a dower house and various other dwellings, a racecourse, six villages, four public houses, about twenty-five large farms and seven derelict mines.

It was this state of affairs that mainly accounted for the West of England's readiness in 1894 to accept the very satisfactory, not to say generous terms of take-over offered by the Commercial Union, which was primarily interested in developing the fire side of the West Country firm and promptly closed down its life fund to new entrants.

During the years that followed, the life fund continued to diminish more or less regularly as various investments were sold to pay claims, but the Commercial Union hung on to the Haldon estate with reasonable success. At the time of the West of England purchase the value of the estate stood in that company's books at only £89,965. Thus the results of its eventual sale in 1918 were thoroughly satisfactory and the Commercial Union shrewdly divested itself of an incubus outside the normal sphere of an insurance office's activities at the precise moment when land and timber were fetching greatly inflated wartime prices.

This, however, is not quite the end of a somewhat fortuitous adventure into estate ownership. In the process of winding up the West of England's life fund, which was completed in 1949, N. R. Gatenby, the Group's Actuary, was faced with solving a great variety of problems, which had their gayer and their graver moments. But perhaps the most fascinating of his experiences was his expedition to Devonshire to investigate certain mineral rights in the Teign Valley that had been retained as a pure speculation when the rest of the Haldon estate had been sold. The minerals were of greater value than the merely nominal book value assigned to them, because there were records of a dozen or more serious mining ventures in the district which produced high grade ores of barium, silver, lead and iron, and which had only failed owing to the uneconomic mining methods of the nineteenth century. It was firmly believed locally that the old mines merely scratched the surface of the existing mineral deposits and that there remained a big future for their exploitation on modern lines.

In the winding up of the fund the interests in these mineral rights were transferred to the Commercial Union's Life Fund. So the story of the Haldon estate remains to be completed, though prospects of rich strikes and successful workings in those particular areas under the soil of the Teign Valley, where runs the Commercial Union's writ, are matters that belong to a future which is both vague and speculative.

# CHAPTER XI

## Aftermath of War—1919-1929

I

FROM the problems and uncertainties of the war the Group emerged with a measure of success that Board, shareholders and management in 1914 could never have imagined remotely possible. The Fire Fund, for instance, had increased in size by about six-sevenths, and likewise the Life Fund; the Marine was up by five-sevenths; the Accident Fund had been much more than doubled. The first year of peace showed no break in the Group's fortunes.

"I have the pleasure of placing before you accounts today so good and so remarkable," Holland-Hibbert told the shareholders in reviewing the activities of 1919, "that I am sure they will not invite and certainly not incur adverse criticism." And none, indeed, was forthcoming. The total premium income for that year was £12¼ million after deduction of reinsurances. The total dividends on the £5 shares amounted to 18/6d. free of income tax.

Roger Owen had led the business safely and successfully through the war and early in 1920, after thirty-five years of service, decided that the time had come for him to retire. But he was held in such high esteem by the directors that they took the unusual course of electing him Chairman for the ensuing year and permanent Deputy-Chairman subsequently. This was a token of genuine affection, but it was also a mark of the Board's shrewd common-sense, for at the time of his resignation as General Manager Owen was generally regarded as the most prominent figure in the British insurance

149

world. One of his colleagues said of him that "his knowledge of insurance in all its intricacies, his remarkable power of grasping difficulties, his broad outlook, his ability to brush aside the things that did not matter, and to hold on to those that did, his power to work and his joy in it—these have made the name of Roger Owen and have contributed so much to placing his Company in the proud position it now holds."

Though he was very much a man who kept himself up to date in commercial tendencies and was always looking ahead in a changing world, Owen conformed to the Victorian and Edwardian tradition of business etiquette and attire. There are still men in the head office at Cornhill who can recall his small, but dignified figure, clad in a frock-coat, walking out of the building at the end of the day and doffing his silk hat to women members of the staff. Outside on the pavement a City of London policeman was usually awaiting his appearance and would hold up the traffic to let him cross the street. *Autres temps, autres moeurs*; the post-war years were to sweep away these graces and mannerisms of another age.

The Board found it no easy problem to fill the vacancy left by Owen. Joseph Powell had been Deputy General Manager for twelve years, but was now in his sixties. It was eventually decided to appoint two Joint General Managers—T. M. E. Armstrong and Joseph Powell, the dual appointment coming into force in May, 1920. Armstrong had entered the service of the Ocean as a junior clerk in 1886, had been promoted to the position of its Assistant Secretary in 1893 when only twenty-three, and been appointed Manager of the company when it was acquired by the Commercial Union. He was well qualified for his new position. He possessed a wide experience of both accident and fire insurance, boundless energy, a capacity for leadership and a remarkable eye for detail. He was an admirable complement to his colleague, who had width of vision and a natural aptitude for cultivating business relationships and good will.

Unfortunately, this partnership was to be very brief. The need for a post-war overhaul of the Group's organisation had become urgent and, as the younger of the two men, Armstrong turned his attention to outstanding problems overseas. In 1920 he made a long tour of India and the Far East, and in 1921 and 1922 he travelled through South and Central America and the West Indies. His reports on this second tour of inspection have been preserved in the Group's archives and from them it is obvious that nothing escaped his eye. The political state of the countries, the condition of the markets, the financial circumstances of the agencies, the relations between separate branches of the Group's companies—all these matters were described in detail. And appended to his notes on each specific country was a " Who's Who " of all the personalities he met, whether officials of the business or agents and clients.

In the course of these travels and in dealing with the heavy volume of work that awaited him on his return Armstrong seriously over-taxed his strength. It seems that his doctor cautioned him to take things easily for a time and go off on a long holiday. This he did in August, 1922, but being the type of personality that he was, he decided to take his family on a walking tour of North Wales. There, while ascending Snowdon, he died of heart failure at the compara-tively early age of fifty-two.

Armstrong's death was a serious loss at what was, as will soon be seen, a far from easy period in the Group's history. The Board found it difficult to replace him and eventually decided to leave Powell as the sole General Manager. To lighten his work, however, they recreated the appointment of Fire Manager, which had been in abeyance since 1908, the Fire Department, unlike other departments, having been directly controlled by the General Manager and his Deputy. The Board's choice for this position fell on Herbert Lewis, Manager of the Union. Lewis made such a success of this appoint-ment that three years later, when the idea of a Joint General Managership was again entertained, he was promoted to share the principal executive work with Powell; and finally, when Powell went on the Board in 1930, he became sole General Manager.

There can be no doubt that Lewis was the kind of personality required at the helm during the time that he held these senior appointments. He was a man of incisive character and mentality. He cared little for the social graces of life and inspired respect rather than affection in his colleagues and among his business associates. He was extremely efficient and hard-working and he drove his ship onwards with relentless energy through that difficult period of crises, depression and uncertainty that was to last during most of the years between the two world wars.

2

In the months immediately following the war it seemed as though the golden years of an earlier age were returning to the world and its business. The fundamental dislocations in international trade, and the effects of a rapid change-over from the artificial conditions in finance and industrial productivity, shaped and maintained under government control, did not show themselves at once. It was as though the brakes to human enterprise had been suddenly removed and forces long pent-up swept quickly forward to repair the ravages of war and reconstruct the needs and amenities of civilised life.

The boom in industry and resultant prosperity were nowhere more marked than in the United Kingdom and Western Europe, though these conditions were also experienced in other areas of the world. The trading results of the Commercial Union Group continued to reflect in 1920 the roseate picture of 1919. That record year of 1920 saw the signing of the Versailles Treaty which at the time added its impetus to human optimism, but was to have disastrous results later.

In 1921, however, the first signs of a long depression appeared. The malaise became almost ubiquitous; nearly every country was affected by it in a greater or lesser degree. And it is impossible to show in understandable relief and proportion the repercussions which it had on a world-wide insurance business, unless its main causes and salient features are briefly recalled.

The post-war boom in Western Europe and the United Kingdom originated in the vast depletion of stocks of peace-time goods and the necessity to replenish them. Large purchases had to be made in " dear money " countries such as the United States; prices were consequently forced up and manufacturers made higher profits. In turn the manufacturers took on more labour and, faced with higher wage costs and the need to expand their plants, borrowed money at increasing rates of interest. Ultimately, the demand for consumer goods diminished at the same moment as prices reached an impossible peak. Sales fell, credit became restricted, there was wide-scale insolvency in industry and a rapid growth in unemployment.

This was the state of affairs by 1921. The next phase, in very general terms, was Europe's effort to reconstruct its devastated areas and its war-shattered economy. These were problems that only governments could attempt to tackle and this they proceeded to do through the issue of successive loans. By 1926 the productive capacity of the leading European countries was thus restored to a pre-war level though the United Kingdom, with diminished export markets, the loss of investments in Russia and the defaulting of interest payments on war-time loans in other countries, experienced greater difficulties over recovery. This was not made easier by the effort to bring the pound sterling to a par with the dollar in 1925—a policy which made British goods more expensive in terms of other currencies and which was eventually discarded in 1929 when, under the National Coalition Government, the country went off the gold standard.

Though Europe's productive capacity was restored by 1926, the governmental measures did not in actual fact liquidate the war's economic effects. Enormous international debts had been incurred in addition to war debts, many of which were never repaid. The paper currencies of countries bore widely varying relationships to gold and international trade thus became increasingly difficult.

Moreover, inflation in Central Europe, especially in Germany, accelerated by the immensely heavy burden of reparations imposed by the Allies, reached such fantastic proportions that in October, 1923, nearly 15½ billion paper marks represented a single German gold mark, and a new Rentenmark equivalent to 1,000,000,000,000 was introduced by the German government. Successive attempts, such as the Dawes and Young plans, to solve the German problem of reparations and the general problem of war debts failed to achieve satisfactory results, and in the end the Young plan and German reparation payments came to be abrogated. But this event, and the extraordinary financial position which arose between the United States and her creditors in the thirties, fall outside this period and will figure in later pages.

3

The start of these post-war economic difficulties was quickly reflected in the insurance market and was referred to by the

Commercial Union's Chairman, Sir James Leigh Wood, in his review of the group's activities during 1921. Commenting in particular on the results of fire underwriting, both at home and abroad, he said:

"The fall in income, due to the economic conditions affecting commerce and industry, is most striking for, with the single exception of the year 1908, there has been no break in the Company's record of continuous increase during the past twenty-four years. Heavy losses, falling on the reduced income, carried the ratio to 57 per cent—as in the year of the great San Francisco earthquake."

The significance of the Chairman's reference to San Francisco lay in the fact that the fire losses of all companies in the United States during 1921 reached nearly £75 million, the highest since the famous earthquake year, and that three-fifths of the Group's entire decrease over its fire underwriting was incurred in the United States.

Even more serious was the drop in premium income derived from marine underwriting. This was caused principally by the diminution of international trade which had laid up a very large amount of shipping and had also greatly reduced the value of ships and cargoes. Inevitably, too, there was heavy competition for the small volume of business available. These conditions were exacerbated by the fact that underwriters were having to pay heavy claims over the cost of repairs which had been deferred during the war.

Almost as adversely affected were the Group's life assurance activities. In the accident field, however, progress was more than maintained. Car insurance, as well as plate glass and burglary business, were developing and these more than offset decreases in employers' liability revenue, resulting from the reduction of wages in industry, and in live stock operations which had been affected by a considerable fall in the value of cattle and other animals.

Throughout the next eight years the Commercial Union and its associated companies were to encounter the effects of the almost continuous succession of crises and depressions in trade at home and abroad already described in this chapter. Wide-scale unemployment in the United Kingdom, and the General Strike of 1926, militated against the development of accident insurance, especially in the workmen's compensation field, and to some extent retarded the growth of life assurance. On the other hand the strike led to a temporary but considerable demand for "Riot" cover although, perhaps because of our national characteristics, claims were few. The difficulty of dealing with the Group's profits in foreign, especially European, currencies, increased from year to year. Progress of fire and accident business in the United States, by far the most important revenue-bearing country in those spheres, continued to be seriously hampered by restrictive legislation and extremely heavy claims resulting from conflagrations, earthquakes, and hurricanes.

As to the marine market, there was some improvement after 1925 as a result of an agreement between underwriting companies and Lloyd's over hull business. Even so, many underwriters incurred yearly losses. The Commercial Union, however, made a gradual recovery in this market after its loss in 1921, though it failed to recapture completely its immediate post-war success. Its net marine premium income for 1929 was less than six-sevenths of that for 1919 and its Marine Fund had dropped appreciably in size.

Despite all these adversities the overall picture of the group's experience during the decade after the First World War is one of considerable achievement. For though the rate of progress was slowed down as compared with that registered in the earlier years of the century, the advance of its interests in all fields, except the marine, was more than well maintained. The growth of its Life Fund was particularly remarkable. Just under £8 million in 1919, it exceeded £17 million in 1929. In the same period the Accident Fund rose from some £3¼ million to nearly £6 million and the Fire from just under £6 million to nearly £8 million.

The secret of this performance in such a period of stress and tension lay largely in the massive resources and elasticity of a business transacting every type of insurance, and operating in almost every corner of the world, so that losses in one country or in one particular sector of activity were almost inevitably compensated by gains elsewhere. This position of strength was, of course, largely founded on the big amalgamations carried out before the war, one supremely interesting example of which was the Ocean's contribution to the accident business which even as late as 1929, when other members of the Group had also made considerable progress in that field, accounted for over five-eighths of the total net premium income of some £8¼ million.

But the earlier stockpiling of interests was by no means the only cause to which can be attributed the way in which the Commercial Union Group pressed its way forward through those years. The policy of expansion was continued and some shrewdly timed acquisitions were undertaken at home and abroad. A great effort was also made to recover and develop markets in Europe and to extend activities in the British dominions and colonies as well as in the Far East. To these and other events we may at this point turn our attention.

4

Shortly after the Armistice an opportunity presented itself for the purchase of the Edinburgh Life Assurance Company. This very reputable business, whose interesting career will be referred to more fully in the next chapter, had had a difficult passage through the war and, though it was beginning to make a recovery, its board and management decided that the days of prosperity for proprietary life companies were numbered in the face of competition from the mutual life assurance societies on the one hand and the pressure of great composite offices on the other. Negotiations resulted in an outright purchase of this Scottish office by the Commercial Union for some £220,000 and it was then reconstituted under the name of the Edinburgh Assurance Company to enable it to transact fire and accident as well as life business. Another Scottish concern, the West of Scotland, specialising with two associated companies in fire, accident and marine reinsurance, was taken over in 1924. Part of this purchase was undertaken in cash, but a still larger part was covered by the creation of a new debenture issue of £450,000.

Another notable acquisition during this period was that of the British General, the history of which is recounted in the next chapter. In the arrangement, which brought this composite business under the Commercial Union's aegis in 1926, 99 per cent of its shares were purchased by an issue of £1,400,000 5 per cent debentures and a cash payment of £542,000. Principally to meet the expenditure involved over this merger the Commercial Union's capital was increased from £2,950,000 to £3,750,000 at the end of 1926. The acquisitions in the United Kingdom that followed were comparatively minor affairs, though they strengthened the business in the marine and accident fields. The Travellers' Insurance Association, taken over in 1928, was a company that had been formed in 1910 and specialised in baggage insurance, chiefly in the United Kingdom and Europe. The Live Stock and General Insurance, an office established in 1878, was absorbed in 1929.

Despite fluctuations in exchange rates the Group more than restored its position in Europe during the twenties. In France a branch replaced for the first time the various agencies which had hitherto been used. This was in 1920 when the agency arrangement with the firm of Haine and Morant was terminated and a branch was established with William Haine as manager. He was a member of the Antwerp family which had been the Commercial Union's agents for Belgium since 1869; he had received training both at the London head office and in New York. A new general agency was established in Italy in 1922 and activities were so well developed there that a branch was created at Milan in 1927. The Commercial Union and other companies in its group had maintained links for many years with Scandinavia through agencies, but towards the end of the twenties their position there was more directly and firmly strengthened. In 1927 a small Danish company, dealing in fire and accident underwriting, was established as a subsidiary of the Palatine, trading first of all as the Thor and subsequently as the Vidar. In 1928 the Commercial Union purchased the Victoria Fire Insurance Company of Stockholm. Founded in 1898, the Victoria had hitherto confined its activities to Sweden, but the Commercial Union proceeded to widen its scope, especially in foreign insurance business, and to such an extent that by the end of the following year its net premium fire income equalled nearly a quarter of the parent company's similar income from the whole of Europe.

The pathway back into Germany was strewn with inevitable obstacles. It will be recalled that during the war the Union's subsidiary company, the Aachen-Leipziger, was taken over by the Frankfurter and that by the agreement regarding this made by Herbert Lewis at Rotterdam a balance of 500,000 marks owing to the Aachen-Leipziger under reinsurance arrangements was to be paid to that company by the Frankfurter and deducted from the purchase price due to the Union, leaving a net sum of 1,437,000 marks for payment to the Union after the war. The Board of Trade and the Union had pressed during the negotiations leading to this agreement for an immediate payment of this sum to be deposited in a bank in a neutral country. But the German government had refused to approve this and a compromise was come to whereby the Frankfurter deposited the balance of the purchase price with the Disconto Gesellschaft in Berlin and the Union deposited the share certificates with the Rotterdamsche Bankverseeninging in Rotterdam.

It is easy to be wise after the event and to speculate on what would have happened if in 1916 the Union had simply allowed events to take their course and had refused to sell its subsidiary. However, when after the Treaty of Versailles in 1920 it lodged its claim for payment under the relevant clause of the Treaty with the Reparation Claims Department, it was faced with the problem of the rapidly deteriorating mark. The case which the Union tried to make was that the debt due to it became payable during the war and that, although its execution was not suspended on account of the declaration of war, it was suspended by the *state* of war because the German government refused immediate payment. Furthermore, it submitted that the general principles of the peace treaty entitled it not to suffer the heavy loss accruable if the debt was paid at the depreciated value of the mark. The Union also argued that another consideration should be taken into account—the balance over the reinsurance arrangements in favour of the Aachen-Leipziger expressed in marks payable, in accordance with an article in the peace treaty, at pre-war rate of exchange. In effect, this balance was payable to the Frankfurter and it did not seem just that the Union's debt to the Aachen-Leipziger or Frankfurter should be discharged at the pre-war rate while the Frankfurter's debt to the Union was payable at the post-war depreciated rate.

The Weimar government rejected the Union's claim as put forward under these various considerations. The Union then proposed to lodge a new claim through the Mixed Arbitral Tribunal, but eventually, dissuaded by counsel's opinion, gave this up. In January, 1922, the exchange of the certificates and the purchase money was made by the two banks, and the payment which the Union at last received, including interest, was 1,770,000 marks in almost worthless paper currency.

Very different from this was the Commercial Union's post-war relationship with the Frankfurter over the taking over of its Berlin branch. An amicable arrangement was come to between the two companies whereby the Frankfurter charged a war-time management fee to the Commercial Union, but offset this against 50 per cent of the branch's profits between 1914 and 1919. This led to the signing in 1925 of a partnership arrangement with the Frankfurter, into which the activities of the Commercial Union's Hamburg branch, successfully established since 1922, were merged. For five years this partnership was continued with marked success and accounted for a very large share of the Commercial Union's profits on fire and accident business in Europe. But then, in 1930, the Frankfurter suddenly became insolvent and the results of that event must be left for description in later pages.

Meanwhile, the Commercial Union had established another successful partnership in Central Europe. Shortly after the war Dr. Gustav Ullman, the principal founder of the Anglo-Elementar, visited London to seek financial assistance for his company. Founded in Vienna by a group of Austrian and Hungarian industrialists in 1897 with a share capital of 5 million A.sch., this concern had been so successfully developed as to become the leading Austrian industrial fire business by 1914. Unfortunately, the break-up of the Austro-Hungarian Empire after the war and the depreciation of currency had seriously affected the company's fortunes. Ullman, therefore, needed to stabilise his business with foreign capital and in London found a response from the Commercial Union and the Excess. Between 1920 and 1922 the Commercial Union acquired over 5,000 of the company's 20,000 shares; in 1926 it took over the Excess holding of some further 5,000; and in 1927 it purchased a further small lot.

The partnership between the Anglo-Elementar and the Commercial Union was successful in every way. Branch offices were opened in Prague, Budapest and, jointly with the Commercial Union, in Zagreb. An office was also opened in Trieste and business was transacted in Poland and Rumania through subsidiary companies—the Silesia of Bielitz and the Britania of Bucharest. The business was widened out to include almost every field of accident underwriting in addition to fire insurance. Close reinsurance relations were also established, the Commercial Union gaining a substantial share of the Anglo-Elementar's reinsurance treaties and, in addition, using the Anglo-Elementar as a medium for the acceptance of surpluses from South America and Belgium.

Altogether, this was an admirable *mariage de convenance* and, though it was to be temporarily dissolved in the thirties, it has since been happily revived, as we shall see, in recent years.

5

Beyond the United Kingdom and Europe—or for that matter even within those confines—the Group's activities were beginning to reach a complexity in the twenties on a scale so intricate that anything in the way of a fully comprehensive account of them becomes impracticable. But certain events and developments may well be selected for their particular interest and importance and for the light which they throw on a kaleidoscope of constantly growing dimensions.

It is not perhaps without interest to note the way in which the Group extended itself immediately after the war in what had been the Ottoman Empire, but was now a British "sphere of influence", and how in that area, at first referred to as the Near East and later the Middle East, it was employing agencies at Basra, Baghdad and Jaffa. At Constantinople and at Smyrna, too, the pre-war agencies were revived, but only for a brief space of time owing to events recorded in a subsequent chapter.

In the Far East new and ominous changes were clouding the political horizon and in China the rise of the Kuomintang was accompanied by a wave of xenophobia. This came to a head in May, 1925, at Shanghai, when the police of the International Settlement fired on a student mob in the Nanking Road. Despite these conditions the Shanghai branch continued to be active and, in particular, undertook extensive underwriting for the British American Tobacco Company. In 1928, however, this side of its business was lost, conditions in the Treaty Ports became even more unsettled, and the fortunes of the branch began to decline. However, extraordinary as it may seem at this distance of time, the extent of the group's hold on the Chinese mainland still continued to be considerable and, in fact, a sub-branch under supervision from Shanghai was established at Harbin in 1926. A prospect of more stable conditions in China was opened up after the Kuomintang had broken its association with communism and when, in 1928, "the Young Marshal", Chiang Hsueh-liang, who had succeeded his father as Manchurian War Lord, hoisted the Kuomintang flag in the four provinces under his control. At this time it was hoped that Manchuria, which had remained comparatively free from disorders even before "the Young Marshal's" arrival on the scene and which was rich in material resources, might look forward to a prosperous future. But such was not to be the case for the very fact that the area now became formally reunited with China, under the nominal authority of the Kuomintang, started a crisis over the two Manchurian railway zones under Russian and Japanese control respectively. Through the state of interregnum that followed, with three nations disputing their interests in that area, the activities of the sub-branch at Harbin were seriously dislocated in August, 1929. It then suffered a sudden and unfortunate blow when its manager and a colleague were captured by bandits, while on a tour of inspection some three hundred miles north-east of the city, and the Commercial Union had to pay a substantial ransom to secure their freedom.

From this region of ferment it may be a pleasant contrast to turn away to the peaceful atmosphere and growing prosperity of Australia. In the first decade after the war the Group's affairs there made good progress and were augmented by several acquisitions. Of these the most important was that of the Australian Mutual Fire Insurance Society in 1920. This was a Sydney business, founded in 1872, with branches in various other states beside New South Wales. On the fire side it had been closely associated with Australia's co-operative building movement. It was also interested in the accident field which it had entered in 1909. From 1920 onwards its range of activities was widened out to include marine underwriting and, geographically, to take in the Pacific Islands. Other accessions in this period included the purchase in 1924 through the Union of the fire, marine and accident business of the Australian Provincial Assurance Association, established at Sydney since 1910, with branches in various other states and also in New Zealand, and in 1927 the Australian States Insurance Company.

In addressing the Commercial Union's shareholders at the annual

M

general meeting in 1926 Charles Seligman, that year's Chairman, referred to the purchase of the Jamaica Co-operative Insurance Company, a small but reputable West Indies office. He went on to say:

"Mr. Owen attended its annual general meeting two months ago, and the reports he brings back are very favourable. It must be a source of satisfaction to the shareholders, as it certainly is to his colleagues on this board, that Mr. Owen should still enjoy such good health and vigour that he is able to make two journeys in successive years to Jamaica, the first to negotiate and conclude the purchase of the Jamaica Co-operative, and the second to consolidate his good work of the previous year."

A pleasant, if somewhat apocryphal, story relates to Owen's purchase of this small concern which, incidentally, has been maintained up to the present day as one of the independent offices within the Group. It seems that Roger Owen was taking a pleasure cruise in 1925 and that the ship in which he was travelling put into Kingston Harbour on a day in March. Owen went for a stroll along the harbour front and happened to see a building with the sign of *The Jamaica Co-operative Insurance Company* posted on it. He had never heard of the existence of such a company and, professionally intrigued, entered the building and asked to see the manager. The result of their interview was that Owen walked back to his ship a few hours later with a provisional agreement for the purchase of the company in his pocket.

# CHAPTER XII

---

# The Edinburgh Life, The West of Scotland, and The British General

### I

THE three businesses of leading importance that came into the Commercial Union Group during this final phase of expansion in the first quarter of the present century were the Edinburgh Life Assurance, the West of Scotland and the British General. Each of them made its particular impact on the Group's activities, as brief accounts of their preceding histories will readily show.

Of these three offices the most venerable was the Edinburgh Life. Founded in 1823, it was among the oldest existing British companies transacting solely life, endowment, and annuity business at the time of its purchase by the Commercial Union. Its fifty-six founders had nearly all been men of the law and included seven Advocates, thirty-seven Writers to the Signet, four Solicitors in the Supreme Court and two Writers. Finance was represented by a banker and five accountants. Their original intention was to provide a service of life assurance throughout Scotland to members of their own professions. The shareholders were to be limited to those professions and it was a condition that each shareholder should also become a policy-holder. The issued capital was £500,000 divided into 5,000 shares of £100 each and an interesting feature of the issue was the restriction of any individual holding to a maximum of thirty shares.

The first board consisted of a President, a Vice-President, twelve "Extraordinary Directors" and fifteen "Ordinary Directors". The "General Court" included all these office holders; the ordinary directors constituted the "Court of Directors" which met weekly. All the original directors, extraordinary and ordinary, were lawyers, bankers or accountants, but within a few months the board's composition was widened to bring in men of distinction in other walks of life and about the same time the idea of limiting the issue of shares and policies to certain professions was also discarded.

One of the first results of the widening of the board was the appearance on the list of "Extraordinary Directors" of Sir Walter Scott. He was already a shareholder and had also taken out a life assurance policy for £2,000. Writing in his diary on December 13th, 1825, he recorded in humorous vein his impressions of the annual meeting of the General Court:

> "Went to the Yearly Court of the Edinburgh Assurance Company to which I am one of those graceful and useless appendages, called Directors Extraordinary—an extraordinary Director I should prove had they elected me an ordinary one. There were there moneyers and great oneyers, men of metal—counters and discounters—sharp, grim, prudential faces—eyes weak with ciphering by lamplight—men who say to gold, Be thou paper; and to paper, Be thou turned into fine gold. . . . My reverend seigniors had expected a motion for printing their Contract, which I, as a piece of light artillery, was brought down and got into battery to oppose. I should certainly have done this on the general ground, that while each person could at any time obtain sight of the Contract at a call on the Directors or Managers, it would be absurd to print it for the use of the Company, and that exposing it to the eyes of the world at large was in all respects unnecessary, and might teach novel Companies to avail themselves of our rules and calculations—if false, for the purpose of exposing our errors—if correct, for the purpose of improving their own schemes on our model. But my eloquence was not required, no one renewing the motion under question; so off I came, my ears still ringing with the sound of thousands and tens of thousands, and my eyes dazzled with the golden gleam offered by so many capitalists.
>
> Walked home with the Solicitor—decidedly the most hopeful young man of his time."

The young "Solicitor" was the Solicitor-General for Scotland, John Hope, who afterwards became Lord Justice-Clerk.

Scott's association with the company lasted for three years and it came to an end as the result of the financial embarrassments that overtook him in 1827. During those three years he was working with prodigious energy on his *Waverley* novels and completed *Peveril of the Peak, Quentin Durward, St. Ronan's Well, Redgauntlet, The Betrothed, Talisman,* and *Woodstock.*

The affairs of the company prospered rapidly and its field of activities was quickly extended. A board of local directors and a branch were established at Glasgow and agents were appointed in eleven other Scottish towns and cities, including Aberdeen, Dundee, Inverness and Perth. A printed book of instructions issued to these early agents contained advice and suggestions which make quaint reading to-day, and questions which the agents were asked to answer about proposers for assurance were extremely elementary by modern standards:

" Is he temperate or free? "
" Is he thin? "
" Is he middle sized? "
" Is he lusty? "
" Is he bloated? "

In 1836 the directors celebrated for the first time the annual meeting of their company with a dinner at Barry's Hotel in Edinburgh and thereby started a custom of " festive meetings " which has lasted to the present day, though this yearly event has long since become a pale shadow of repasts that were consumed in the thirties of the last century when the habits of Scottish gentlemen were, to put it mildly, extremely convivial. A minute book of these occasions has been preserved in the archives of the Edinburgh Life and it certainly merits more than a passing reference even though this involves a digression from the business of life assurance into the realms of gastronomy.

The dinner of 1837 is an excellent example of the kind of meal that our ancestors were capable of surviving in the first year of Victoria's reign. A report on the menu was presented to the guests before they were allowed to dine, but as it ran into more than a thousand words, some condensation of its contents is required. The first course consisted of Turkey and Spring Soups, accompanied by Cayenne, Sliced Lemons and Iced Punch. " The Course of Fish " included Turbot served with lobster sauce and melted butter, Soles, Sperlings, Stewed Cod and Oysters. The diners were advised to take a glass of sherry before this course, to offset the acidity of the punch, and to continue drinking this till towards its close, when champagne was put before them. It was suggested that two glasses of this should be tried before the arrival of the third course. This third stage of the meal was the meat course, the principal features of which were grouse pie, roast saddle of mutton " rather underdone to suit the taste of an intelligent Calculator ", dressed calf's head, roast turkey, Dumfries ham, a curry, fillets of chicken with mushrooms, cutlets with two sauces, sweetbreads with tomato sauce and " to suit the abstemious appetites, Veal patties, *with no Sauce at all* ". Sherry and champagne were provided through most of this course, but were replaced by hock towards its end.

In " The Game Course " that followed there was a choice of woodcocks, pheasants with bread sauce, partridges with toast and butter, and wild duck with *sauce de gourmands*. The wines previously introduced were all left " within reach ", but claret and port were strongly recommended as a more relishing alternative. A savoury omelette followed the woodcocks, a *parmezan fondeau* the pheasants. " In removing this Course, the Wines above mentioned," the report stated, " are still within call but some may, perhaps, incline to take refuge, at this stage, in a small glass of Glenlivet, or *l'eau de vie.*"

The dessert was " limited to ices, chestnuts, anchovies and olives ", between which was served a *chasse diner* of Curacoa and Mareschino, and the meal was finally rounded off with tea and coffee.

These gargantuan feasts continued till 1840, but in that year it was hinted by the General Court to the special committee of directors responsible for ordering the menu that " they ought to keep in mind that this is a Life Assurance Society which has a deep interest in the health of their members—and that according to the received medical maxim of the present day, the *plainer* the repasts, the *safer* the risk ". And from then onwards the minutes of these " festive meetings " make no detailed reference to what was consumed in the shape of food and wine.

It was not long before the Edinburgh Life crossed the Border and its first agent in England appears to have been at Newcastle-on-Tyne. He was George Wailes, a local solicitor, appointed in 1836. In the following year a London office, supervised by a local board of directors, was opened. The Newcastle agency was converted into a branch in 1873. A booklet issued by the company in 1908 shows that by then it was firmly established in London with a City office and with a West End office in Piccadilly. Other branch offices in England were at Manchester, Liverpool, Birmingham, Bristol, Cardiff and Leeds. In Scotland itself there was a branch at Dundee, in addition to the long established branch at Glasgow, while in Ireland activities were covered through an office in Dublin.

By that year the company's life assurance and annuity fund amounted to nearly £4¼ million. Though it had been constituted as a corporate body by a special Act of Parliament in 1845 and its original Contract of Copartnership had been revised several times to meet the requirements of an expanding business, the constitution of its board with a President, Vice-President, Extraordinary Directors and Ordinary Directors, remained the same as when the company was founded. The only change lay in its membership which had become progressively grander with the years, including a large representation of the Scottish aristocracy among the Extraordinary Directors and of men distinguished in the arts and scholarship among the Ordinary Directors.

When the Duke of Montrose presided over the annual General Court on March 14th, 1914, he was able to record a year of excellent progress. But the war and a struggle for survival, even though successful in its outcome, forced the board to realise that the days of prosperity for proprietary life offices were numbered and, as we have already seen, the Edinburgh Life accepted an offer of acquisition by the Commercial Union shortly after the Armistice in 1918.

2

Though the West of Scotland was a comparative newcomer as a Scottish office, it had the distinction of being the first fire insurance company established in Glasgow. It was also an interesting example of a business that owed its success in the main, and throughout its independent career, to the vision, leadership and energy of one man.

In 1886 George MacGregor, then serving on the staff of the

Glasgow office of the Scottish Union and National Insurance Company, conceived the idea of endowing Glasgow with a fire organisation of its own at a time when such a company would be likely to attract strong local support. He approached one of the leading men in the city's commercial life, William Jacks, and made such an impression on him that Jacks backed his project, gathering together a group of business friends, most of them industrialists, who founded the West of Scotland Fire Office Ltd., as it was first called, at the end of 1886, and became its first directors.

MacGregor's efforts over the formation were rewarded by his appointment as Manager. As such he remained till 1917 when he was elected to the board and became the company's Managing Director. Six years later his hold over the company's affairs was so strong that its board appointed him Chairman as well as Managing Director. And when the Commercial Union purchased the West of Scotland, it wisely left MacGregor to continue in this dual role until his death in 1934.

The company's authorised capital was £250,000 in 50,000 shares of £5 each. The original memorandum of association provided that not more than £1 per share should be called up unless authorised by special resolution. This was never done. The amount payable continued to stay at £1, and even in 1919, when a final issue of shares was made, the total amount actually paid up was only £50,000. The reason for what at first sight seems an excessive under-capitalisation becomes apparent when one takes into account the particular character of the West of Scotland's policy and activities. It started life as a non-tariff office, but in 1891 became a member of the Fire Offices' Committee. This step was adopted as a preliminary to the cultivation of facultative reinsurance business—a policy which met with a fair measure of success and resulted in a comparatively large and profitable transaction of business principally in London and Liverpool, where offices were opened in 1892 and 1895. When at a later date a system of reinsurance by treaties between individual offices supplanted this earlier method of facultative reinsurance, the company entered into treaties with several other British offices. In connection with this earlier policy an associated business, the Scottish Re-Insurance Company Ltd., was founded in 1894 for the purpose of passing on to it by way of reinsurance the first surplus lines of the

West of Scotland. The greater part of its income was, in fact, derived from the treaty business retroceded by the parent company, and no business was at any time accepted direct from other offices.

With the West of Scotland's growing expansion a branch was established in Edinburgh in 1898 and another at Manchester the following year. Other branches were opened in Bristol and Birmingham, but do not appear to have been successful and were eventually closed. In 1903 a decision was made to move into other fields of insurance and in 1904 the company's name was changed to the West of Scotland Insurance Company Ltd. Accident business was the first of the new fields to be developed, burglary insurance being the first venture and, later, from 1907 onwards employers' liability was undertaken. Soon afterwards other classes of contingency business were dealt with and these eventually came to include motor insurance. The company entered the marine market in 1916 by means of quota share treaties.

Meanwhile, the West of Scotland had extended its operations to Europe in 1909, appointing agencies at Gothenburg, Antwerp, Copenhagen and Constantinople. Further afield, it started up activities in Canada and Australia. But it seems to have overstretched itself in these earlier overseas ventures and most of them had been given up as unprofitable by the time that it joined the Commercial Union in the twenties, though by then it had interests in France, Belgium, Holland, Egypt, India, the Far East and Mexico.

With the outbreak of the First World War, and the consequent severance of business relations with enemy countries, the principal markets for the placing of reinsurance business were closed. The West of Scotland decided that this situation offered an opportunity for the formation of a British company, which might participate in the absorption of reinsurance treaty contracts with German and Austrian companies terminated by the war and late in August, 1914, founded the Home and Foreign Re-Insurance Company Ltd. with this end in view. This business was conducted in the same way as that of the Scottish Re-Insurance Company, working solely for its parent company. Both these subsidiaries participated equally in the reinsurances of the West of Scotland. Their results from year to year were similar and satisfactory.

3

The acquisition of the British General, a non-tariff office, by the Commercial Union at the end of 1926 was an event that caused considerable interest in the insurance world. The fact that it was non-tariff required a dispensation from the tariff offices in regard to the period in which its rates could be continued. Its size and standing, referred to in the preceding chapter, had been attained within a remarkably short space of time—a mere twenty-one years. It has been said earlier that the first quarter of the present century was a period of amalgamations unique in the history of British insurance. The interesting fact about the British General is that, starting in 1904 with a paid-up capital of only £5,321, it achieved its singularly rapid growth almost entirely through taking over other businesses.

What was the secret, it may well be asked, of its ability to do so? The answer lies to some extent at least in its origin which consisted of the simple process of paying the liquidator of a moribund Midland concern of not much standing, called the Northern Homes and General Insurance Company Ltd., £100 for its goodwill, books, records and furniture. This set a precedent for subsequent operations for, instead of purchasing live offices, which would have involved the taking over of somewhat expensive organisations, the British General specialised during its formative years in buying the better portions of businesses which had already suspended activity. This policy avoided the need for heavy increases of capital, the cost of these expensive absorptions being written off out of subsequent premiums. It is not altogether surprising, therefore, that the British General was sometimes referred to in insurance circles as "The Salvage Merchant".

Pursuing this role, the company acquired in 1910 the current policies of the Clayworkers' Mutual Assurance Company—an arrangement that gave it an entrée into the brickmaking and allied trades which it subsequently developed in considerable measure. The first important absorption was that of the Northern Equitable in 1914. This was an influential Glasgow concern which had reached liquidation not because its business was bad, but because its rates were too low. The take-over was regarded as decidedly risky in certain quarters, but it completely justified itself and gave the company a strong footing in Scotland—and at a much cheaper cost than could have been achieved by more ordinary methods of development. Another Scottish office, the Cosmopolitan, was taken over in the following year, and in 1917, when the London and Midland foundered, the British General picked up the best sections of its business.

It was in 1920, however, that the company really broke out into the open in its advance to major importance. In that year it showed a record increase in premiums, interest earnings and underwriting profits, and what was equally valuable to its fortunes was an agreement it came to with the Scottish Temperance Life Assurance Company. This office, founded in 1883, had established a high reputation both north and south of the Tweed and its life fund stood at over £4 million. By the agreement the British General took over the whole of the Scottish Temperance capital, while the Scottish Temperance, for the benefit of its policy-holders, subscribed for 100,000 British General shares. A working arrangement was simultaneously made, by which the British General passed to the Scottish Temperance all its life business and the Scottish Temperance was to influence to the British General all its fire and accident business. Though this agreement was re-arranged in 1924, when it was decided to convert the Scottish Temperance into a mutual office, the association was in the main continued.

In 1922 the British General was making a number of small purchases, which included the National Accident Compensation, used for reinsurance, the Traders and General, excluding its marine and foreign business, and the National Benefit, then in liquidation. These were casualties of the early years of post-war trade depression. So, too, was the ill-fated City Life absorbed in 1925. Shortly before it joined the Commercial Union Group the British General had also acquired a controlling interest in the British and European (established in 1908), the intention being to develop it as a reinsurance affiliate.

This almost continuous process of partial and wholesale acquisitions, started with great caution and subsequently pursued with larger and more daring strokes, brought the British General, in the course of twenty-one years, into every field of insurance. In addition to its headquarters in London's Cheapside, it came to establish a West End branch in Cockspur Street and twenty-seven branches in the United Kingdom. It extended itself overseas with branches in the United States, Canada, Australia and India and with agencies in France, Belgium, Holland, Egypt and Newfoundland.

One notable development in the career of the British General was not connected with its successive acquisitions. In 1924 it came to an arrangement with the Britannic Assurance Company of Birmingham whereby the whole of that company's fire and accident business was reinsured with and managed by the British General. This was a mutually convenient arrangement because it enabled the Britannic to offer a full assurance service to their life policy-holders, thus keeping out their competitors, and at the same time provided the British General with a good type of fire and accident business.

During a long period of this association the Chairman and Managing Director of the Britannic, J. A. Jefferson, also sat on the board of the British General. Since Jefferson's death in 1956 the successor to his office, Frederick A. Powell, has continued this link. The importance of the association between the two companies has steadily increased; in 1925, the fire and accident income of the Britannic slightly exceeded £18,000; in 1959 it exceeded £1,120,000.

It has been said that the passing of the British General into the hands of the Commercial Union created considerable interest at the time. In the event, however, its affairs were not in such good shape as they appeared on the surface. In fact, it required extensive reorganisation by its new owners and it was not until the late thirties that it started to make a satisfactory contribution to the profits of the Group.

# CHAPTER XIII

## Events of the Twenties

### I

IF we take into account the size and complexity of the Commercial Union Group, still rapidly developing during the first decade after the First World War, it will come as no surprise that it became increasingly involved in the kind of disasters that make newspaper headlines at home and abroad. But what is certainly a matter of interest is the way in which the Group managed to emerge from some, at least, of them without really heavy losses.

Of such events was the fate that overtook the city of Smyrna in September, 1922. The Group's liabilities over this disaster were extremely heavy and caused serious concern to the Board and management. But, as matters turned out eventually, its losses were negligible.

The Smyrna disaster was an indirect result of the war and the Treaty of Sèvres. By this treaty, concluded in 1920, the victorious allies deprived Turkey of her pre-war empire and, *inter alia*, placed Smyrna and the Ionian hinterland under Greek administration for five years. So far as the Smyrna area was concerned, the treaty had been anticipated in 1919 at the Paris Peace Conference by the Council of Three, which had authorised the occupation that duly took place in May. At first the Greek forces contented themselves with the occupation of Smyrna alone. Later, however, they advanced inland for nearly two hundred miles and it seemed as though the defeated remnants of the Turkish army, bottled up in Anatolia and in apparently hopeless plight, would offer no serious resistance. But neither the Greek government nor its general staff had taken into their calculations the formidable Kemal Ataturk, who had held the British at bay in Gallipoli and shown outstanding ability in the Palestine campaign. In the face of this Greek invasion Ataturk rallied his fellow countrymen, established his "National Government of the Turks" and formed a new army. In August, 1922, he took the field and attacked the Greeks at Afium Karahissar. This battle resulted in a heavy defeat for the Greeks, and the remnants of their army, completely disorganised and utterly demoralised, started to stream back towards Smyrna. By September 8th the majority of these remnants had reached the port and been evacuated on ships waiting to take them back to Greece. The Turks took possession of the city and port the next day without any effective opposition.

So enraged was the Greek nation by this disaster that a revolutionary junta, with a dominating military element, took control. It forced King Constantine to abdicate in favour of his son, George, turned the government out of office, and organised a public trial of those it considered responsible for what had happened. As a result of the trial five ex-ministers, and the commander-in-chief of the expedition, Hadjanesti, were taken to a field on the outskirts of Athens and shot.

Following closely on the retreating Greek soldiers, and ahead of the advancing Turks, thousands of Greek and Armenian refugees from the interior of Anatolia had poured into Smyrna. Their number was never exactly known, though estimates varied between 200,000 and 300,000. They packed the mile-long quay, hoping against hope to embark on such ships as remained in the harbour. But when the first Turkish troops appeared, they fled in panic to the back part of the city where they crowded indiscriminately into any building that offered a hiding-place.

Meanwhile, reports from war correspondents had been appearing in British and foreign newspapers to the effect that the Greek troops had devastated the countryside and burned towns and villages during their retreat to the coast; and from the early days of September insurance brokers in London had been offering substantial premiums for war risk cover on properties in Smyrna. Some of these were believed to have been accepted by Lloyd's underwriters. The Commercial Union, however, and its associated companies, like most other insurance offices, had declined all such offers.

Four days after the Turkish occupation the first news of an outbreak of fire in Smyrna was received; and three days later the horrifying fact was learned that practically the whole of the city, except the Turkish quarter at the northern end and a small section at the extreme north-west corner, had been burned down.

How had this appalling destruction started or, of even more importance, who might have started it? The first messages from correspondents on the spot put the blame on acts of incendiarism by Turkish soldiers. Later reports accused the Greeks. Finally, the new "Turkish Grand National Assembly" at Angora issued a statement that the fire was the work of Armenian incendiaries.

Out of the welter of conflicting reports one fact seemed to emerge with definite certainty at this stage. This was that the fire had not been accidental. Understandably enough, this fact was of the greatest importance to the underwriting companies which, in view of the clause in their policies excepting loss or damage arising in connection with war, riot, civil commotion, and similar perils, refused to admit liability and called on claimants to prove that their losses were not connected with any such circumstances.

The claimants, of course, were not disposed to take the insurance companies' view that the fire was not accidental. They sent in their statements and, when these were not accepted by the companies, inevitable disputation started. In July, 1923, a number of writs were issued by certain claimants and it became obvious that at least one or more test cases would eventually take place. Millions of pounds were involved and the insurance companies formed a "Smyrna Committee" to defend their interests. On legal advice they also discontinued their branches or agencies in Turkey. Had they not done so, they would have been faced with defending themselves in Turkish courts and, under all the circumstances, it was hardly to be expected that the decisions arrived at would have been unbiassed.

The Commercial Union Group, acting like other companies, closed the agencies which it had revived at Constantinople and Smyrna. The parent company was involved and so, too, were the Union and the Palatine. An assessment in September, 1923, showed that the total gross liabilities of the three companies approximated to £752,000 with claims to date of some £561,000; the net liabilities totalled nearly £352,000, with claims amounting to some £236,000. The Union's position was the most serious of the three and it had already received gross claims amounting to some £313,000 and net claims of nearly £170,000, representing much the highest percentages —at 92 per cent and 82 per cent respectively.

Altogether, the Group's liabilities were probably as high as those of any companies involved. On the other hand they were spread out, generally speaking, among a large number of small claimants. For this reason it escaped appearance in a test case, though the Board and management must have followed with considerable anxiety the two particular actions, which were the first to come to trial and which were eventually fixed for the end of November, 1924.

Of these two actions one was brought by the American Tobacco Company against the Guardian Assurance, the other by the Societé Anonyme des Tabacs d'Orient et d'Outre Mer against the Alliance Assurance. The American company claimed some £168,000 for loss of tobacco and other goods, the French company some £3,000 for loss of tobacco leaves in bales. The court decided that the hearing of the second action should immediately follow the first and that the evidence taken in one case should be available in the other.

The hearing in London started on December 1st before Mr. Justice Rowlatt and occupied fourteen days. Rarely, perhaps, has such a variety of personalities and nationalities been assembled together in an English court to give evidence. Among those appearing for the plaintiffs were Colonel Mouharrem Bey, chief of the Turkish General Staff when Smyrna was occupied, Major Cherefeddine Bey, a Turkish cavalry officer who led his army's vanguard into the city, the Chief Engineer of an Anatolian railway, Colonel Nicholas Vanvacopoulos, commander of a detachment of Greek troops which reached the outskirts of Smyrna on September 10th, and a number of Greek, Italian, French, Jewish, American and Czecho-Slovak nationals. Evidence for the defendants was given by Sir Harry Harling Lamb, British Consul-General at Smyrna, an Armenian priest, a British Brigadier-General, who happened to have been in Smyrna on his way back to England from Constantinople, a Greek sister in charge of a Smyrna hospital, an Armenian nurse, Major H. R. Maxwell and Company-Sergeant-Major Fripp, of the

Royal Marines, who had been landed in the port with a detachment of 200 troops from the *Iron Duke*, and a number of civilians and merchants of various nationalities.

The evidence given on both sides of these two actions was bewildering and confusing. It was quite impossible to deduce from it any exact picture as to how, when, or where the fire originated, or who might have started it. Counsel for the plaintiffs made a great point of stressing that the words "in connection with" in the policies could not have the effect of "during". And in his summing up the Judge agreed to this, indicating that in no part of the clause was the existence of a casual connection between the fact and the damage dispensed with. But he went on to say that the causation was not simple, but manifold.

"It is not," he explained, "to be likened to a chain, but to a net. In this exception I find included the remote, the indirect and the contributory cause, a catalogue which seems to me to include every string in the net; so much so that I do not think the words 'in connection with' add anything to the comprehensiveness of the phraseology."

The final passage of his judgment was a masterly condensation of all the facts that had emerged:

"The military occupation of Smyrna brought about a state of affairs in which there was the opportunity in the absence of sufficient policing for looting and outrage, and when, in the triumph of one race and religion over another, there was the exultation which would tend to make the outrage ruthless. The fire arose out of the looting and outrage. Can it be said that the fire was not occasioned even indirectly or remotely, and that it was not even contributed to, and was not, as a matter of cause and effect, even connected with the military occupation of Smyrna? I do not think it can; and without reference to the words 'incendiarism directly connected with' the other matters, which words only occur in the Policy of one of the two Plaintiffs, I think judgment, in both cases, must be for the Defendants with costs."

Both the plaintiff companies appealed in May 1925, but unsuccessfully, against Mr. Justice Rowlatt's verdict, and with the failure of other actions in two European courts, one of the most unusual episodes in the annals of fire underwriting litigation came to an end.

2

Infinitely the most spectacular and most horrifying disaster of the twenties was the Japanese earthquake of September 1st, 1923. This, together with the fires that followed in its wake, razed the greater part of Tokio, Yokohama and other cities to the ground. The number of persons who perished was never exactly known, but in Yokohama alone, where a series of tidal waves sweeping in from Tokio Bay added to the destruction, some 23,000 out of a population of 400,000 lost their lives. A contemporary estimate placed the losses of property, buildings and shipping at £186,500,000.

It was a greater disaster than the fate which overtook San Francisco and may with some certainty be regarded as the greatest single disaster, due to a natural phenomenon, of modern times. But more than a passing reference cannot be accorded to it in our narrative because the Commercial Union Group escaped from its consequences with negligible losses. Of these the most serious was the destruction of its branch building on the sea-front at Yokohama. As to its under-writing losses, the Group was safeguarded against claims by clauses in the various companies' policies excepting the results of earth-quakes, and the only sums paid out consisted of refunds of premiums for the year to foreign companies which amounted to little more than £10,000.

Throughout these years a succession of tornadoes and hurricanes afflicted various parts of America and, more especially, its eastern coast-line. Next to the Royal Group the Commercial Union and its subsidiaries undertook the largest amount of tornado business by British companies in the United States. Experience had long since shown that in America it was necessary to write this type of business in order to protect one's fire clients and that on the whole it proved profitable. But the losses in any one year could be heavy even though covered by the premiums. In 1925, for instance—a year when only minor hurricanes were experienced—the parent company, together with the American Central, the California, the Commercial Union of New York, the Palatine and the Union, paid out nearly 457,000 dollars to cover clients' losses.

In the following year, 1926, there occurred one of the worst hurricanes that ever hit the eastern coast. The Marine Department, as well as the fire side of the business, was heavily involved in this disaster which took a severe toll of shipping as well as of property on land. This hurricane swept along the southern shores of Florida in September and across the Carribean Islands, but it was Miami which received its full force.

One has to picture Miami as it existed in 1926. It was then a comparatively new town with skyscraper office buildings and a beach lined with "cottage" residences owned by millionaires. It was, in fact, a bathing resort for the wealthy, rather garish and ostentatious, and quite unlike those older American summer camps that had been developed much earlier on the shores of Long Island, Connecticut, and Rhode Island, as the summer playgrounds of families listed in the Social Register.

Such was the place that caught the worst of the hurricane or, rather, two hurricanes in rapid succession. The first rushed through the resort at the speed of one hundred and thirty miles an hour for nine hours. The second whirled down from the sky shortly afterwards at a speed of a hundred miles an hour when nobody was expecting a further visitation.

In the town itself wooden houses were ripped apart or broken into splinters, concrete buildings were loosened from their foundations and a recently completed 18-storey skyscraper was so badly twisted that it had subsequently to be demolished. Yachts and shipping in the harbour were lifted bodily into Royal Park and the rest were engulfed. The new docks were reduced to ruins. In Miami Beach many of the residents were killed by collapsing houses or drowned in a tidal wave. In the nearby districts the damage and loss of life were almost as great, while at Moore Haven, directly west of Palm Beach, the levee holding back Lake Okeechobee broke in three places and the countryside was flooded to a depth of twelve feet.

"There was no warning and people had no chance to escape," wrote an eye-witness of the destruction at Moore Haven. "Those who are alive today saved themselves by swimming or by clinging to the wreckage of flimsy structures that collapsed under the first impact of the water. A few made their way to two-storey buildings which had remained standing. We saw bodies of men, women and children floating about, but we made no effort to recover them, first seeking those who were still alive. Only one child of a family of seven was saved. Of another family of six, only the father was saved."

In Miami and the district immediately adjoining it over one thousand persons died, about one thousand persons were injured, and thirty-eight thousand became homeless. The damage to houses and property in Miami alone was estimated at between £10 million and £20 million.


3


In the whole of its career until 1927 nothing could have been a greater stroke of irony than an event which overtook the Commercial Union in that year. This was the collapse of its head office building in Cornhill just before midnight on Saturday, August 6th. If such a misfortune had been suffered by any other business than a great insurance office, it might perhaps have received rather less attention in the press and by the general public. There was, however, nothing wrong with the building's construction and the collapse was due to excavations that were being made on an adjoining site for the foundations of the new head office of Lloyds Bank.

Though steps had been taken to underpin the Commercial Union's premises, these excavations seem to have been driven too deep alongside the western wall of the building. The first ominous signs of impending trouble appeared after a storm on the Saturday morning when cracks in the wall became visible and started to widen. Some fifty workmen on the site laboured throughout the day and against time to reinforce the underpinning with timber and concrete. They worked on into the night, but by eleven o'clock it was evident that nothing could stop a collapse. The men withdrew to safety, and the caretaker and his family, who occupied the flat on the top floor, hurriedly left the building. Forty minutes later the wall began to bulge outwards, cracks spread along the third storey, and windows started to fall outwards. The entrance to Cornhill had by now been cordoned off, but a great crowd of spectators, gathered by the steps of the Royal Exchange, held its breath when a loud rumbling noise heralded what was to happen.

PLATE VII

*From the lithograph by John Nicolson*

THE FALL OF THE HEAD OFFICE
BUILDING IN CORNHILL, 1927.

A report in *The Times* gave a vivid and concise account of the building's last moments:

"A few minutes before 12 fresh fissures were seen, people were urged to turn back, and then the top floor gave way. An electric light had been left burning and the wire fused as the masonry poured down. The whole building appeared to heave . . . and the end fell away with a loud roar which was heard for a considerable distance. Clouds of dust filled Cornhill and spread over the Royal Exchange to the Bank of England. When they had subsided it could be seen that the end of the building had been ripped out as effectively as if a bomb had torn away the structure."

*The Times'* report went on to describe the scene when daylight came:

"It could be seen that only about one fifth of the Commercial Union Assurance Company's premises had disappeared, but the collapse had involved every storey. Rooms had been cut across their middle. A stack of chimneys stood untouched above the highest floor, where the wreckage of a kitchen had been left. An iron girder hung precariously from the roof level. Below was the wreckage of offices. . . . From the lower floors thick girders hung downwards, bent and distorted by the weight of stone which had crashed down upon them. Everywhere there was a tangle of pipes and wires."

The sensation caused by this event was not confined to the City. It was nation-wide and made headline news in the provincial as well as the national papers. For several weeks Cornhill was closed to traffic as the foundations of the western end of the street had also subsided and the street's surface was suspended on nothing more substantial than pipes and cables. At one time it was even feared that the Royal Exchange was in danger of collapsing. But this and many other alarming rumours about the safety of other large buildings in the locality had little substance in reality.

Nevertheless, anxiety and consternation about the increasing size of modern buildings, and the subsoil on which they were built, were reflected in a spate of articles not only in the popular press, but also in technical and commercial journals. Understandably enough, the particular nature of the subsoil in the Metropolitan area was singled out for attention and an article in *The Review* of August 12th summarised the considerable mass of speculative information which was disturbing the public:

> "London offices," it stated, "are built on London clay, the several natural drains of which running through the City have in the course of centuries been covered in and are now known only by their outfalls into the river—the bed of the Wallbrook is within twenty yards of the Commercial Union site, and it is said that there are two other streams, the Langbourne and the Sherbourne, also within 'working distance'—and these natural drains have within recent years (within the last generation or so) been supplemented by huge artificial drains in the form of tube railways, as well as shallower excavations, sewers etc., none of which are effectively filled in following construction and repair. In these factors there is apparently sufficient cause for the formation of cavities under roads and buildings."

An interesting result of this event in the insurance market was a sudden demand for "subsidence" underwriting. Within a few days these risks were being accepted at widely varying rates. In the issue of *The Times* for August 12th reference was made to an instance where as much as £5/5/- per cent for twelve months was understood to have been paid, whereas six days later the paper mentioned the writing of a risk at the nominal rate of 6d. per £100 for the same period. The rapid growth of this comparatively new class of underwriting formed the subject of a special article in the *Financial Times* on August 23rd:

> "Insurance in connection with the collapse of buildings," the article noted, "through subsidence and otherwise have lately become a marked feature in the operations of the London Insurance market. This special type of indemnity has developed on considerable lines and also on scientific principles, and the influx of business is a bright spot in a market which at this season is usually dull.
> Many important buildings in London have been insured since the collapse of the Commercial Union Assurance Company's in Cornhill. Although the aggregate value represented in these special policies is not determined, it is known to have already extended to several millions.
> Before this spectacular occurrence, there has been little demand for this class of business, notwithstanding the fact that it has been an insurable interest in London for many years. Nothing has happened to draw special attention to this risk compared with this event,

although some impetus was given to insurance at the time when the stability of public buildings in the City was a matter of general discussion, as in the case of the Monument and St. Paul's Cathedral.

Insurance propositions now under consideration have resolved themselves into many different forms, and no attempt has been made by underwriters to adopt a uniform policy on the principle of fire insurance, and they are guarding themselves against risks where the proposer may have special reasons for insurance unknown to the assurer. In dealing with highly valuable property a favourable surveyor's report is required, and policies representing extensive liabilities are usually subject to limited liability."

As the alarm and despondency occasioned by the Cornhill event died away, the demand for subsidence insurance also tended to diminish, but it has since continued to be practised on a small scale and, in particular, surveyors' investigations and reports on subsidence risk have been developed to a degree of technical efficiency which was certainly not the case before 1927.

So much for the general repercussions of this unexpected affair. As far as the company itself was concerned, temporary quarters were found in Adelaide House and there the staff moved, taking with them everything in the way of files, documents and archives that could be salvaged from the wreck. Order was established out of chaos in a remarkably short space of time and the control of the far-flung business seems never to have been seriously impaired.

Some difficult problems, however, had to be solved by the Board and management over the reconstruction of their head office. Of these the most delicate was the question of the legal liability of Lloyds Bank. The idea of instituting legal proceedings against another financial institution, with which they were on friendly terms, was most distasteful to the directors. Instead, a series of discussions between representatives of both boards was initiated and early in October an amicable arrangement was come to at a final meeting between W. W. Paine, a director of Lloyds Bank, and Alfred Shepherd, a director of the Commercial Union. Duly ratified by both boards, the arrangement provided for an immediate payment of £80,000 by the Bank to the Commercial Union, an indemnification of the Commercial Union against the liability of claims made against it by any parties for losses resulting from the collapse of its building, and the assignment to the Bank by the Commercial Union of any claims which it might have against other parties in respect to the damage sustained.

The other principal problem was whether to reconstruct the building, a large part of which still remained standing, or to demolish it completely and replace it with a new and modern structure. Sir Aston Webb, one of the most eminent architects of the time, who had been President of the Royal Acadamy from 1919 to 1924 and a member of the Commission appointed to investigate the state of St. Paul's Cathedral, was brought into consultation on this matter. The recommendation eventually made by his firm was based on a simple calculation taking into account the high value of City land. His son, Maurice Webb, discovered that in the old structure nearly one-fifth of the entire site at ground floor level was occupied by the brickwork required for walls and piers and that extremely valuable space was consequently rendered unavailable. From this the conclusion was obvious—with modern engineering resources far greater advantage could be taken of the superficial area of such an important site.

Acting on this recommendation, the Board gave orders in October for the demolition of the old building and, as soon as this had been completed, the foundations and retaining walls for the new structure were put in hand by Holland, Hannen, and Cubitts, the firm which had erected the original building. The task of erecting the superstructure was then taken over by Trollope and Colls. This they completed in the remarkably short time of twelve months, and in November, 1929, the Commercial Union took possession of its new head office.

To City workers this alteration in the skyline of Cornhill and Lombard Street brought also a local improvement in communication between the two thoroughfares, for advantage was taken, with the agreement of the City of London, to alter the position of Change Alley running between the Commercial Union and the new Lloyds Bank headquarters. This tortuous lane was straightened out, making the new site practically rectangular and improving the public passage way.

Externally, the façade of the new building, surmounted by a statue symbolising Prudence, combined elegance with simplicity and was gracefully decorated with emblems, some of them adopted from

Greek legends, symbolising the hazards of fire, life and marine underwriting. The bronze front doors were another outstanding feature of the new home of the Commercial Union. Internally, the offices were so constructed as to admit the maximum amount of daylight and were admirably streamlined in the best sense of that word.

The building remains today as a principal landmark in Cornhill and continues to deserve the tribute which a writer paid to it at the time of its completion:

"The Commercial Union building is not only British, but also an achievement of which Londoners may be proud. Its architecture is modern, in the sense that it deals frankly and competently with a building problem of a kind which tradition has not even dimly anticipated. The design does not, in spite of its efficiency, encounter the pitfalls of the 'mechanical fallacy'; it succeeds, as a good building should, in humanising the details of everyday existence. And the building is, in its well-considered balance and unity, expressive of the inherent stability of a great business enterprise."

PART FOUR

# Years of Consolidation
## 1930-1945

# CHAPTER XIV

# The First Phase
# of Unification—1930-1939

I

FOR the Commercial Union Group the thirties were years of challenge. The record of its activities during this period needs to be told in relation to two factors of salient importance. The first was the deepening of the world-wide economic depression leading onwards to major political disturbance in the international field and to the Second World War. The second was a development in the insurance industry which, in the case of the Commercial Union Group, was to impose a particularly onerous and protracted operation.

The partial recovery of international trade in the later twenties was more apparent than real and the whole flimsiness of its structure collapsed in an unpleasantly dramatic way with the sudden financial slump that overtook the United States in 1929. The principal cause of this American débacle was the extraordinary situation that had arisen over the payment of reparations, war debts and post-war debts incurred by European countries. America had become the chief creditor country of the world. The United Kingdom alone had contracted to pay her £920,000,000 over a period of sixty-two years. Her other allies of the war also owed her vast sums of money and, to meet these debts, exacted as much in the way of reparations from Germany as that country could afford to pay in cash. But this was a fast dwindling source and eventually a fantastic state of affairs arose by which Germany could only cover the enormous imposition through borrowing from the United States. If the debtor countries of Europe had been permitted to settle their debts to the United States by a great one-way flow of trade across the Atlantic, this would have helped to solve the problem. But the United States had reached such a stage of industrial output that she did not require large imports from Europe and imposed a customs barrier that kept them out.

Such, in part, was the cause of the collapse. Next, however, followed its result. America began to cease extending further loans, gluts of unsaleable goods accumulated in Europe and elsewhere, and within three years international trade was to shrink by two-thirds.

Sir Robert Horne was Chairman of the Commercial Union in 1931, and his speech at the annual general meeting included an ably reasoned statement on the economic situation. A prominent banker and a former Chancellor of the Exchequer, he used the meeting as a public platform for expressing his own viewpoint. The speech created considerable interest at the time and as a contemporary commentary on world finance deserves requoting, in part, thirty years later.

"A year which the majority of people in all parts of the world were glad to see come to an end," was how Sir Robert described 1930. . . . "So far as general business is concerned, it was one of the most disheartening periods in the memory of anybody now alive. Few industries escaped from its dismal influence, and the sombre statistics of trade show how in every country, in greater or less degree, commerce was reduced to disquietening dimensions.

"The low prices to which commodities fell created disturbing effects in countries of primary production. In some it gave rise to political upheaval; in others, to financial dislocation; while most of them suffered from both these evil consequences. Such untoward conditions could not fail to have their effect in multiplying the troubles from which the manufacturing countries were already suffering, and, throughout last year, the world-picture presented anything but an encouraging aspect.

"The business of insurance, though it is one of the steadiest amongst the branches of human activity, could not escape from the adverse influences which I have indicated.

"On the face of it, the catastrophic decline in wholesale prices is the most acute trouble from which the world is suffering. . . . The price of commodities is expressed in terms of gold, and, when we say commodities have fallen in price, it also means that the value of gold has risen in relation to commodities. The scarcer gold is the lower becomes the price of goods. In the present state of things may it not be true that, instead of there being a glut of commodities, there is a scarcity of gold? Such an explanation seems to be the only one which rationally accounts for the fact that practically all commodities are at one and the same time in a similar position of alleged over-supply.

"Moreover, the existing conditions as known to us seem to support this theory. I do not mean that there is sufficient gold in the world to meet the needs of trade and commerce, but that all the gold that is necessary is not being made available. The great bulk of gold today is held in America and France. The United States has nearly half the gold in the world and France today possesses three times as much as England; and neither of these nations is lending in the measure that the world requires.

"International trade has as one of its features that the creditor nations of the world lend their surplus to the debtor countries to enable them to carry out the developments by which they thrive and pay their debts. Such lending creates a demand on the part of the borrower for goods from the rest of the world and stimulates trade. On the other hand, when lending is restricted, demand is diminished; prices fall; and this in turn lessens the purchasing power of the debtor countries and their ability to borrow.

"After the War was over, America did lend largely abroad; but at the time when the boom on the New York Stock Exchange began she practically ceased to do so, and, indeed, owing to the high rates of interest offered by the speculators of Wall Street, she attracted still more of the gold of the world to her shores. Since the slump occurred, American lenders have been too apprehensive, or too cautious, to indulge in external loans; and the gold which has accumulated in the United States is higher today than at any previous time. Similarly the French investing public, after the losses which they suffered through pre-War loans to Russia and Turkey, have been very hesitant about lending outside of their own country; and any incipient courage they possessed has been chilled by the fate of the Young Reparations loan which was taken up very largely in France and has suffered considerable depreciation. . . .

"I have indicated my view as to the world position. There is, however, a domestic situation which we in Britain must confront with clear-sighted courage and solve for ourselves. Nobody else can solve it for us, and if we refuse, because of its uncomfortable aspects, to apply our minds to it we may easily drift to disaster. We have a vast War debt which costs us a huge sum in interest every year. It adds greatly to our cost of production and weakens our capacity to compete in the external markets of the world. Some of our chief rivals in trade have adopted the device of getting rid of a considerable portion of their obligations by depreciating their currencies through inflation and thus reducing the amounts of their debts.

"Such a course was judged to be closed to us because of the importance, both from the financial and commercial point of view, of sustaining the credit of London as the monetary centre of the world, and putting the pound sterling in a position to buy as large a quantity as possible of the food and raw material which we purchase from overseas. This, however, as was very imperfectly realised, involved our taking the only alternative course of cutting off every form of unnecessary expenditure, both public and private, and making all the savings possible to pay off our debt, the weight of which was automatically increased by appreciation in the value of the pound. By such an alternative alone was it possible to curtail the costs of production in this country to a point which would enable us to sell our goods in the export markets of the world.

"It must be obvious to all of us that we have not seriously followed this plan, and that, instead of restricting our expenditure, we have been expanding it on social services which, even if good in themselves, the country has not been able to afford. The inevitable consequences have followed. The expanded services have involved more expenditure followed by higher rates and the most severe taxation in the world. These, in their turn, have, by increasing the cost of production, weakened our competitive power in external markets. Failure to sell our goods has resulted in the retrenchment or closing down of manufacturing establishments, with a consequent increase of the numbers out of work, while mounting unemployment, with its additional charges and burdens upon the community, has carried the spiral movement of rising costs to higher flights."

Within a few months of Sir Robert Horne's speech to the shareholders of the Commercial Union conditions rapidly worsened. By the end of 1931 there were 2,900,000 unemployed persons in the United Kingdom. Expenditure on the dole was rising at the same time as the yield from taxation was falling. The failure of the Austrian Creditanstalt and the great German Danatbank, in which a large amount of British money had been invested, added to the embarrassments of the United Kingdom. Foreign money began to be withdrawn from the City of London and the Bank of England was obliged to seek loans again from the United States and France. Both countries, however, insisted on the balancing of the British budget as a condition of such assistance. Since this would have involved, among other cuts in expenditure, a reduction of the dole, the Labour Government, then in power, split up. The so-called National Government under Ramsay MacDonald succeeded it. In September, 1931 the United Kingdom abandoned the gold standard.

Within just over a year thirty-five other countries followed the British example. Still later, in 1933, the United States went off gold, and devalued the dollar by 40·94 per cent in 1934. Belgium devalued her franc by 28 per cent in 1935. France, Switzerland, Holland, Italy and several other states devalued their currencies in 1936. And those countries which clung to gold increased their control of currencies and prices.

If we look back on those lean and unhappy years, it is possible to detect a gradual adaptation of international trade to this process of devaluation. In the later thirties some revival was beginning to take place across the artificial barriers that nations and groups of nations had set round themselves. It is possible that time and peace would have brought their solution. But time and peace were running out. Italy's invasion of Abyssinia in 1935 led to sanctions being imposed on her. The Spanish Civil War, lasting from 1936 to 1939, promoted hatreds far beyond her frontiers. From 1937 onwards China and Japan were locked in struggle on the Chinese mainland. And, finally, Hitler's invasions of Austria and Czechoslovakia were a prelude to his invasion of Poland and the outbreak of the Second World War.

2

It is interesting to notice how closely the annual results of the Group's activities reflected these events. The Fire Department was the most seriously affected of all. It immediately felt the financial crisis in the United States where a large bulk of its income was normally derived. By 1932 the decrease in losses there failed to keep pace with the falling income and, due entirely to this factor in one country, the Group's fire account showed a loss, small though it was, for the first time in many years. By 1936 there were signs of a recovery. The trade recession in the United States was on the way out and there was a considerable expansion of the Group's fire underwriting there as well as in the United Kingdom. Unfortunately, this upward movement was retarded by the depreciation that year of the principal European currencies. By 1937, however, the upward movement went ahead at home and abroad and the only areas where seriously unfavourable results occurred were, understandably, China and Spain. From then till the outbreak of war the Fire Department's recovery was well maintained.

The experience of the Accident Department followed more or less similar lines. But it was able to throw off the effects of the American recession more quickly—a fact accounted for in the main by the truly remarkable strength of the Ocean's casualty business there. In Europe also the Ocean's accident underwriting was confined to Holland and Belgium with the result that it was not so seriously hit by the depreciations of the leading currencies.

An important event of this period in the United Kingdom was the passing of the Road Traffic Act in 1930. The number of accidents on British roads had inevitably increased with the growth of motor vehicles and the time had arrived when some form of compulsory insurance was becoming essential in the interests of owners, drivers, passengers and pedestrians. Nevertheless, the placing of this piece of legislation on the statute books was not particularly welcome to accident underwriters.

"Unquestionably the passing of this Act," stated Sir James Leigh-Wood, the Commercial Union's Chairman in 1932, "has made it incumbent upon us to accept many risks which, but for the liability imposed on motor owners by the Act to effect insurance, we should have preferred not to accept. Motor cycles are a frequent source of accidents, and indications are that the relatively small premium, which was probably sufficient for the selected business we transacted prior to the passing of the Act, is insufficient now that every owner of a motor cycle has to obtain insurance."

So heavy, in fact, were the losses on motor cycle third party risks that insurers were forced to raise their rates in the following year. Throughout the thirties the experience of this new form of compulsory motor insurance was difficult and, though in the year before the war it had come to rank with workmen's compensation as the largest sector in volume of business transacted by the Accident Department in the United Kingdom, it was certainly not the largest profit earner.

Considering the parlous state of international trade and the laying up of ships, the Marine Department weathered this period remarkably well. Its results in 1930 were excellent and it also rode on an even keel through 1931. Two difficult years followed, but from 1934 onwards it made good progress. Several causes contributed to this achievement. The Joint Hull Committee, consisting of representatives of the insurance offices and Lloyds, had got well into its stride and was exerting its influence over the stabilisation of the rates structure. During the period of trade depression the costs of repairs to ships tended to fall. In the years immediately preceding the outbreak of hostilities there was a good amount of profitable underwriting of war risks. But perhaps the most important cause was extremely able management—firstly by A. L. Page up to his retirement as marine underwriter in 1931 and, later, by A. L. Kennedy from 1932 onwards.

It was during Kennedy's period as underwriter that the Commercial Union embarked on the most ambitious adventure in marine insurance that it had ever undertaken. In 1935 the two principal steamship companies concerned with trans-Atlantic passenger traffic combined to form the Cunard White Star Line, one of the objects of the amalgamation being to carry through the building of two liners with such size and speed that they could maintain regular weekly departures from both sides of the Atlantic hitherto requiring three vessels.

The building costs of the "Queens", as they have since become familiarly known, were extremely heavy and a serious problem arose as to their insurance. The *Queen Mary* had been commissioned by the Cunard Line before the amalgamation with the White Star and she lay for some time on the stocks on Clydeside as "No. 534". There was heavy unemployment on Clydeside at the time and the government was eventually induced to take an interest in the progress of "No. 534" for this reason. The immediate problem involved was the underwriting of the building risk. £4,500,000 for a single ship was an amount that the market was not ready to write. An arrangement was come to whereby the Board of Trade wrote £1,780,000, and the market, led by the Commercial Union, the remaining £2,720,000. This was accomplished by agreements entered into between the Cunard and the Commercial Union on the one hand, and the Commercial Union and Board of Trade on the other, whereby a policy was issued through the Commercial Union for the amount not absorbed by the market, and this amount was then reinsured by the Board. The company thus, in effect, managed the Board's line for them. When completed and ready for service in 1936, the *Queen Mary*, with a gross registered tonnage of 81,237, entailed a sea-going risk of £4,800,000, of which the Board of Trade took up £1,800,000, and the market, again led by the Commercial Union, £3,000,000.

The building risk of the *Queen Elizabeth* was computed at the same amount as for her sister ship, but in her case the market, once more led by the Commercial Union, wrote a far larger proportion at £3,760,000, the Board of Trade writing only £740,000. When completed in January, 1940, her gross registered tonnage was 83,673, and her sea-going risk—she was at once commissioned as a troop ship—stood at £5,600,000. Of this the market, again led by the Commercial Union, underwrote £2,144,000 and the Board of Trade £3,456,000. Today the value of each of the "Queens" is considerably increased and the market, still led by the Commercial Union, absorbs the whole of these risks. The remarkable success of these two great ships—with their origins in the years of depression—will always rank high in the history of British marine enterprise and their success is a tribute to the high craftsmanship of British shipbuilding, to imaginative ownership, and to the audacity and strength of the British marine insurance market.

Except for a slight decrease of income in 1938 the record of the Life Department during the thirties was one of good progress. Its activities continued to be almost entirely confined to the United Kingdom and were, therefore, unaffected by the changes in overseas currencies. In bad times, too, people are more anxious to provide against the possibility of even worse fortune. But here again first-class management was largely responsible for a steady expansion of business. This can be illustrated by the growth of the Commercial Union's Life Fund from some £18 million in 1930 to over £28 million in 1939. The British General's Life Fund had been maintained as a separate unit and this also rose from just over £800,000 in 1930 to well over £2 million in 1939.

The funds of the three other departments tell their tale. That of the Fire Department stood at around £7,056,000 in 1939 and was lower by some £400,000 in comparison with 1930. The Marine at just under £1,412,000 in 1939 had increased by nearly £420,000 and the Accident at £5,990,000 was some £66,000 over the 1930 figure.

The general picture of the Group's career during these challenging years is one of slow and hard-fought progress. Once again, and as in the twenties, the Group's resiliency during a period of external stress and tension owed much to its massive resources and the far-flung character of its enterprise. The true sign of its underlying strength lay in its total assets which in the thirties increased by some £10 million, reaching a total exceeding £70 million by the end of 1939.

3

Retrenchment and elimination of redundancy were obviously called for in these inter-war years of depression and crisis. But the principal reasons for the wide and intense unification of activities, that started in the late twenties and was pressed forward in fuller measure during the thirties, were connected with other issues. The Commercial Union was not the only head of a group of composite insurance offices which ceased to add further to its empire after the late twenties and which from then onwards began to co-ordinate and unify its structure. Most of the other large-scale British insurance businesses acted likewise, though it may well be repeated here that this progress of integration involved the management of the Commercial Union in a particularly onerous task.

Several causes had contributed to the sudden decline during the late twenties of the rationalisation in the British insurance industry that had been taking place since the turn of the century. But the principal cause, and the one that emerges with abundant clarity, was that the size of the larger groups had reached a point where any further amalgamations would have entailed associations too immense at that period to offer any incentive. The time had, in fact, arrived for the larger groups to stop expansion and start consolidation.

To the incisive mind of Herbert Lewis these requirements had been apparent even before the day in 1926 when he had joined Joseph Powell in the management of the business, reaching that position just as the acquisition of the British General was being completed. If we glance back at the state of affairs as it then existed, we can more readily appreciate the changes which were subsequently pressed forward in the thirties.

Through successive acquisitions and mergers at home and abroad the complexity of the Group's structure had outgrown the capacity of the head office in Cornhill to administer with anything like full comprehension and efficiency. In the United Kingdom, for instance, the parent company alone possessed two main branches in the City as well as a West End branch, eight other offices in the London area, twenty-one area branches in the provinces and, administered through them or directly from the head office, some seventy offices in smaller centres. Between them the other members of the Group disposed of many branches and offices in the United Kingdom. Taking into account the fact that the majority of these branches and offices were engaged in underwriting fire, life and accident policies, the proliferation of activities and staff needs little imagination to visualise. There was also no adequate centralisation or grouping of policy in relation to rates, risks and claims.

While he was still Fire Manager, Lewis had taken an initial step to clear up anomalies in his own sphere of United Kingdom operations by obtaining approval for the establishment of a Central Survey Bureau in 1925 and the appointment of a chief surveyor for the inspection of fire risks throughout the country. As General Manager, and actively supported by W. F. Todd, then Accident Manager of the Commercial Union, he made a still more comprehensive over-haul of accident underwriting on the home front. In 1931 the Glasgow branches of the Commercial Union and the Scottish companies, although still operating independently, were brought together in a new building in St. Vincent Street and at the same time an Accident Claims Department was set up there which, under a claims super-intendent, functioned for a local Group of all these companies. The innovation was so successful that "Central Accident Claims Departments", functioning for all members of the group in specific areas, were established in Dublin, Liverpool, Bristol and Edinburgh during the following year. Similar units were created at Belfast in 1933, Birmingham in 1935, and Cardiff in 1936.

Todd was an enthusiast over these projects. Their object, as he would frequently reiterate, could be summed up in three words—"efficiency, service and economy". As time went by, their beneficial results were to spread outwards into other fields of the organisation in the United Kingdom and to set a pattern of even wider co-ordination, as we shall see in later pages.

The tangle of interests overseas was infinitely more extensive and intricate than the thickets in the home country. Herbert Lewis brought all his energy to its unravelling and his first step with this end in view had been to visit Australia and New Zealand in 1928. He spent some four months in the two countries, reaching Australia early in February and leaving New Zealand early in June.

In that year the total net premium income of the Group in Australia exceeded £1,000,000. It was, therefore, an important sector of the Group's activities, but the favourable conditions, which had existed for many years, had recently been modified by growth of competition leading to increased expenditure in the acquisition of business and also by the establishment in certain states of state insurance departments.

Six of the allied companies, in addition to the parent business, were by then engaged in Australia—the Ocean, Union, Palatine, British General, Edinburgh (transacting marine business only), and the Australian Mutual. Lewis found their relationship, or lack of relationship, to each other far from satisfactory and described the state of affairs in no uncertain terms:

"Each of the Allied Companies has its own management and

organisation and there has been a lack of co-operation between the various units, so much so that on occasion different policies have been advocated in Tariff Association meetings by individual companies of our group. In the case of the Commercial Union there is no control of its Australian business, the Branches in each State being practically independent and reporting direct to London.

"My investigations on the spot showed me that while, as a result of Head Office admonitions, there had of late been more frequent consultation between the Allied Companies, this was haphazard and often prejudiced by personal considerations. In these circumstances the Commercial Union had lost prestige in the Tariff Associations and was not exercising the influence to which it is entitled."

Before he left Australia Lewis, with his customary firmness, reorganised the structure of the Group's organisation there. All the then allied companies, except the Ocean, were brought under the control of a resident manager at Melbourne. Their respective branches and general agencies in the different states were left to remain independent of each other, but all of them were placed under the authority of Melbourne which from then on became the medium of communication with London. A. H. Russell, who had successfully run the Union's branch in Australia since 1902, was appointed to this new position of resident manager and F. L. Morey was put in charge of the Ocean with its chief office, as it then existed, at Sydney. Four years later the merging of the Group's Australian activities was taken a stage further and the Ocean also was brought into group control from Melbourne.

In New Zealand Lewis found the insurance position similar in many respects to that in Australia except that the competition was less severe. Besides the parent company only two other members of the Group were then engaged in underwriting there—the Union and the Ocean. Lewis toyed at first with the idea of bringing these New Zealand interests under the control of Melbourne, especially as the general supervision of the Union's branches in New Zealand had been vested in Russell since 1925. But on second thoughts he decided against this, recording that "there is a certain resentment against control from Australia and the imposition of this would lower the prestige of our representative as compared with that of his colleagues". The link with Australia was, therefore, severed and the

Union was brought under the supervision of the Commercial Union's main New Zealand branch office at Wellington and its manager, Gordon Reid. The Ocean's activities in the Dominion were for the time being kept independent, but within a few years they too were placed under the supervision of the Commercial Union's main branch in the Dominion.

From New Zealand Lewis sailed for the United States, where he visited San Francisco, Chicago and New York during June and July. There had already been some co-ordination of business activities in the North American continent, but even so the maze of interests there infinitely exceeded in intricacy anything existing elsewhere in the Commercial Union's empire. The proliferation of interests with which Lewis had to deal can be understood if it is described in some brief detail. The Group was operating in all fields of insurance except life. Engaged in fire underwriting were the parent company and the Palatine, Union, British General, California, American Central, and Commercial Union of New York. Casualty business was being transacted by the Ocean and its subsidiary, the Columbia, whilst ocean marine underwriting was written exclusively by the Commercial Union. The California and the American Central, with their own boards and directors, were still largely independent, in policy and working arrangements, from the rest of the Group; and the Ocean was also very much a law unto itself in its own highly specialised domain. The other companies had been more closely brought into line with the Group policy and organisation, but as they were administered under three separate geographical departments—an Eastern controlled from New York, a Western controlled from Chicago, and a Pacific controlled from San Francisco—there was no clear centralisation on New York.

It was this particular anomaly of geographical departments that Lewis, ably assisted by F. W. Koeckert, who had succeeded Whitney Palache as United States manager in the preceding year, began to clear up during his 1928 visit. The Western Departments, covering the states of Illinois, Indiana, Iowa, Kansas, Kentucky, Michigan, Minnesota, Missouri, Nebraska, North Dakota, Ohio Oklahoma, South Dakota, Tennessee and Wisconsin, was moved *en bloc* from Chicago to New York. Only a small office, for transacting local business, was left at Chicago. At the same time the offices and agencies in Colorado, Wyoming and New Mexico were placed under the control of the San Francisco branch. This involved a drastic piece of reorganisation.

Before he left for England Lewis also started to deal with the American Central. He instructed its President to bring the company's policy and methods more closely into line with those of the Commercial Union, and he transferred its activities on the Pacific Coast to the California.

During the thirties Lewis continued to make frequent visits to the United States, their main purpose being to streamline the business there. In 1930 the California's activities were placed directly under the control of the Commercial Union, whose Pacific Coast manager was appointed its President; and the staff and offices were brought together under one roof at San Francisco. In the same year the whole of the American Central's organisation was placed under control from New York.

In 1931 and 1932 the unification of management of the various companies was taken a stage further. A "master pool" was established for the purpose of pooling and distributing on a proportional basis the net premiums of all the members of the Group, and arrangements were made for common membership of the boards and local boards in New York. Finally the Ocean became fully integrated into the United States organisation in 1936 when H. Collins, its manager, received the additional appointment of deputy manager, under Koeckert, of the Commercial Union's fire companies.

During his visit to the United States in 1928 Lewis had found time to spend a few days in Canada. Here again he discovered the same problems of proliferation and, though they were on a smaller scale, they were in one aspect at least—the appearance on the scene of the American subsidiaries—even more peculiar. The activities of the Commercial Union and Palatine were being controlled from Montreal; those of the Union and the Canada Accident were also controlled from the same centre, but under different management. The Ocean had its headquarters at Toronto. The British General was represented in Montreal by a manager responsible to London. The American Central was operating in Quebec, British Columbia, Alberta, Saskatchewan, Manitoba and Western Ontario. The California was engaged in British Columbia, Alberta and Saskatchewan under the control of the Commercial Union's branch manager at Winnipeg and Vancouver.

"The representation of the Commercial Union Group in Canada is somewhat complicated," was Lewis's comment on this situation. "There has not hitherto been that amount of consultation and co-operation which is desirable between the various companies and I think it would be advisable to look further into this question on some later occasion."

And look into it he certainly did during the next few years. By 1931 all companies of the Group except the Ocean had been brought under the control of a central management in Montreal. In 1934 the Canada Accident's activities were extended to inland marine and transportation. Finally, in 1938, the Ocean's operations were integrated into the organisation managed from Montreal, its main office being transferred there from Toronto.

Elsewhere than in Australasia and North America the problem of unifying and consolidating the Group's interests were less complicated. The only other region, where any extensive pruning and grouping needed to be undertaken, was South Africa and its adjoining territories. Here, however, considerable reorganisation had been carried out in the twenties and in 1929 the Union and Palatine had come under the control of the Commercial Union. In 1930 the old premises of the Colonial at Cape Town were pulled down and the Group's main office, built on their site, was opened in 1932. From then onwards the area controlled from Cape Town came to include the four provinces of the Union, Northern and Southern Rhodesia, South West Africa, and Portuguese East Africa.

In any account of these overseas activities during the thirties some brief reference at least should be made to Central Europe, for it is a matter of some interest that British insurance business was profitably and securely maintained there even after Hitler's rise to power.

In Germany the collapse of the Frankfurter in 1930 did not spell the end of the Commercial Union's régime in the Reich. A successful branch was built up by the company's English representative, W. Penney, at Frankfurt and by its German manager, Georg Stelzner. It developed fire and accident underwriting in various parts of the country and for some period was engaged in German trans-Atlantic business. In conjunction with a German office, the Neptunus, it also extended itself into the consequential loss market, which at that time was not highly competitive. In fact, it had a flourishing career right up to the outbreak of war when it passed into the hands of the Aachen-Leipziger. The Palatine, too, did profitable direct business through its agents, Adolf Mengers and Co. of Hamburg, within the Hanseatic cities and the districts of Schleswig-Holstein and Lauenberg, but in 1939 its portfolio was transferred to the Deutsche Sach of Hamburg.

The Commercial Union's successful association with the Anglo-Elementar of Austria, started in the twenties, was still further developed in the thirties, and particularly in accident business where new fields, such as motor insurance, were coming to the fore, and older fields, such as burglary and third-party insurance, were making advances. But after Hitler marched into Vienna and the Anschluss was proclaimed in March, 1938, it became evident that the British interest in the Anglo-Elementar could only endanger its position as Austria's leading industrial insurance company and advantage was taken of an offer by a German office, the Colonia of Cologne, to acquire the business.

## 4

These developments in Europe bring us to the outbreak of the Second World War. But meanwhile the management of the Group's affairs had passed into other hands. In 1935 Herbert Lewis, who had entered the business as a junior clerk in the Union over fifty years earlier, decided that it was time for him to retire as General Manager. Though now in his late sixties, he was still extremely vigorous and the Board realised that none of his near contemporaries in the business possessed in comparable degree his own qualities of leadership and drive. Eventually they adopted a plan whereby, as Sir James Leigh-Wood explained it, "Mr. Lewis will be relieved of much of the daily toil of executive work and will have time to devote himself with greater freedom to the problems coming under the heading of higher administration." The plan was to elect Lewis to the Board and, furthermore, to make him its "working chairman", while at the same time he was to have alongside him a "chief of staff with the title of manager".

This arrangement was a novelty in more ways than one, for the new manager was the youngest man yet appointed to such a position. Though only just over forty, John Makins had already gained wide experience of insurance work both abroad and at home. He had entered the service of the group at Aachen in 1910 and from there had been transferred to Paris. After service in the First World War with the Royal Artillery he had returned in 1919 to work for the next five years in the Foreign Fire Department at the Commercial Union's head office. Then, in 1925, he was posted to Kobe as manager of the Japan branch. Thence he proceeded in 1926 to Shanghai as assistant manager of the China branch.

Early in 1927 Makins had been assigned to New York and in September that year became appointed Assistant United States Manager in order to ensure a fuller cohesion between the London head office and the New York management. This position was no sinecure. The Group's large and complicated interests in America were, as we have seen, passing through a most difficult period at that time, culminating in the financial crisis of 1929. Thus Makins's appointment to the second most important place in the American organisation, and one which to some extent carried with it the status of an English counsellor, required considerable qualities of diplomacy and moral courage. Altogether, it was a difficult and delicate assignment, but so well handled that it brought its reward in 1931 when Makins returned to Cornhill and was appointed Fire Manager of the Group.

From 1935 to 1938 the older and the younger man worked admirably together since they shared similar views about the management of the business and the streamlining of its structure. Makins was rapidly playing himself in during those three years and the Group's affairs were responding well to a touch that combined the wisdom of age with the freshness of new ideas. In June, 1938, the partnership ended, when Lewis finally retired. The Chairmanship then reverted to its former status and Makins was invested with the General Managership. He continued to engage himself with the unification of interests at home and abroad during those fateful months before September, 1939, and was also occupied with preparing for the problems that would have to be faced if war came. In the summer of 1939 he visited the United States where much of his attention was absorbed in discussions over the writing of war risks. Back once more in London, he hastened forward plans for the further grouping of work in the provinces and, in particular, the establishment of new central accident claims departments in Manchester, Leeds, Newcastle, Hull, Nottingham, Leicester, Southampton and Sheffield. These plans reached completion, as events turned out, two months after the war started. The war was, in fact, to expedite, through shortages of staff, the process of the Group's unification.

# CHAPTER XV

---

## The Group's Contribution
## to the War Effort—1939-1945

I

IF the part which British insurance played in the First World War was important, the part which it played in the Second World War—a total war—was vital. There are few published records about the history of insurance in this second war and an account of the Commercial Union Group's contribution to the national effort during that period is, therefore, of some historical interest.

Reports from Spain and Abyssinia had prepared the British public, and for that matter the world at large, for the effects on land of total war. Guernica had provided an ugly and impressive example of destruction from the air. The risks to life and property on land were moreover matched by the risks at sea to shipping. And those who could remember the results of the German blockade of Britain in the First World War needed no imagination to envisage the effects of another blockade infinitely more serious owing to the deadlier weapons and wider ranging capacities of modern submersibles.

Though the British government was slow in taking steps to introduce legislation regarding insurance against these potential perils on land and sea, it was commendably thorough-going when it finally did so. On August 4th, 1939, the War Risks Insurance Act was passed through Parliament. The Act dealt comprehensively with measures for insurance of ships and cargoes, insurance of goods in the United Kingdom, and a wide variety of supplementary problems.

So far as damage on land was concerned, the 1939 Act was designed to cover commodities. Its importance will be appreciated if one considers the position in which merchants would have found themselves on the outbreak of war without such a cover. No underwriters could be expected to write the potential losses on large quantities of materials and food and the obviously prudent course for any business man to adopt was to keep down his stocks of merchandise to the lowest possible level. But, however wise this precaution would have been on the part of the individual merchant, it would have spelt disaster from a national point of view. It was essential that both before and after the outbreak of war the largest possible stocks should be built up to maintain the war effort and sustain the population. The 1939 Act brought about a commodities war risk insurance scheme whereby the private insurance of stocks on land was prohibited and everyone who sold anything was compelled to take out cover with the Board of Trade. Thus a government monopoly in this field was established. But as it would have been impracticable for the Board of Trade to operate the scheme, the fire underwriting offices were employed as the government's agents to collect the premiums and pass them on to the Board. From the outset of the scheme the Commercial Union Group was heavily burdened with this agency work and it set up a special department to cope with the inflow of premiums and to give advice to clients.

From 1941 onwards the Group's responsibilities on behalf of the Board of Trade were still further increased. The War Damage Act was passed in that year and this extended the government's scheme to cover buildings, business plant and equipment, and private chattels. Buildings under this new Act were insured direct by the Government through income tax, but everything else was placed in the hands of the fire underwriting offices as agents. In that first year of the Act's operation the Group was involved in dealing with premiums amounting to some £10,000,000.

The volume of this work grew with every year of the war, and so did its complexity. The War Damage Act had been well enough framed, but it covered such a vast assortment of human needs and possessions that bewildering anomalies were continuously cropping up and much time on the part of the special department was taken up with consultations with the Board of Trade. In his recent history of Lloyd's D. E. W. Gibb quotes a good example, in regard to tombstones and coffins, of the kind of problems that had to be solved.

> " Was a tombstone, asked one of the brokers, a building or a chattel? If it was a building it would come under Part I of the Act and insurance would be compulsory. If it was a chattel it came under Part II and the insurance was optional. The Board of Trade considered the point and decided that the tombstone was a building. But what of the coffin? Did that go with the stone? No. On the same authority it was a chattel falling under Part II of the Act, so there was no necessity to insure it. The stone and the coffin must go separate ways."

By the close of the war in Europe the Commercial Union and its subsidiaries had issued over one and a quarter million policies under the government war risk schemes.

Several of the Commonwealth nations introduced similar schemes to that adopted in the United Kingdom and the overseas branches of the Group afforded assistance in their operation. On the accident side of its business the Group also rendered services to Commonwealth governments. In India, for instance, its various branches acted as agents for the government in the operation of a war injuries compensation insurance scheme introduced in 1943. Under this scheme employers in certain industries were obliged to insure themselves with the government again liability for war injuries. The Group's services were given in return for expenses only. The date of the introduction of these measures is significant; the Japanese were advancing through Burma and were approaching the gateways into northern India.

For several months before the outbreak of war the Commercial Union's Marine Department had been a member of the War Risks Cargo Pool set up as the result of an arrangement made by the Board of Trade with the marine market, whereby underwriters accepted war risks offered to them in the same way as they would in normal times, but reinsured risks of King's enemies with the government. On the outbreak of war, however, the marine clauses of the 1939 Act came into force, and the Board of Trade opened its War Risks Insurance Office. In this second war the arrangements between the government and the marine market were very different from those

P

adopted in the first. The government, profiting from its experiences between 1914 and 1918, had rightly decided that it would not repeat the old methods which left the Board of Trade to accept all the bad risks, allowing the insurance companies to take all the good.

In brief, the marine clauses of the War Risks Insurance Act divided cargo risks into two categories—voyages to and from the United Kingdom and voyages between two countries overseas. It was agreed by the companies that if they quoted rates for the first category, these would not be less than the government's rates. The advantage of this arrangement was that the government was not subjected to competition by rate cutting and at the same time foreign insurers, who might not wish to cover their risks with the British government, could take out policies with the British insurance companies. In the second category underwriters could quote what rates they liked.

These arrangements worked extremely well throughout the war. The Marine Department of the Commercial Union acted as agents of the Board of Trade over the underwriting risks on voyages to and from the United Kingdom and its Underwriter and Adjuster of Claims served on many official bodies including the War Claims Committee and the Food and Supply Committee. It is a matter of sufficient interest to record that, though not being able to quote lower rates than those of the Board of Trade on the first category of voyages, it nevertheless transacted a considerable amount of business in that sector—a sure testimony to its reputation in the market for efficiency and close personal attention. In the second category its underwriting of cargo risks rose to very high proportions, as we shall see later. Such, indeed, was the intensity of marine underwriters' work in the war that it led to an important development. Under the auspices of the Institute of London Underwriters an "Institute Combined Policy" was introduced, the whole of the administrative work over the compilations of the lists of underwriting offices being carried out by the Institute. This saved so much time on the part of underwriters that what was a war-time innovation has since become an established practice.

The Marine Department's contribution to the war effort was not confined to its work for the British government and the British mercantile marine. It played a prominent part in operating what was called the "Norwegian Master Cover". This was started after the German occupation of Norway and its basic purpose was to underwrite all Norwegian ships on their own original conditions. The premiums were payable by their Norwegian owners out of profits on war-time voyages and claims for losses were paid by the British underwriters. A similar scheme was undertaken for Dutch shipping after the occupation of the Netherlands.

For the ordinary civilian not engaged on essential war work in the United Kingdom no government scheme protected his dependents if he was killed by enemy action. The Group's rates offered for this extra coverage under its life assurance policies were generous. At the start of the war the extra annual premium charge was fixed at £1 per cent and in October 1943 this was reduced to 5/- per cent and removed altogether from January 1945. The total claims for loss of life through enemy action, which the Group paid out between the start of the war and December 31st, 1945, amounted to some £580,000. Another and most important contribution to the national war effort was the Life Fund's subscriptions to the various government war issues. By the end of the war they had come to exceed £8,000,000. In addition, the Group as a whole had invested nearly another £12,000,000 in government securities—a striking example of the part which insurance concerns played in the winning of the war.

Nor was this all. In the dark days of 1941 when Britain stood alone against the might of Germany, and America's "Lend-lease" had not yet been formulated, it became essential for the British government to find money to pay the United States for urgently needed war supplies. An ingenious loan agreement was entered into for this purpose between the government and the Reconstruction Finance Corporation of the United States. This provided a sum of £106,000,000 based on the deposit as collateral of British owned securities in the United States. A considerable amount of this collateral consisted of the capital stock of 41 British insurance companies operating in the United States—some £45,000,000 in all—and the share certificates of the Commercial Union's holdings in its subsidiaries in the United States were duly deposited with the government.

"What eventually happened to these securities?" is a query which will almost certainly occur to the reader. The answer is that the

British government found it possible to repay the loan about six years after the war—to be precise on October 1st, 1951—an act which owed its feasibility in no small degree to the post-war dollar earnings of the British insurance companies in the United States. Released from pledge, the securities were then returned by the government to their owners.

2

Looked at departmentally, the problems and experiences of the Commercial Union and its associated companies on the home front varied considerably. In the early months of the war, for instance, the group had to meet claims on a heavy outcrop of fires due to an unexpected cause—the nightly black-out. Dwelling houses were a particular menace now that their windows were heavily shrouded. Left temporarily unoccupied, if a family was out for the evening, they showed no signs of an outbreak of fire until it had reached such a stage and obtained such a hold that it was too late to deal with.

Another serious effect on fire income came with the early air raids and accumulated throughout the war. The report of the Fire Department on activities in 1940 put the matter succinctly:

"The loss of property through enemy action has meant the loss of insurance coverage. As an example, in the raid on London on December 29th no fewer than 1,166 warehouses within one mile of the Royal Exchange were destroyed or so badly damaged as to render further fire insurance unnecessary."

Without the War Damage Act there can be no doubt that the losses from German bombing, and especially incendiary raids, would have been insupportable even for such a strong group of businesses as that represented by the Commercial Union. Even so, there was a great extension of ordinary risks to property due indirectly to war-time conditions and it was a surprising achievement of the Fire Department and of the branches throughout the country that progress in work and results was maintained throughout the war.

In the accident sector experience was rather more erratic. There the disappearance of private cars from Britain's roads brought increasing loss of revenue with every year. But this was more than counterbalanced by the large growth of activity over workmen's compensation due to the continuous expansion of industry as it became harnessed into the war effort.

The achievement of the Life Department was nothing less than remarkable. At the annual meeting of the Commercial Union's shareholders, which took place shortly after the end of the war in Europe, John Gilliat, the then Chairman, in commenting on its work said:

"It is significant that the 1944 net new business figure, £227,274 in excess of the 1943 total, and 86 per cent of our best pre-war result, has been realised at a time when nobody in the Company's service remains in whole or even part-time employment for the primary purpose of securing new Life business."

Loss of staff to the armed services and to special war-time appointments was among the many problems that confronted John Makins and his colleagues on the management. The long years of war drained away their personnel and imposed a strain on the men and women left behind at a time when the burden of work for the government was added to an increase in general activity. Makins' experience over the co-ordination of the group's interests in the United States had, as we have seen already, been used to good effect at home in the years immediately preceding the war. Under his aegis schemes for further co-ordination and reduction of unnecessary effort in the United Kingdom were carried a stage further during the war. In 1942 a Central Accident Claims Department was created in London which at first acted both for the Head Office and also for claims in the London area. Still more far-reaching was an overhaul of home fire underwriting. Since 1934 a scheme for group underwriting had functioned successfully at Aberdeen. In 1943 preliminary steps were taken to extend this scheme to the whole country with the result that at the beginning of 1944 there was a pooling of the home fire business of all the allied companies. The beneficial effect of this change became apparent almost immediately.

Throughout the war Cornhill was maintained as a centre of the Group's administration. But arrangements were made for a dispersal of specialist head office staff to premises in Totteridge and Bickley, these places being selected in the interests of the employees concerned. Except for a few broken windows and very minor damage from incendiary bombs to its roof the head office came unscathed through the war. And elsewhere in the home country the branches were fortunate in escaping loss of buildings or serious damage. The one outstanding casualty was the West of England's historic office at Exeter. This was almost completely destroyed in the Baedeker raids of 1942. As mentioned in an earlier chapter, it has since been completely rebuilt.

### 3

The course of this Second World War inflicted far greater losses on British business interests overseas than did that of its predecessor. It is hardly necessary to recall that most of Europe was a closed book to us after the summer of 1940 and that after the over-running of Greece in 1941, Spain and Portugal remained as the only friendly and unoccupied continental countries to which we had any ease of access. With Japan's entry into the war at the end of 1941 we began to be deprived of our possessions and protectorates in the Far East and our trade with China came to an end. These vast losses of trading territory made their impact felt on the fire and accident sectors of the Group's revenue. But it is an interesting fact that the impact made little more than a dent. By the end of 1941 the overseas revenues of the fire and accident departments actually showed considerable increases. The overseas fire revenue continued from then onwards to increase throughout the war. The overseas accident revenue suffered some reduction in 1942 and 1943, most of this being due to loss of income from private car insurance. But it rapidly picked up again in the last two years of the war. Growth of business in the United States and the major countries of the Commonwealth accounted for this satisfactory progress. Workmen's compensation in particular was being actively developed in those countries owing to war-time conditions, and in the United States especially the Ocean and its subsidiary, the Columbia Casualty, were making rapid strides forward in most branches of casualty business.

Strangely diverse were the situations in the overseas possessions of European countries brought about by the German occupation of the

Continent. Perhaps the most interesting of all was its effect on the Belgian Congo. That vast colony of a small country now came into the limelight. Separated from Belgium it took sides with the Allied cause and became an invaluable source of raw materials such as copper, iron, tin, radium, gold, industrial diamonds, rubber and palm oil. It also played an important part in air and road communications northwards through the Sudan into the Middle East. And English and South African travellers passing through its territory on their various war missions were amazed to find in the heart of the African jungle a luxurious modern European city such as Leopoldville, the Congo's capital, and other well developed towns like Elisabethville and Stanleyville.

A story of war-time adventure in 1940 attaches itself to the Commercial Union's associations with the Congo and it relates especially to the Le Jeune family who had for many years been associated with the company's interests in Belgium.

Here it is necessary for the moment to return to the earlier years of that association. The Commercial Union was almost certainly the first insurance company to write business in the Belgian Congo. In 1869 Stanislas H. Haine had been appointed the company's first agent in Antwerp. A certain Charles Le Jeune was at that time a friend of Stanislas Haine and Le Jeune happened also to be a friend of King Leopold II. It was this link which led to the company's appointment of him to conduct such insurance services as were necessary in the pioneer days of the territory, which was at that time privately owned by the Belgian King.

For many years this work brought in only a slight amount of revenue and both in Cornhill and Antwerp it was regarded as not more than a sideline to Belgian underwriting. Until as late as 1927 the Congo insurances had been written through the Commercial Union's home foreign department as "Transatlantic business" from Stanislas H. Haine in association with Charles Le Jeune (Assurances) of Antwerp. But in that year some glimmering of the bright prospects opening up in the Congo had become apparent to the younger Le Jeunes and they reached an agreement with the Commercial Union to act as its general agents throughout the territory and also in the neighbouring territory of Ruanda-Urundi. From then onwards business was accepted in Antwerp, but it emanated from sub-agencies in the two territories—in particular from the Cie Fonciére du Katanga at Elisabethville.

After the outbreak of war the Le Jeunes decided to transfer control of these activities to the Belgian Congo itself and Alick Le Jeune intended to go to Elisabethville to establish a new office there. Unfortunately for him he was caught up in the German invasion of Belgium, but his brother, Charles, managed to escape and eventually reached Leopoldville where he set up an office and reconstructed the company's portfolio.

Benefiting from the enforced exclusion of the Belgian market, the agency prospered throughout the war and was subsequently developed into a fairly considerable organisation, dealing with fire, accident and marine underwriting, and equipped with sub-agencies operating in the principal centres. Bearing in mind the vast potential resources of the Belgian Congo, the prospects for progress of this venture started in the last war seemed fascinating enough, as indeed V. E. Masters found them when, at that time an Assistant Manager of the Group, he visited the territory in 1951. But in recording his impressions he sounded a note of carefully tempered optimism:

"We cannot ignore the difficulties which beset the Agency, the difficulties of native labour, of the distance between the several large centres, the lack of facilities which are accepted in Europe as essential, and we must bear in mind the unorganised state of the insurance market, the influence of the Belgian brokers, and the difficulties of conducting a satisfactory business in a territory of such extraordinarily rapid growth. We must remember that the father of one of the young clerks in the Agents' Marine Section is proud of his former cannibalism."

4

In an organisation so far-flung geographically as the Commercial Union Group it was inevitable that some members at least of its overseas branches would be swept up in the maelstrom of war.

As the Germans drove towards Paris in the summer of 1940 the three British members of the staff remained in Paris, and one was interned at St. Denis. Haine went to Bordeaux and lived on in

France till 1941. News of his death in that year was deeply felt by the management and senior members of the staff. He had been associated with the Commercial Union for more than fifty years and for over twenty years had managed its Parish branch with outstanding ability.

Japan's entry into the war in 1941 resulted in the immediate closing down of the branch in Yokohama. J. A. Dixon, the manager, was interned in a concentration camp. He was subsequently removed to Yokohama prison and placed in solitary confinement. For sixteen days he was subjected to cross-examination. Then this unpleasant experience suddenly ceased and he was merely detained until released at the end of July, 1942, in time to catch a ship home as an evacuee two days later. He and his wife found their way back to England in October. Asked on his return about his treatment by the Japanese while in prison, Dixon laconically described it as a " weird mixture of cruelty and kindness."

At Shanghai the manager of the China branch, E. Lester Arnold, was interned. Some time later, however, he was released to comparative freedom—only to find himself employed in the ironical position of assistant to the liquidator over the winding up of the branch's business. When this had been completed, he was interned again until the end of hostilities in the Far East. In Hong Kong the local branch manager, R. L. S. Webb, and his European assistant, were sent to a concentration camp at Kowloon. Webb was released at the end of the war, returned to England to recuperate, and went back some months later to reopen his branch.

The fate of the Singapore branch and its staff deserves more than a passing reference. The city capitulated at sundown on February 15th, 1942, some nine weeks after the Japanese had started to invade Malaya. "It was an unforgettable experience for those who were there," a member of the staff was to record after the war, "the sky blood-red with the reflection of fires, and the tropical atmosphere heavily charged with dust from shattered buildings."

The manager of the branch, A. C. Potts, was evacuated by sea just before the capitulation. So, too, was his wife and the wives of two other members of the British staff. Potts eventually made his way back to England via Ceylon. His wife and the other two women were placed on a separate ship and lost their lives. Of the seven other

British members of the branch six had been absorbed into the Malayan Defence Forces; they took part in the retreat and became military prisoners of the Japanese. The other member, C. W. Warren, remained at his post in Singapore to the end, being also an officer in the local A.R.P. organisation, and was sent to an internment camp at Changi convict prison. His wife and the wives of two of the other branch officials, who had courageously decided to stay on, were sent to a separate women's internment camp at Changi. All of them— prisoners of war and internees—suffered three-and-a-half years of harsh treatment from their captors. All of them survived, though their health was seriously affected and they were brought home as soon as possible after V.J. day to recuperate.

Among those of the staff who fought right through the Malayan campaign was the present branch manager at Singapore, Alistair Mackenzie, who was awarded the Military Cross. His wife saw service as a nurse and received the O.B.E. Another decoration, the British Empire Medal, was awarded to a Chinese member of the staff "for courage and devotion to duty as Group Warden during the air attacks on Singapore in 1941-1942". The recipient of this decoration was Cheong Chong Yew. He rendered devoted service to the restoration of the branch after the war and is now its Chief Clerk.

## 5

The toll at sea was infinitely greater in this Second World War. The British, their allies and the neutral nations lost nearly 5,100 merchant ships totalling more than twenty-one and a half million gross tons. The dice against us were far more heavily loaded than those between 1914 and 1918. After the summer of 1940 our North Sea blockade came to an end and we also had no bases on the Southern Irish coast as in the earlier war. The German surface- raiding warships and U-boats, with a much greater range of move- ment than formerly, were able to roam the Atlantic with far more freedom and from the ports of the French northern and western coasts. Whereas in the first war we had Italy as our ally in the Mediterranean, she now confronted us there as an enemy. Whereas Japan was our ally in the first war, she did immense damage to our shipping in Far Eastern waters from 1941 onwards. Moreover, we had to contend with air attack, with a three dimensional instead of a two dimensional war at sea.

For reasons mentioned earlier in this chapter the Commercial Union, like any other British office dealing in marine insurance, could have avoided altogether the writing of war risks on hulls and cargoes. In any event it had to quote higher rates than the government's. But the company decided to accept such risks from the outset and the Marine Department's handling of them was accomplished with a fine mixture of courage and expert judgment firstly under A. L. Kennedy and, after his death at the end of 1941, under his successor, Glanvill Smith, who had been assistant underwriter since 1933. In fact, the department's revenue continued to mount progressively higher through those very years of the war at sea when our losses were heaviest—that is to say up to the end of 1942, a year which was perhaps the worst period of the whole war from the marine point of view. In that year German submarines were concentrating on the Atlantic before the United States had fully deployed her sea-power and, especially in and around the Caribbean, were doing immense destruction to ships and cargoes. Of course, the department raised its rates, but even so the risks and losses were great and were only sustained by extremely able assessment and readiness to persevere after a succession of adversities.

"The acceptance of war risks," stated John Gilliat, the company's Chairman when hostilities came to an end, "is an abnormal exercise of our functions and, though the premiums are large, the hazards are many and the outcome necessarily uncertain; therefore, whilst the results of our underwriting have been satisfactory, we welcome the return to more normal conditions."

From 1943 onwards, when the Mediterranean was cleared and the British and American navies were successfully combating the submarine menace in the Atlantic, the volume of revenue steadily decreased as the rates for war risk coverage were constantly reduced and a large quantity of shipping was requisitioned by the allied governments.

The heaviest claim met by the Marine Department during the war was not insured on the high seas. On April 10th, 1944, a cargo steamer, the *Fort Stikine* arrived at Bombay. The harbour was crowded with shipping. The *Fort Stikine* carried in her holds a large quantity of cotton and 1,400 tons of explosives. On the following day it suddenly caught on fire. Frantic efforts were made to get the flames under control. They were unsuccessful and when the fire reached the holds, two terrific explosions shook the port and city. In the harbour itself the burning cotton was blown in all directions, setting fire to and destroying nine other ships. In the city enormous damage was done to property and buildings partly through the blast and partly through the extension of the fire beyond the harbour. Five hundred persons lost their lives and a further thousand were injured.

The magnitude of this disaster was not revealed to the world at large till after the war. It caused the Government of India to draw up a scheme for the relief of persons who had suffered injury or damage to property. The fire underwriting companies agreed to make a voluntary contribution of 12½ per cent towards the liability assumed by the government over the damage to property on land insured with them. The total claim was established at £12,000,000 and the Commercial Union Group paid over a substantial sum as its share in the contribution. The Marine Department was much more heavily involved in the loss and partial destruction of ships and cargoes, the total cost of which to the whole marine market came to some £6,000,000.

Among the most tragic war losses at sea over which the Marine Department became involved was an incident in which the *Queen Mary* figured. In October, 1942, she was crossing the Atlantic from New York to Gourock. Escorting her was the light cruiser *H.M.S. Curacao*. One of the duties of escorts was to circle their protégées from time to time. During one of these movements the *Curacao* cut across the bows of the *Queen Mary* and the great ship, unable to slacken speed in time, smashed through her. The *Curacao* foundered almost immediately, taking most of her crew to the bottom with her.

It was difficult to apportion the blame over this unhappy event and the case eventually went to the House of Lords which decided that one-third of the loss should be borne by the *Queen Mary's* underwriters and two-thirds by the Admiralty.

6

From this Second World War the Commercial Union Group emerged stronger than ever. At the end of 1945 its Fire Fund exceeded £8 million, its Marine Fund £2 million, and its Accident Fund £7 million. The Life Fund stood at over £33 million. The Group's total assets had risen to more than £85 million.

Much has been said in this chapter about the contribution that the whole business made to the winning of the war at home, abroad and at sea. But special mention should be made here, and before we pass onwards into times of peace, of the members of its staff who joined the fighting services. From the head office and from branches and offices in the United Kingdom and the Commonwealth 2,734 went into the war. Out of their number 145 perished on land, at sea and in the air, and 70 received awards and decorations. In the United States, too, 350 members of the various companies of the Group played an active part in their nation's war effort.

PART FIVE

*Years of Progress*
*1946-1958*

# CHAPTER XVI

---

## *Insurance under New Conditions*

THIS history now enters into a period familiar to almost everyone who may read it. For this reason there is not the same need to recount in detail, as in the case of the years that followed the First World War, the social, economic and political events through which the Commercial Union Group has progressed since 1946. Let the story tell itself with its own particular reflections of developments and change. But it may be as well to remind ourselves of a few basic facts that have affected trade and industry at home and overseas and, consequently, the insurance market so inextricably bound up with them.

Firstly, there is the miracle of the world's recovery in so short a space of time from the enormous expenditure in life and property of a war fought on a total scale. It has been estimated that over 22,000,000 persons, military and civilian, perished in the conflict and that over 34,000,000 were wounded. An American assessment of the total costs of war materials produced by or for the belligerents has placed them at $1,154,000,000,000. In Europe especially the material damage was enormous. In forty-nine of Germany's largest cities nearly 40 per cent of houses were destroyed, and over 60 per cent of Berlin was reduced to ruins. In Britain nearly 3,300,000 properties were destroyed or damaged by air attack. In France nearly one-fifth of that country's houses were devastated by the end of the war and it was estimated by the French War Damage Commission that the total cost of the conflict to the nation was equal to 45 per cent of her entire wealth.

International trade had been brought to a virtual standstill. The nations of Western Europe had for the time being been almost entirely put out of action as manufacturing countries exporting to the world, while the United States, with a productive capacity easily able to fill the vacuum, could not fully do so because the rest of the world had insufficient dollars to pay for her goods. And Britain's attempt to put the pound sterling on a parity with the dollar ended in failure with its devaluation in the autumn of 1949.

Despite all this, international trade and commerce recovered their stability much more effectively within the first decade after 1945 than within a similar period after 1918. So far as Western Europe and North America were concerned, the lessons of the First World War had been learned. The treatment of Germany was less harsh and exacting and the chain reaction that would have been caused by excessive reparations was thus largely avoided. In the immediate aftermath of war the European economy was buttressed by the United States through the establishment of the International Bank for Reconstruction and Development and the International Monetary Fund. Later, in 1947, came Marshall Aid, followed by the establishment of the Organisation for European Economic Co-operation and of the European Payments Union, leading in due course to a rehabilitation of Western Europe, the beneficial effects of which were to spread outwards through the world at large.

On the other hand the period was to see the descent of the Iron Curtain, splitting Germany into two and also removing from the Western or Capitalist orbit into the Communist sphere Poland, Czechoslovakia, Hungary, Rumania, Bulgaria and the Baltic States. The advent of a Communist State in China was to intensify this division of the civilised world into two separate economic camps and, though in recent years some resumption of trade between the two camps has begun to take place, insurance underwriters of the Western world have not been able to re-establish themselves on Communist soil.

Another symptom of change in international relations, which will become apparent in this survey of the Commercial Union Group's activities, has been the secession from the influence or possession of the so-called "colonial" powers of vast tracts of territory in the Middle East, in Africa, in the Indian sub-continent, in Malaya, in

Indonesia and elsewhere. The results of the granting and, in some cases, the seizing of independence have varied considerably between one new nation and another. Generally speaking, however, there has been an extreme upsurge of nationalist consciousness vented in legislation inimical to foreign trade. But it is an interesting and remarkable fact that the Commercial Union Group, as indeed other large British insurance businesses, has held its own in most of these countries and even extended its interests in some of them.

Lastly, a phenomenon of recent years has been the wide-scale development of industry in the great producing countries and the accelerating demands for the modern amenities of life among their wage-earning classes. To these demands have been added the growing requirements of semi-developed and under-developed communities. The unprecedented increase in air travel, in car ownership, in television are among the many changes that pose problems and opportunities alike to modern underwriters. More than all else, perhaps, the advent of atomic energy has presented issues of far-reaching complexity. These issues challenge underwriters in nearly every section of insurance and, as a leading composite office, the Commercial Union Group has, as we shall see, played its part along with others in insuring the hazards from this new form of power both at home and overseas.

# CHAPTER XVII

# The Changing Scene in Britain

I

AMONG the important changes that came to affect the pattern of life in the United Kingdom after the war was the nationalisation of the country's key industries. The effects of these measures, all of which were carried through between 1947 and 1949, have been diverse in their application, especially in the insurance market.

Coal mining was the first of the industries to be nationalised and the National Coal Board came into existence on January 1st, 1947. In this case the insurance market, including the Commercial Union Group, lost its long-standing association with the industry. No colliery buildings or plant have since been insured, the Board carrying its own losses. But shortly before the ownership of pit props was transferred to the Board from the Timber Control Department of the Board of Trade, there was a fire at West Hartlepool destroying half a million pounds' worth of timber and for a year the insurance of pit props was underwritten by the market with the Commercial Union as leading office. This seems to have been the only case where any property of the National Coal Board has been insured. It was, moreover, only a temporary measure. The mines continue to be the nation's property and the nation continues to be responsible for any losses in them.

The British Transport Commission was established exactly a year after the National Coal Board. As far as the railways were concerned, the only insurance policies placed widely throughout the market were for the Eastern, North Eastern and Scottish regions and these insurances have been continued, the Commercial Union again being the leading office. The insurance policies of the former London Passenger Transport Board were also continued and the Commercial Union Group shares in this insurance, although not as leading office.

The nationalisation of road transport under the Road Haulage Executive, itself a body responsible to the British Transport Commission, was to have a rather different and more varied history. From the outset the Executive decided to insure its property against fire and certain classes of accident business in the market, and the Commercial Union Group played its part in this coverage through a market pool, the Road Haulage Insurers Committee.

Next on the list of industries to be nationalised came the country's electricity services, these being brought under the British Electricity Authority on April 1st, 1948. After long negotiations with the insurance market this body resolved to cover all its property and interests under a special scheme provided by the whole market. To implement this extremely important collective contract an organisation called the Associated Insurers (British Electricity) Management Committee was appointed. This has continued to function most successfully since it was set up and the Commercial Union Group has been prominently associated with it, John Makins having been largely responsible for carrying through the negotiations that led to its formation in 1949, and having subsequently presided over its activities as Chairman till 1958. Furthermore, the Chairmanships of the organisation's advisory panels have been held by senior officers of the Group.

The vesting date for the gas industry was May 1st, 1949. Nationalisation in this sphere was carried out with a marked emphasis on regional autonomy and the Gas Boards have continued to function with considerable commercial independence. All of them, in greater or less degree, have sought security for their property and interests in the insurance market against both fire and accident risks. The Commercial Union Group has maintained interests with several of them and, as a result of long standing relations with gas enterprises in the West Country, it leads the market in the underwriting of the South Western Gas Board's insurances.

Such in general terms have been the effects on the insurance market and the Commercial Union Group of the nationalisation of Britain's key industries. Socialist legislation, however, has also been felt in other ways. The National Health Act, for instance, and the introduction of the new social security services in 1948 were to take the underwriting of the country's hospitals out of the market and make this the responsibility of the nation. National insurance was also to cause some temporary slowing down in the growth of personal accident business.

More far-reaching still in the accident underwriting field were the first results of the Industrial Injuries Act introduced in 1948. This relieved employers of the liabilities imposed on them by the Workmen's Compensation Act. Insurance over such risks became unnecessary and an inevitable fall in income from this source started to set in. The Act also produced a difficult complication, referred to diplomatically by the Group's Chairman, Colonel J. Leslie, in his address to the shareholders that year.

"Our Workmen's Compensation Policies also covered the Insured's Common Law liability to workmen and, as this liability still remains, the necessary cover has been continued under all policies at an adjusted rate of premium."

The number of accidents notified with a potential Common Law liability continued to increase. By 1953, however, the Group's experience over Employers' Liability business was becoming brighter. This was partly due to the application of general increases in rating, to offset the rising volume of claims, and partly to improvements in methods to prevent accidents. It was also due to the upward swing of wages and the Group's progress in securing new business in this field. This progress has been more than maintained in recent years and, though some of the problems caused by the Industrial Injuries Act have not yet been solved, it is an interesting example of how British insurance can absorb or assimilate legislation and produce new techniques to deal with it. The effect on certain companies specialising in Workmen's Compensation Insurance was to lead them to branch out into other fields of underwriting such as fire, with a resultant increase in competition for business.

It should, perhaps, be added here that the Commercial Union and its associated companies in the United Kingdom have actively interested themselves in promoting safety in industry and are represented on fifteen local Industrial Accident Prevention Groups formed in 1957 under the auspices of the Royal Society for the Prevention of Accidents.

2

The pattern of insurance in the United Kingdom during the last decade or so has been as much affected by social changes as by political events. In this respect our way of life has followed developments more or less similar to those that have been taking place in various other parts of the world and we shall see something of their effects both at home and abroad in a later chapter. But here a passing reference may well be made to certain matters, familiar enough though they may be to anyone who has lived in Britain since the war.

The days of petrol rationing seem very remote. Yet in actual fact it was not abolished until June 1st, 1950. Even before that date the number of cars on our roads was steadily increasing, but since then their number has swollen to enormous proportions following the economic recovery of the country. Since the year when petrol rationing ceased, the Commercial Union Group's premium income from motor insurance at home has increased at least sevenfold. Though more vehicles in circulation have meant more premiums, they have also meant more accidents and this fact, coupled with changing designs of engines and bodies, has resulted in an ever increasing spiral of claims' costs borne by the insurers. However, greater prosperity and higher earnings in general have tended to influence the courts to award higher damage for Third Party claims. To meet this continuous upsurge in claims British accident underwriters have experienced serious difficulties in setting their premiums at a suitably commensurate figure, but it is a fact of some interest that British premiums have been maintained at a level substantially below that of most European countries.

In common with other British insurers, the Commercial Union

Group has been associated with movements to protect the general public against accidents and has played a part in the work of the Motor Insurers' Bureau from its formation in 1946. This organisation's principal object was for the protection of persons injured in accidents caused by uninsured motorists, but its scope has been widened to give sympathetic consideration to persons injured by unidentified motorists.

No less than citizens of other countries the British have taken to air travel in a big way since the last war. The Group is not directly interested in underwriting aircraft, but the rapid growth in air travel has had a considerable bearing on the development of its personal accident account. With the great advance in aeronautics air travel has become no more hazardous than travel by more traditional means, and the flying risk is now generally included without additional charge as a normal part of the cover in the personal accident policies of the Group's companies.

Since the post-war revival of television the installation of television sets in British homes has grown with fantastic pace from year to year. The Group has pioneered the development of television insurance in the United Kingdom and the great increase of its premium income from this source in recent years is an interesting example of television's impact on the insurance market.

The most far-reaching industrial development of the fifties was the advent of atomic energy. The immensity of the problems involved in covering atomic energy installations made it obvious that the knowledge and resources of the entire insurance market should be marshalled together. In 1956, therefore, to facilitate the underwriting of atomic insurance, there was established under Sir John Makins as Chairman the British Insurance (Atomic Energy) Committee—a consortium of tariff, non-tariff and mutual insurance companies with full support from Lloyd's. Under this organisation the insurance of atomic installations is undertaken and pooled between all its participating members. This British organisation has at all times been in close touch with similar organisations overseas in several international conferences, and meetings with experts in other European markets have taken place.

Though atomic energy is being developed in the United Kingdom under the best possible rules of safety, it nevertheless involves grave risks because any escape of radioactive substances from a reactor or other confines is liable to cause serious injury to persons and damage to property. Operators, therefore, can look to underwriters to provide third party indemnity up to the statutory limit of £5,000,000. In addition, the values of reactors and other property on an atomic power site may run into sums in the region of £50,000,000 or £60,000,000. Not only do insurers have to cope with these immense sums, but they are also faced by new perils, of which in these early days they have little practical experience.

Nevertheless, the British insurance market has faced up to this challenge. The Commercial Union Group has always been in the vanguard over this entirely new venture and it continues to remain there. It is strongly represented on various committees which sift the intricate data and appraise the underwriting hazard in connection with nuclear reactors.

## 3

An alarming phenomenon in the years immediately following the Second World War was the mounting incidence of fires in residential property, in factories and in warehouses. In 1946 Britain's bill for fire damage was reported in *The Times* as having exceeded £12 million; in 1947 it nearly reached the £20 million mark. "Fire wastage", to use a term coined in the insurance market, became a matter of concern to the government, as well as to industry and commerce, and something had to be done about it, especially in view of the post-war shortage of buildings and commodities. At this point the insurance market came forward with a valuable scheme in the nation's interests. The Fire Offices' Committee, of which the Commercial Union Group is a member, approached the various government departments concerned and, in consultation with them, established in 1946 a body now well-known as the Fire Protection Association.

With the rapid growth of industrial productivity in very recent years and the large sums entailed in materials, plant and products, damage and loss caused by a single event can be far greater than twenty years ago. This is particularly true of modern engineering workshops and motor car and aircraft assembly plants. Floor and roof acreage are far more extensive than they used to be. Division walls have been almost entirely eliminated to avoid obstruction of the production line. There is, of course, a danger in generalising about such developments or of simplifying the problems presented. In greater or less degree, however, these factors seem to account for at least four of the major fires which, between 1957 and 1959, have overtaken works belonging to firms with household names in such industries. The Commercial Union Group had led the market in underwriting three of these works and, in conjunction with its market co-insurers, paid claims, for property and consequential loss, totalling several million pounds.

Among disasters that have overtaken older properties during recent years in the United Kingdom, and over the losses sustained thereby the Group has taken its share in meeting claims, the most spectacular perhaps was the fire that broke out in London's famous poultry market at Smithfield in the early hours of January 23rd, 1958. It was certainly the most disastrous fire of that year.

"The territory was unfamiliar to the fire-fighters and the conditions were dangerous", to quote a subsequent report in the Fire Protection Association's Journal. "Before it broke through the surface the fire was carried through numerous cold air pipes and ducts in an underground maze of windowless compartments with limited access and restricted ventilation. Fire-fighting operations were made particularly dangerous by the dense clouds of smoke produced by large quantities of insulating materials, bituminous sheeting, granulated cork and slab cork. Above ground ice conditions turned the water to sheets of ice and froze the uniforms of the firemen. Two thousand firemen worked in shifts for several days to have the fire under control; two firemen lost their lives and many were seriously injured."

The precise cause of this disaster, which destroyed vast quantities of poultry in addition to the buildings and stalls, was to remain unknown.

# CHAPTER XVIII

---

# Developments Abroad and
# Marine Events

I

IMPORTANT as was the Group's growth of business at home
after the last war, its progress abroad was still more marked.
Reviewing for the shareholders this progress even within three
years after the war's end, Colonel J. Leslie, who had recently been
elected Chairman, referred to the fact that "the international character of insurance is recognised by those familiar with the workings of
the insurance world, but to the layman it is not apparent, and it may
help you to appreciate it if I tell you that, of our £29½ million Fire
and Accident premiums, no less than £19½ millions, or two-thirds,
is in respect of business transacted outside the borders of this country.
. . . Generally, the resilience of our overseas business has been
remarkable, and it is very encouraging for the future to find that
after all the vicissitudes of the last ten years our company's
reputation in the world for security and service stands as high as
ever."

The resumption of relations with Europe was surprisingly rapid.
Almost immediately after the entry of the allied troops into Paris in
1944 a delegation of four, representing the British insurance companies and Lloyd's, and including John Makins, had been flown out
there by the Royal Air Force to discuss with their French opposite
numbers problems arising from the freeing of France from enemy

occupation. Incidentally, as reported in the press at the time, this delegation of four were the first British civilians to arrive in Paris after its liberation. Relations with Belgium and Holland were also re-established after their liberation. One at least of the causes of this quick resumption of pre-war business was the loyalty displayed by the Group's agents and branches throughout the long period of enemy occupation of their respective countries. Perhaps the most astonishing instance was in Denmark. When German troops had suddenly occupied Copenhagen in 1940, Aage Ferdinandsen, the Group's Danish manager, promptly removed the names of the Group's British companies from the entrance to the Vidar offices. The Vidar itself continued to operate throughout the war as a Danish business and the fact that it was owned by the Commercial Union Group seems to have been overlooked by the Germans. Thus, with its offices, staff and portfolio intact, the Vidar became an immediately effective medium for the other companies of the Group when Denmark was liberated in 1945.

Resumption of business relations with the ex-enemy countries of Europe presented different problems altogether. The Group's long-standing associations with fire and accident underwriting in Germany were not resumed, though it started again to transact marine business through Mund and Fester, who have been its agents in Hamburg since 1861. With the descent of the Iron Curtain Hungary and Czechoslovakia were lost to the British insurance market. On the other hand activities in Italy were successfully opened up again after a settlement of pre-war debts. But quite the most interesting development of the Group's interests in Europe after the war was to be its re-acquisition of controlling interests in the Anglo-Elementar of Austria.

It will be remembered that after Austria's occupation by Germany the Board and management in Cornhill had decided to take advantage of an offer by the Colonia of Cologne to sell to that company the shares representing some 55 per cent of the total capital of the Anglo-Elementar held by the Commercial Union. But after the liberation of Austria the company found itself deprived of its portfolios in Czechoslovakia, Hungary and Yugoslavia, and its subsidiaries, the Silesia and the Britania, were confiscated. In Austria itself it came to suffer from the stigma of its German associations; it was forbidden to

have a board of directors and was placed under a public administrator.

Fortunately, the public administrator was Dr. Bittner, who had
been in charge of the company's fire business before the war and at
the end of it occupied a position equivalent to the general managership. Under Bittner's energetic guidance the Anglo-Elementar was
gradually restored to its status of a leading industrial fire company in
Austria.

In the autumn of 1955 V. E. Masters, at that time an Assistant
General Manager of the Commercial Union Group, happened to visit
Austria and shortly after his arrival in Vienna was approached by
Bittner on the matter of the Commercial Union's interest in the
Anglo-Elementar. Bittner advised him that, with the recent signing
of the State Treaty and the restoration of Austria's sovereignty, the
shares sold to the Colonia had passed into the ownership of the
Austrian state, that a number of offers had already been made to
the Minister of Finance to purchase these shares, and that if the
Commercial Union wished to resume its holdings in the company,
there was no time to lose in starting negotiations.

Masters thereupon secured an interview with the Minister of
Finance, Dr. Kamitz, who promised him the first refusal to buy the
Anglo-Elementar shares. He also saw Dr. Heinrich Wagner, head of
the Aufsichtsamt, who offered him such assistance as he could over
the re-acquisition. Enquiries at the British Embassy confirmed his
own opinion about the satisfactory state of the Austrian economy
and its excellent future prospects. On returning to London he recommended an early decision to negotiate with the Austrian government
and by November of the following year the Commercial Union re-
established its former association with the Anglo-Elementar through
purchasing its former holding of shares—a holding which has since
been increased.

The Anglo-Elementar has grown from strength to strength in
recent years. Through its medium the Commercial Union has continued to develop valuable contacts with fire, accident and marine
business in Austria. By 1958 the company's premium income
exceeded that of any other members of the group in the European
field—nearly £1½ million in the accident sector and some £385,000
in fire business.

After Austria the European countries, in which the Group most successfully widened its influence during the post-war period up to 1958, were Belgium, Holland, Italy, Portugal and Denmark. Between 1946 and that year the accident net premium income from Europe rose from £273,000 to nearly £3,400,000 and the fire income from some £250,000 to over £1,130,000. As in earlier years, the Ocean played a dominating part in the growth of the accident account.

This description of the European scene would be incomplete without a reference to one particular development—the impressive growth of co-operation between the underwriting markets of Western Europe. This is, of course, a reflection of wider trends in the Western European economy, but it is interesting as showing the inextricable links of insurance with the expansion of international industry and commerce. With the advent of the Organisation for European Economic Co-operation it soon became obvious that insurance must play a vital part in the growth of trade between the countries involved. The Commercial Union Group has for a number of years been associated with the insurance sub-committee of O.E.E.C., and V. E. Masters, now one of the Group's Deputy General Managers, has served on it as one of the Vice-Chairmen since 1955.

2

Life on the North American continent rushes along at a tempo which is unparalleled elsewhere. Business is conducted on a vaster scale, the developments and rewards of industry are pressed forward more rapidly, and nature combines with man to produce success on the one hand and disaster on the other with a larger and more spectacular flamboyance than in most other parts of the globe. The impact of such conditions on American insurance has become apparent enough in past pages of this history. It has continued to make its influence felt as strongly as ever in recent years.

Fire wastage in the United States increased more rapidly after the last war than in the United Kingdom and, over and above this, the fire underwriters' problems were not lessened by the frequency of havoc-making wind storms and hurricanes. In 1950 the Eastern States were struck by hurricanes that damaged houses and property to the extent of 400 million dollars. In 1954 three tornadoes, to become famous under the names of Carol, Edna and Hazel, resulted in widespread destruction. The claims presented to the insurance industry as a whole over these 1954 events exceeded 200 million dollars. The Commercial Union Group received over 25,000 claims, which cost it more than £650,000 to settle. Less spectacular and, therefore, attracting less attention were numerous similar storms which year by year came to represent a substantial proportion of the Group's total losses in the United States. And here it is sufficient to say that, whereas a century ago the violence of American hurricanes was no less than it is today, the damage to property is infinitely greater owing to the vast growth of the continent's built-up areas.

As in the United Kingdom, part at least of the increase of fire wastage in the United States was accounted for by the development of the automobile and aircraft industries. The largest single claim ever sustained by the Group was occasioned at Livonia, Michigan in 1954 through a fire that almost completely destroyed the hydromatic gear works of the General Motor Corporation.

In casualty business the march of events showed similar characteristics. The turnover of the Ocean and Columbia mounted rapidly from year to year. A large amount of this was accounted for by automobile business, but it was exactly in this field that extremely heavy claims, especially over third-party risks, came to be an unwelcome experience.

Added to these problems in the forties and fifties were the general growth of competition in the American insurance market and the difficulties promoted by State insurance legislation. They spelt the necessity for continuous contact at a high level between the Group's headquarters in London and the United States management, as the frequent visits to New York and further afield by Makins, in his capacity as General Manager, provided ample evidence.

Further reorganisation and integration of the Group's diversified American interests became imperative and the various reports which Makins presented on his return from these visits show the complexity of the problems involved. He made his first post-war tour of the United States in the late summer and early autumn of 1947. Koeckert, whose able management has been referred to earlier, had now approached the age of retirement as chief executive in the United

States. Makins decided that this was a suitable moment to bring about a scheme of closer integration. He, therefore, advised that Koeckert should become the General Attorney of all the British companies—the Commercial Union, the Union, the Palatine, the British General and Ocean—and Chairman of the four American subsidiaries—the Commercial Union of New York, the American Central, the California and the Columbia Casualty. As a complement to this change he recommended Harry Miller's appointment as Manager for the four fire companies and as President of the Commercial Union of New York and the American Central.

In October, 1948, Makins was again in New York in connection with these changes that had been put into force earlier in the year. His main purpose on his next visit at the beginning of 1950 was to say farewell to Koeckert who had finally retired at the end of 1949. Koeckert was then seventy and had been at the helm of affairs for twenty-two years. It was decided to postpone placing any one officer in his overall position of authority. Complete responsibility for the management of the fire interests was vested in Harry Miller, while L. S. Jones was given a similar position in relation to casualty business. An interlocking of their activities, and thus of the whole of the American régime, was brought about by making them deputies to each other in their separate spheres. A sidelight on this somewhat unusual and ingenious arrangement was the growing trend in the United States towards "multiple line" underwriting.

To keep in touch with the effects of this reorganisation Makins revisited the United States in the autumn of 1951. But he did not go there again till 1953 when he combined his visit with a tour of Canada, his period in the two countries lasting from late in January to early March. His tour through the United States on this occasion was a diverse affair which had more to do with certain aspects of underwriting on the continent than with Group reorganisation. From New York he went on to Atlanta and other places in the South, where his main pre-occupation was with the problems of fixing limits for windstorm business which, as we have seen, was causing the management considerable anxiety. He also attended the centenary celebrations at St. Louis of the American Central, stopping off on the way at Chicago, Buffalo and Hartford for conferences with officers and staff.

The mounting growth of windstorm claims was again one of the causes that brought Makins to New York early in 1954 and 1955, but his principal reason for going there was to review the progress of the integration programme and to carry forward a stage further the re-arrangement of executive duties. This applied particularly to the specialist departments and ancillary services such as personnel management, printing and publicity, accounts, investments, supply facilities and office methods. The work of officers in the field was also revised and intensified. In 1956 consultations with Harry Miller took place in London.

Makins's final visit, as General Manager, to the United States was undertaken in the autumn of 1957. On this occasion he put the finishing touches to a protracted and difficult scheme of reorganisation, in which he carefully blended the importance of human values and relationships with the major issues confronting a wide-scale business in a vast territory. Deaths and retirements now made these finishing touches possible. Already the Group's continental activities had been streamlined under three main branches covering the Metropolitan, Southern and Pacific Coasts areas. Earlier, too, fire operations had been pooled, as we have seen, among the seven fire companies and casualty business between the Ocean and Columbia. But from January 1st, 1958, complete integration of the entire American organisation was established under one management at New York and with the appointment of Harry Miller as chief United States executive. Fire and casualty activities were pooled among the nine companies, and from now onwards the three main branches and all ancillary and specialist activities were controlled from New York.

The General Manager's frequent visits to the American scene throughout this period were supplemented by tours of investigation on the part of other senior officials of the management. The great importance of the American sphere to the British insurance market is matched by its accumulating problems and risks; and only constant surveillance of such a sphere can permit a British insurance group to maintain, let alone develop, its business there.

Between 1946 and 1958 the Group's net premium income from the United States rose in round figures from £3,193,000 to £12,200,000 in the accident sector and from £4,712,000 to £12,080,000 in fire underwriting.

R

3

During these years frequent visits were also made by the General Manager to Canada, and he and other senior officials undertook lengthy tours by air and sea through Australia, New Zealand and South Africa. The population and affluence of these Dominions were now growing far more rapidly even than in the inter-war years. In fact, their national status and international importance were already established. An impressive sign of their industrial, commercial and agricultural expansion was the increasing size of their insurance markets. Here again progressive schemes of integration of the Group's activities and operating companies were to take advantage of new opportunity.

Indeed, the rise in results from accident and fire underwriting in their territories was to be little less than prodigious. In Canada, for instance, the net accident premium income rose from some £594,000 in 1946 to over £3,200,000 in 1958, while in the same period the net fire premiums rose from some £320,000 to nearly £1,237,000. In Australasia the net premium income increased in round figures from £530,000 to £3,500,000 and the fire from £450,000 to £2,000,000. The main contribution to the results from the African continent was supplied by the Union of South Africa and the territories adjoining it. These results showed a net accident premium growth from some £356,000 to £1,444,000 and in the fire sector a growth from £83,000 to £301,000.

On the other hand the Group's rate of progress in Asia was seriously impaired. In that continent the march of events towards and beyond independence was to exert its effects more adversely on British insurance interests than on most other British business activities. The granting of Dominion status to India and Pakistan in 1947 was followed by India's proclamation of herself as a republic in 1950 and by Pakistan proclaiming herself as an Islamic republic within the Commonwealth in 1956. Burma and Ceylon gained their independence in 1948. The federation of Malaya as an independent nation within the Commonwealth took place in 1957. Outside the Commonwealth the Dutch East Indies had become the United States of Indonesia in 1949.

During the first flush of independence it was inevitable that these countries would display nationalistic tendencies in their business affairs. They had thrown off the yoke of foreign government; they would now throw off the yoke of foreign commercial enterprise. India went so far as to nationalise all life assurance in 1956, though this had little effect on the interests of the Commercial Union Group, which had only practised such underwriting there in a very limited way. However, the tendency in most of these new nations was to introduce legislation inimical to foreign underwriting and encouraging to indigenous insurance enterprise.

It is difficult at this point of time to predict the future of British and other foreign insurance companies under these changing conditions in Asia. But in a quickly contracting and growingly interdependent world, and with the need to attract capital for social and industrial development, it seems possible that there may be second thoughts on the value of limiting or impeding foreign enterprise in insurance. Certain it is that in the accident sector at any rate the Commercial Union Group has under difficult circumstances made a surprising degree of progress, mostly in India and Malaya, and more recently in Indonesia. The goodwill shown to British interests by the Indonesian government is an interesting and welcome feature of the Asian scene. A sign of this was the approval given by that government to the establishment of a Commercial Union Group office in Djakarta in 1959, when the control of its Indonesian interests was removed to the Indonesian capital.

Elsewhere—in Central and South America and the West Indies—political conditions combined with natural phenomena, such as the 1951 hurricane, which inflicted the greatest disaster on Jamaica that has been experienced in its known history, to retard progress in fire underwriting.

If we take an overall view of the Group's development abroad during these years, the picture is extremely interesting and significant. Though its rate of progress financially in the United States was slowed down, the actual growth of income from that country continued to be very large indeed and provided the main bulk of its overseas revenue. The rate of progress in Europe was excellent, and that registered in the English-speaking countries of the Commonwealth was quite outstanding compared with earlier years. The results from Asia showed a slowing down in rate of progress, but were far from unsatisfactory under all the circumstances. During a period of continuous change and crisis in international relations the Group augmented its annual overseas net premium income from some £9½ million in 1947 to over £33½ million in 1958.

4

In many respects marine underwriting, whether transacted in the London market or overseas, is inevitably an even more sensitive barometer of the fluctuations in international trade and politics than in any other form of insurance. The experience of the Group's Marine Department since the end of the last war certainly bears out this statement.

Throughout this period, as in earlier years, the main bulk of London underwriting was concerned with hulls, whereas in foreign underwriting, or in other words the business done by the Group's branches and agencies overseas, the emphasis was on cargoes, except in the case of the United States, France and Norway, where hull business formed the larger part of transactions. For this reason a more accurate and interesting picture of the course taken by maritime commerce will emerge if we look at the two sides separately.

The rebuilding of their merchant fleets was one of the first preoccupations of the maritime nations during the years immediately following the war. By 1948 there was a great resurge in the volume of world trade and in the world tonnage of shipping. The boom was not confined to cargo carrying vessels. Passenger traffic was coming into its own again and typical of the new liners that were commissioned that year was the *Caronia*, insured for £4 million. By 1951 most European countries possessed shipping tonnage comparable with or even exceeding those of 1939 and the world's shipping was actually 27 per cent higher in volume than the pre-war figure. The substantial rise in profits recorded by the Marine Department that year was largely due to its London underwriting, in which it had scored the advantages not only of the growth in numbers of insurable hulls, but also of their increasing values.

The tale of success continued despite the now mounting costs of repairs in British, American and European shipyards, some heavy claims incurred over the loss of several large liners, and other claims through the serious gales and floods of 1952 along the British, Dutch and Belgian coasts. In his 1954 report to the Board Glanvill Smith, who was still in office as Marine Underwriter, stated:

"We continue to lead the majority of the large Liner and Tramp Fleets of the world and have the confidence of the rest of the market in our decisions."

That year of 1954 had not, however, been an easy one for London underwriting. The end of the war in Korea had brought with it some reduction in the commissioning of ships at the very moment when British yards had launched their highest tonnage since 1930. There were, moreover, many obsolete vessels still in commission and these constituted a potentially heavier risk to the insurer.

For the next three years the Group's Marine Department continued to maintain its satisfactory results in the London market. In 1958, however, the ominous trends in the shipping trade, which had started to reveal themselves four years previously, began to exert a more serious effect. The old law of supply and demand confronted ship-owners. There was a surplus of ships and a dearth of commissions. Harbours in Britain and many other parts of the world started to become congested with laid-up vessels ranging from war-built tonnage to others which had recently been completed. A fall in the value of hulls resulted and, though there was an inevitable decrease in the Marine Department's profits that year, the quite substantial revenue earned was undoubtedly due to sound underwriting.

Fundamentally, the fortunes and fluctuations in cargo underwriting, so much of which was effected overseas, were governed by the same principal factors as that which prevailed in hull coverage— the state of international trade. In other respects the variations were considerable. Post-war inflation and the high cost of commodities at first maintained cargo underwriting at a good profit level. By 1954, however, the fall in the costs of commodities, the introduction in many countries of currency restrictions limiting imports, and the influence brought to bear by certain governments on merchants to insure with indigenous underwriting companies began to be felt in foreign business. In Asia especially the problems experienced through government influence and legislation were extremely difficult and certain countries introduced measures of compulsory reinsurance of cargoes with government sponsored companies.

Despite these difficulties and also the constant growth of competition in cargo underwriting, the Group's overseas marine branches and agencies managed between them to add substantial increases to yearly premiums between 1955 and 1957. But in 1958 the same conditions overtook cargo as hull underwriting. Added to these there was a decline in the Group's cargo operations in Indonesia, where its Dutch agents had been compelled to leave their business. The brightest spot in overseas cargo transactions that year was Europe, where an increase of income resulted from several agencies and the figures of the Anglo-Elementar were included for the first time.

So much for the principal developments in the Group's marine operations during these years, but the picture would be incomplete without some reference to certain events on sea and land. The new nation of Indonesia has figured several times in this part of our history, and a state of affairs arose towards the end of 1957, which culminated in a warm gesture of friendship towards British interests from Indonesia. On December 6th, after some days of unrest, which included strikes and the "unofficial" seizure of Dutch Offices, the Indonesian Government announced that it had taken under its control all Dutch shipping companies, and ordered all Dutch ships to remain in port. This order was later confined to vessels of the Dutch mercantile fleet in Indonesia, but various other vessels, including British, were seized from time to time for alleged illegal trading. Some Dutch vessels were rescued by the Dutch Navy, and three were released with the connivance of the rebel government. On March 20th, 1958, the Indonesian government announced that it was handing back all these Dutch vessels to the Dutch company's own management, but that they would be barred from Indonesian coastal trade. The number of ships held at this time was thirty-six, valued for insurance purposes at some £11,000,000.

The reasons leading to this decision were extremely interesting. Almost the whole of this Dutch fleet operating in Indonesian waters was underwritten in the London market, which sent out a deputation to Djakarta to explain the position to the Indonesian government. When, as a result of prolonged discussions, it realised that the brunt of the loss through confiscation would fall on the British underwriters, it decided not to go ahead with its intention. A. W. Green, at that time the Commercial Union's Marine Adjuster of Claims, who incidentally had been elected Chairman of the London Salvage Association that year, was a member of this delegation, and his technical advice was of great value and helped materially in the successful outcome of the mission.

Casualties to famous liners made newspaper headlines during this period. On March 24th, 1947, the *Monarch of Bermuda* caught fire while being reconditioned in dry dock at Hebburn-on-Tyne. The vessel was very badly damaged and the surveyors estimated the cost of repairs at over £1,600,000. The Ministry of Transport and other interested parties refused to allow the vessel to remain in the Tyne or to let repairs be started at once. At this juncture the liner was towed to Rosyth, it being agreed that she was a constructive total loss. However, this was not to be her end for the underwriters, led by the Commercial Union, intervened and, as a result, the *Monarch of Bermuda* was repaired and in 1949 was sold to the Australian government which renamed her *New Australia*. In 1958 she was transferred again, this time to the Arkadia Steamship Company, and is now a cruising ship known as the *Arkadia*. Another famous liner met her fate in dock when the Canadian Pacific's *Empress of Canada* was burnt out and capsized in the Gladstone Dock at Liverpool on January 25th, 1953. Insured on a value of £1½ million, with the Commercial Union leading the slip, she was written off as a total loss.

Among the major disasters at sea, in which the Group became involved, was the loss of the *Magdalena*. This liner, while on her maiden voyage, became stranded on rocks off Rio de Janeiro on April 4th, 1949. She was refloated, but ran into heavy weather while being towed into Rio. Breaking in two, she became a total loss. The Commercial Union Group had led the slip on the *Magdalena* and with its market associates had to meet a claim by the owners for £2,300,000, though a salvage of £125,000 was made.

Among the most tragic events at sea in recent years was the collision between the new Italian liner, the *Andrea Doria*, and the Swedish ship, the *Stockholm*, on July 25th, 1956. There is no need to recount the details here except in the briefest way. The *Andrea Doria* was inward bound for New York, the *Stockholm* was outward bound for Copenhagen. They collided with each other off Nantucket in thick fog shortly before midnight. The Italian liner listed so badly that her lifeboats could not be lowered. Altogether fifty lives were lost, and the *Andrea Doria* eventually turned turtle and foundered. It will be remembered that the liability for the collision was extremely difficult to prove, but negotiations in London, in which the Commercial Union played a leading part, culminated in an amicable settlement, thus avoiding the need for prolonged legal proceedings.

That the net premium income from the Group's marine operations rose from some £1,161,000 in 1946 to nearly £3,070,000 in 1958—an increase of nearly £2 million in a difficult period of international trade and relations—is a tribute to the Marine Department and its staff at home and abroad. Glanvill Smith, who had been appointed Marine Underwriter in 1942, continued as head of the Department until his retirement in 1954. He was succeeded by his Deputy, G. W. Hogsflesh, who is still at the helm of the Group's marine affairs. Both men have earned the respect of their colleagues in the London marine market and both have served for two years as Chairmen of the Institute of London Underwriters, Glanvill Smith in 1951 to 1952 and Hogsflesh in 1956 to 1957.

# CHAPTER XIX

State of the Business, 1958

THROUGH the Second World War and its aftermath the Group had made remarkable progress both abroad and at home. It may be a comfortable belief that once a business has passed beyond its growing pains and has become a world-wide organisation, backed by powerful assets, nothing can keep it back and only some quite unique disaster could destroy it. Well before 1938 the Commercial Union Group had reached that stage in its career. But it would be a mistake to imagine that its progress could have been maintained, let alone accelerated, without expert and dynamic leadership.

A business of this character needs wise Chairmanship and the guidance of an able Board of Directors; it relies much on the ability of its senior officials and head of departments, several of whose names have figured in recent chapters. But there can be no doubt that in the period between 1938 and 1958 its career received the greatest impetus from its General Manager, Sir John Makins. He had been knighted in 1950 for his services to the insurance industry. These had been many and varied. His Chairmanship of the British Insurance Association occurred at a difficult time, and here it should be mentioned that he served for two years, from 1947 to 1949, in this most important and responsible position. Other voluntary appointments to which he had been elected were the Presidency of the London Insurance Institute in 1944 and the Vice-Presidency of the Chartered Insurance Institute in 1957. He retired from the chief executive position in the Group on May 31st, 1958. In announcing

249

this impending change of management at the annual general meeting in 1957 Colonel Leslie, the Chairman, had paid a special tribute to Sir John's outstanding achievement:

"Sir John," he said, "joined the Company in a junior capacity in 1910 and has thus served for over forty-seven years, during the last twenty years of which he has occupied the position of General Manager. During his tenure of the highest executive office in the Company we have seen the growth of the Fire, Accident and Marine premium income from £14,000,000 to £64,000,000; an increase in new Life assurance business from £6,000,000 to £24,000,000, and an increase in the assets from £67,000,000 to £178,000,000. In addition, he has had the responsibility of guiding our affairs through a world war and the difficult period of adjustment which followed, and he has succeeded in welding the various members of our important group of companies into an integrated unit, whilst at the same time preserving their individuality. It is a record of which he has reason to be proud and for which we have reason to be grateful."

On his retirement Sir John Makins accepted an invitation to join the Board and also to become one of the Deputy Chairmen.

For some months before this F. E. P. Sandilands had been the Group's Deputy General Manager after a successful period in office as Manager of the Ocean, whose impact in particular on the overseas fortunes of the Group has several times been commented on. He now succeeded to the General Managership. There were to be some further changes in the higher management some months later. V. E. Masters and R. P. F. Smallwood, who had been the two Assistant General Managers since 1955, now became the joint Deputy General Managers, and L. H. Hewens, formerly Assistant Manager, was appointed Assistant General Manager with special responsibilities for the home organisation. Shortly afterwards a change in the Secretary's department took place. R. K. Lochhead, Secretary of the Group for twenty-two years, retired in May, 1959. During a distinguished career in insurance he had held the important appointment of Chairman of the Investment Protection Committee of the British Insurance Association from 1945 to 1953. His election to the Board left a vacancy which it was decided to fill by dual appointments, the two Assistant Secretaries, R. A. Bodey and L. S. Cooper becoming the Investment Manager and the Secretary of the Group respectively.

PLATE VIII

FOUR GENERAL MANAGERS

ROGER OWEN        HERBERT LEWIS

SIR JOHN MAKINS        F. E. P. SANDILANDS

The balance sheet for 1958 showed continued progress during a difficult year. The net premium income of the Fire Department, operated by A. W. White as Foreign Fire Manager and A. J. Yardley as Home Fire Manager, reached a figure of over £25,000,000. The net premium income of the Accident Department, under R. L. Hervey who, after five years as Joint Accident Manager, had been appointed sole Manager that year, exceeded £40,000,000. The Marine Department's figure of some £3,070,000 has already been mentioned.

The progress of the Life Department cannot be gauged by similar yardsticks. Its activities in the United Kingdom since the end of the war had gone ahead with astonishing rapidity under N. R. Gatenby, the Actuary and Life Manager since 1943. The diversity in the range of life assurance and its importance in the national economy has increased so greatly during the last decade or so that full justice cannot be done to them in this review. But when it is said that the net sums assured by the Group in the United Kingdom grew from some £9,880,000 in 1946 to nearly £29,000,000 in 1958, some idea of these developments, and the pioneer part which the Group has played in them, may be readily grasped.

In 1958 the Commercial Union's issued capital had been increased and now stood at £7,788,000. As against this, its total assets at the end of 1958 exceeded £190,000,000. It was in fine shape and well poised for the spectacular step that it was about to take in the following year.

# PART SIX

---

# *New Measures and New Men*

## *1959-1961*

# CHAPTER XX

## The North British & Mercantile

### I

ON April 20th, 1959, the Boards of the Commercial Union and the North British & Mercantile announced that "discussions with a view to a merger of interests have resulted in an offer by Commercial Union for the whole issued capital of North British & Mercantile". The paid up capital of the North British at this time was £4½ million, consisting of £2,750,000 worth of ordinary shares and £1,750,000 of preference stock. The merger was to be effected by an exchange of one fully paid 5 per cent £1 cumulative redeemable preference share of the Commercial Union for each £1 unit of the 4 per cent non-cumulative preference stock of the North British and five fully paid Commercial Union ordinary shares for four North British ordinary in addition to 5/- in cash for each ordinary share. This proposed merger was duly ratified and came into force on June 1, 1959.

To finance this arrangement the Commercial Union Group's nominal capital was increased to £13,187,500 by the creation of a further 13,750,000 shares of 5/- each and of 1,750,000 preference shares of £1 each. Three members of the Commercial Union Board, Colonel J. Leslie, its then Chairman, R. C. Brooks, and Sir Mark Turner, and F. E. P. Sandilands, the General Manager, joined the Board of the North British, while three of the North British Directors, C. H. Kleinwort, its Chairman, Sir Thomas Frazer and J. G. Phillimore joined the Commercial Union Board.

The negotiations leading up to this merger had been a well-kept secret. The announcement created a sensation not only in financial circles, but far beyond. The Commercial Union Group's total assets in 1958 have already been mentioned as standing at £191,384,248. The North British Group's total assets in 1958 stood at £127,499,968. Thus the combined business disposed of nearly £319 million's worth of assets—a vast figure even in modern insurance groupings.

With the exception of certain acquisitions by the Guardian Assurance in 1954, 1956 and 1957 there had been no noteworthy mergers in British insurance for some thirty years. 1959, however, was to witness a return of the trend in the industry towards rationalisation that had typified the first quarter of the present century. Four other important amalgamations were to take place that year, but that of the Commercial Union and North British was much the largest. Indeed, so far as the records show, it still remains one of the largest single events of its kind in the whole history of British insurance.

The principal reason for this amalgamation was the importance of consolidating and developing fire and casualty business in the United States, the problems and potentialities of which have been frequently referred to. And here it is worth noting that about £45 million or 45% of the amalgamated undertakings' non-life premium income was derived from that source.

The merger naturally aroused wide publicity including an entertaining comment in the *Post Magazine*:

> "The United States may well be the proving ground for this new insurance inter-planetary missile with its immense power and range, but other territories will soon see that, unlike those giants which were described by Mr. Vuffin in *The Old Curiosity Shop* as 'very weak in the knees', this one is unlikely to show any weakness anywhere."

2

In the coming together of two large groups of companies co-ordination of activities and administration presents a lengthy programme, which will only just have got into its stride when this history appears. In all this the blending of traditions has its interesting aspect, and the traditions of the North British are so distinctive that the size and shape of the combination, as it now exists, cannot be properly assessed without some account of the origins and career of the new partner.

The North British Insurance Company, as it was first called, was founded in Edinburgh as a fire underwriting office on November 11th, 1809. At that time Scottish susceptibilities were sensitive to a growing invasion by commercial interests from south of the Border. In the insurance field especially this invasion had gone some distance and twenty English offices were conducting flourishing business in Scotland. The men who established the company were J. W. Brougham and George Moncrieff, partners in an Edinburgh firm of wine merchants and insurance brokers. Appealing to Scottish national feeling and obtaining the patronage of prominent members of the Scottish aristocracy and landed gentry, they founded the company with what was at that time the very considerable nominal capital of £500,000, taken out in shares of £200 each with £10 paid on each share.

Among the original subscribers was the Marquis of Huntly, who became the company's first President on his return from the ill-fated Walcheren expedition, where he had commanded the Fourth Division. The Vice-Presidents were the Earl of Errol, the Earl of Elgin, collector of the "Elgin Marbles", the Earl of Aboyne, and William Adam, a Scottish Member of Parliament. The "Extraordinary Directors" were mostly drawn from Scotland's landed gentry, and the "Ordinary Directors"—in other words the executive Board—mostly consisted of Edinburgh and Leith merchants.

As Joint Managers of the new company Brougham and Moncrieff conducted their early activities from a flat in Parliament Square, for which they paid a modest annual rent of £30. Their activities, however, were marred by a reverse within seven months of the company's existence. In the evening of June 4th, 1810, George the Third's birthday was celebrated in Glasgow by a display of fireworks. A rocket entered an open attic window in premises, insured by the North British, of a firm of dry goods warehousemen in Glassford Street. The consequences were serious and Robert Wright, an Edinburgh architect and a member of the "Ordinary" Board, visited Glasgow in the company of Brougham to investigate the position. On their return they reported to a special committee of the directors. According to their statement "it appeared that the fire was occasioned by a squib or rocket entering a window on the roof of the building and communicating inflammation to cotton goods of various description which were therein deposited. The fire engines were soon on the spot, but, unfortunately, and to the great disgrace of the Glasgow Police, under whose management they were, they were in such a miserable state of disorder, and the firemen all drunk, it being the evening of His Majesty's Birthday, that they were of no use, and the fire was literally allowed to burn and thereby occasion a loss of many thousands of pounds, which otherwise could only have amounted to a few hundreds."

No wonder the firemen were unable to perform their duty! George the Third was a most popular monarch in Scotland. Multiplied toasts were drunk in his honour at each of his successive birthdays. At a banquet given by the Edinburgh Corporation to mark the occasion a year previously fifty-one toasts were drunk, and fifty-two at another feast later in the year to celebrate his Jubilee. Could the Glasgow firemen be severely censured for emulating the leading citizens of a neighbouring city in manifesting loyalty to their sovereign?

As this event turned out, it was a blessing in disguise. The company's loss, it is true, was almost £6,500; the paid up capital amounted to about £22,000 and the premiums for the year to £2,149. Payment of this sum must, therefore, have caused considerable worry to Board and management, but paid it was and paid promptly. In fact, the promptitude of the settlement was not lost on Scottish merchants and the company's affairs began to prosper to such a degree that in 1812 it decided to secure premises of its own.

This new office of the North British fronted the High Street a little to the north-west of St. Giles and near the Lawnmarket. The building occupied the corner of a street formed to give access to the new city by the Earthern Mound, then in process of accumulation from the rubbish of the Old Town. It was called Bank Street in compliment to the Bank of Scotland which stood at the far end.

For the next ten years the North British steadily developed its resources. Shortly after it had completed the tenth year of its career the long reign of George the Third came to an end; and although the Napoleonic Wars had absorbed an enormous amount of the nation's wealth and the ensuing peace by no means brought plenty, the company's progress continued. When George the Fourth came to the throne, its premium income more than doubled that recorded in its first year.

In 1823 the North British decided to enter the life assurance field. For this purpose its capital was raised in the following year to £1 million in 5,000 shares of £200 with £10 paid up. Of these shares 3,142 were those which had been subscribed for since the company's foundation, and the remainder were to be sold according to demand, £10 per share being set aside from the proceeds of sale as paid up capital. By 1845 they were all disposed of and thus the paid up capital became £50,000.

The next move forward, and a highly ambitious one, was to seek the privilege of a Royal Charter. This was granted in 1824. There can be little doubt concerning the reasons for this success. George the Fourth had been greatly delighted with the outburst of loyalty that greeted him on a visit to Edinburgh eighteen months earlier. He was particularly flattered by the attentions paid to him by Scotland's aristocracy, and as five of their number, and a distinguished five at that, headed the list of office-bearers of the North British, the petition would have had an inevitably favourable hearing.

Having obtained their Charter, the directors seem to have been inspired to fresh endeavours. They decided to invade the English market and sent a deputation to explore the possibilities in the North of England, where the effects of the industrial revolution were getting into their stride. This reconnaissance resulted in the formation of important connections and the establishing of agencies. In Liverpool especially the deputation experienced a most successful reception. Here great assistance was given to it by a fellow Scot— Sir John Gladstone, father of England's future Prime Minister who was then a boy at Eton. It was Sir John Gladstone, specially desirous of promoting the interests of old friends and neighbours whom he had known in his youth at Leith, who made the first opening for the North British in the Liverpool district.

Meanwhile, many influences were at work in Edinburgh. Its population had increased from 100,000 in 1809 to nearly 150,000 in 1825. Gas and water supplies had been introduced into the city. Along with the Tolbooth and Luckenbooths there had disappeared from the High Street the last relics of the Town Guard, the link-boy and the sedan chair. What was more, the New Town was spreading rapidly beyond Princes Street and had reached and crossed the Water of Leith.

The company decided to move with the times and took up larger quarters in Hanover Street. This placed it in the heart of the fashionable quarter of the New Town and also removed it from a site which had become unsatisfactory for conducting business. The front windows of the offices in the High Street had looked out on a spot where public executions took place. Scenes of disorder were frequent. At the execution of a highwayman named Johnston, in 1818, a mob had assailed the scaffold and rescued the condemned man. An armed company of soldiers from the Castle had to be called in before he could be recaptured and hung. The constant recurrence of these gruesome spectacles jarred on the nerves of the directors and staff. In fact, the Board minutes make reference to the subject and on one occasion they record a change in time of a certain meeting to avoid its coincidence with an execution.

The high prospects of the early twenties dwindled in the second part of that decade. There were widespread commercial disasters in 1825 and constantly recurring bread and machinery riots. More direct in their impact on the company's fortunes were extremely heavy fire losses between 1827 and 1829 and during this period no dividends were declared. At the end of the twenties, however, when William the Fourth ascended the throne, the North British was advancing once again. Its fire premium then amounted to nearly £7,900, its life premium income to nearly £25,000, and its Life Fund exceeded £54,000. And though at the end of 1830 the balance against the Fire Department was large, it was more than offset by the profit resulting from the first septennial period of the Life Department.

But the going had not been easy and, as ever in the careers of commercial undertakings, the fearsome question of expansion as against restriction of effort had to be faced. "Expand or bust" appears to have been the maxim guiding the company at this time. In 1832 it established a branch in London only to be set back by an outbreak of cholera there and political strife over the Reform Bill of that year. However, perseverance ultimately prevailed over these circumstances and the company's connections in England and Ireland were later extended, an opening in Ireland having been made in 1835.

The real turning point in the affairs of the North British came with the first year of Queen Victoria's reign in 1837. From then on its progress became assured, though it was on the life side more than through fire underwriting that it began to consolidate its position. In 1842 it purchased for its headquarters a site in Princes Street, Edinburgh, on which it constructed what was to be a conspicuous architectural ornament until it was demolished and replaced in 1908 by a new head office regarded as one of the finest buildings in the street. In 1845 it secured further scope for activities in England and Ireland through an Act of Parliament; and in 1860 through a further Act it again extended its range of business, defined the rights and obligations of its shareholders, and was empowered to transact operations overseas.

3

Armed with these additional powers, the North British entered into a new phase of its career—a phase of expansion abroad and at home. It broke ground in India in 1861 by starting fire business through an agency. Three years later it added life business to its Indian activities. Finally, it established an influential board of local directors in Calcutta, thereby gaining the support of the mercantile community. Simultaneously with this new departure in India the company set up an agency in Canada, later to be converted into the Montreal branch. Here again an influential board of directors was appointed and under its supervision operations were steadily extended in the wake of the Dominion's exploration and development.

At home the North British began to expand its position through a number of acquisitions. The great period of amalgamations in the insurance industry, it will be remembered, was not to come till the turn of the century. It is true that a proliferation of new and unstable offices, started in the middle of the nineteenth century, resulted in a number of mergers. But the North British was almost certainly unique in the scale of its absorption operations at this time. As early as 1855 it had acquired the Morayshire Insurance Company, a small but healthy office. In 1859 it had taken over a much more valuable business in the shape of the Newcastle Fire Office founded as far back as 1783. This institution had a most interesting history of associations with the early days of gas for lighting purposes. It introduced gas lighting into Newcastle and conducted this undertaking as part of its activities from 1817 till 1830, when it sold it to the Newcastle-upon-Tyne Subscription Gas Light Company.

These acquisitions were a mere prelude to the step which the North British took in 1862. This step brings us back full cycle to the Tooley Street fire in 1861. Had it not been for that fire, the Commercial Union would never have existed and, had it not been for the same event, its new partner of 1959 might never have pursued a major rôle in the insurance industry. For it will be recalled that the only other office which materialised from the Mansion House meeting of 1861 was the Mercantile Fire Insurance Company and that within a year this combined itself with the North British.

The Mercantile Insurance Company had just started its operations which were aimed, like those of the Commercial Union, at reducing the mercantile rates of the tariff companies, when it became known to its directors that the North British were willing to adopt a similar policy. Negotiations took place and led to a merger between the two offices, the name given to the combined business being the North British & Mercantile Insurance Company.

It was an interesting and fruitful marriage between Edinburgh and the City of London. While the North British brought to it long experience of fire and life underwriting and a widely spread, solidly established organisation, the Mercantile, a parvenu to insurance circles, had been formed and was being directed by a brilliant coterie of City bankers and merchants. Among their number were John Cater, its Chairman, of J. W. Cater, Son and Co., Edward Cohen of Drake, Kleinwort and Cohen, Pascoe Du Pre Grenfell of Pascoe, Grenfell and Sons, Peter Ralli of Ralli Brothers and John Schröder, later to become Baron Schröder, of J. H. Schröder and Co.

Administratively, the union presented certain problems of dichotomy. These, however, were solved by maintaining two boards of "Ordinary Directors" and two head offices, one in Edinburgh and the other in London, where the company moved to the site in Threadneedle Street which it has ever since occupied. An overall executive control was provided by the appointment of the North British Manager in Edinburgh, at that time David Smith, as General Manager of the joint organisation. Well into the present century, too, the successive Presidents, Vice-Presidents and "Extraordinary Directors" remained predominantly Scottish.

The subscribed capital of the North British & Mercantile was £2 million in 40,000 shares of £50 each with £6/5/- paid up. At the end of 1862 its fire premium income amounted to £119,591, its life premium income to £228,436, and its life funds to £1,441,324.

4

Almost simultaneously with this event the new company extended the life side of its interests by acquiring the United Kingdom Life Assurance Company. From its foundation in 1834 the headquarters of this office was in Waterloo Place, whence it had developed valuable connections in the West End of London. After the acquisition the North British & Mercantile converted the Waterloo Place office into its West End Branch.

This was to be the last acquisition of any importance for nearly thirty years. Life business was pushed forward rapidly during these years, but no attempt was made on any scale to extend it outside the United Kingdom. On the other hand fire connections were pressed ahead vigorously in many parts of the world. An early step was to establish an agency in New York. The company's initial progress in the United States, however, was chequered by the calamities undergone by other pioneers of British insurance on the North American continent. In the Chicago fire of 1871 its losses were £325,000; in the Boston fire a year later £92,000.

Immediately the London Board heard of the Chicago disaster they cabled New York, "Proceed with good risks at advanced rates. Settle losses promptly. Draw at three days' sight. Subscribe 5,000 dollars for sufferers." The cable found its way into the American newspapers; it brought with it a breath of business alacrity compounded with humanity, typical of the best traditions of the City of London. It was not quickly forgotten by the American public, and the promptitude also displayed in the settlement of the Boston claims still further enhanced the company's prestige and connections in the United States. Well before the turn of the century it was firmly established across the Atlantic and in 1897 it formed its own company on American soil—the North British & Mercantile Insurance Company of New York, later to be renamed the Mercantile Insurance Company of America.

In the latter half of the nineteenth century, too, the North British had driven its roots into Canada, where it had a central office in Montreal, into Australia, where its central office was situated in Melbourne, with a branch office in Sydney, and into India, where its central office was in Calcutta. It had also become well-known in Europe, its principal business there having been fostered in Germany, where it had set up a central office in Berlin, and in Austria with a central office in Vienna.

The home organisation had also been extended. North of the Border the Scottish Provincial Assurance had been absorbed in 1889, this transaction giving the company a stronger foothold in Aberdeen and the north-east. Glasgow had long been an important branch and smaller offices existed in Dundee and Inverness. In Northern Ireland there was a branch at Belfast and in Southern Ireland one in Dublin. South Wales was covered from a large branch in Cardiff and all the principal English cities were included in the company's network.

Soon after the turn of the century the North British & Mercantile began to play its own part in the trend towards rationalisation of the insurance industry. By taking over the Universal Life Assurance Company it widened its interests in India and formed a Committee of Management in Bombay. In 1907 it extended its American organisation by purchasing the Commonwealth Insurance Company of New York. This business had been started in 1886. Whether or not it had failed to weather the shock of the San Francisco Earthquake the previous year is uncertain. Boldness of approach to disaster seems to have characterised the North British in taking this step for it had itself lost £660,000 through that calamity.

Finally, the company entered the marine market in 1908 by purchasing the Ocean Marine Insurance Company for £525,000. Founded in 1859, the Ocean Marine had itself acquired two other offices during its career—the City of London Marine and the

National Marine. It was a first-class organisation in its own sphere.

5

At the time of its centenary in 1909 the dimensions of the North British & Mercantile entitled it to a high place in British insurance. If it had not quite entered the hierarchy, it was close to the gateway. Its annual report for 1908 showed a total income of nearly £4,300,000; its assets amounted to more than £20,000,000. To the territories, in which it was doing business at the turn of the century, there had been added New Zealand, South Africa, South America, China and Japan.

The purchase of the Ocean Marine had given it the status of a composite office engaged in all four main branches of underwriting. However, it was weak on the accident side, where it was dealing on a rather small scale in one section only—that of employers' liability. This weakness it proceeded to remedy in no uncertain manner in 1910 by acquiring for £850,000 the oldest existing accident business in the world—the Railway Passengers Assurance Company.

Without undue exaggeration it may be said that the story of the origin and early career of the Railway Passengers Assurance up to 1910 is in effect the history of the early growth of accident insurance. It began, as its name implies, with the underwriting of risks of railway travellers, but eventually spread out into nearly every other sector of accident insurance as each one became developed in turn.

The decade of 1840-50 was notable, perhaps more than anything else, for the momentum of railway development, and from this sprang the conditions favourable to the conception of accident insurance. Until then the pace of travel, as of life in its wider field, had been comparatively slow, and with the railways in the experimental stage it is not surprising that accidents occurred through failure of plant and personnel and by the folly of travellers not yet accustomed to the new conditions.

During 1844 no fewer than 150 new railway undertakings were brought before the public, rivalry being one of the major factors in development and lending impetus to an insane race to exploit this new source of wealth. The following year saw numerous amalgamations. Then in 1848 came the introduction of express trains, with some consequent disorganisation of traffic and many accidents, although it is, perhaps, surprising that the number of accidents was not greater. By 1848 some 5,000 miles of railway track had crept across the face of Britain, providing ever-increasing travel facilities, and in January, 1849 it was reported in the press that "Railway accidents are almost of daily occurrence, generally ending in loss of limb, often of life". During the half year ending 30th June, 1849, 96 persons were killed and 75 injured on all railways open for public traffic. The idea of assurance against death by railway accidents was a natural consequence of these conditions, and various suggestions were submitted to the railway companies, though without success.

The man who conceived the idea that led to the formation of the Railway Passengers Assurance was a solicitor, H. F. Holt by name, who was already interested in life assurance. He sought the assistance in 1848 of friends in the insurance and banking worlds, and negotiations eventually led to the formation of a company through a deed of settlement in March, 1849. The banking house of Strahan, Paul, Paul and Bates took a prominent hand in its formation and John Dean Paul, later to receive a baronetcy, was its first chairman from 1849 to 1855. Holt's firm, Holt and Aubin, were appointed the company's solicitors.

Before the company could start its work, which required the co-operation of the railway companies and the Railway Clearing House, it was essential to get a bill passed through Parliament. By the end of June the Railway Passengers Assurance Company's Act, 1849, had received the Royal Assent.

This was the first of a succession of private Acts governing and facilitating the conduct of the company's business. It provided for the marking of insurance tickets limiting their scope to a particular journey, but did not restrict the company's business to tickets so limited. Commuted Stamp Duty was authorised at a rate of 5 per cent on premiums. A scale of disablement allowances was not prescribed, but compensation for injury was to be such sum (not exceeding the Fatal Benefit stated on the ticket) "as shall be deemed reasonable and liberal compensation for such injury as well as for the pain of mind and body and loss of time and money consequent thereon".

The reason why the co-operation of the railways was essential was that the scheme required advertising in stations, and also the booking clerks would need to offer accident insurance tickets to passengers when they bought their travel tickets. The early tickets were of the same size as the travel tickets. At first it had been in the intention to cover passengers against death or injury only for single journeys; the cost was to be 3d. for a first-class passenger to insure £1,000 in case of death, 2d. for a second-class to insure £500, and 1d. for a third-class to insure £200. In case of injury only, a sum of money was to be paid commensurate with its extent. This discrimination between classes of passengers appears at first sight to typify Victorian class-consciousness. But in actual fact it was caused by contemporary conditions of railway travel. Second and third-class passengers were exposed to greater risks because their carriages were roofless. When, however, the Railway Passengers Assurance finally started out on its venture, it also offered periodical tickets applicable to any class, the annual premium payable for a death benefit of £1,000 being fixed at £1 and for a benefit of £200 at 5/-.

In August, 1849, these periodical tickets became available to certain railway officials whilst engaged in their duties. As an inducement to support the scheme the cover included riding on engines. An exception to "duty" journeys was made in favour of the Secretary of the North British Railway who occasionally travelled to his residence on an engine! Soon after this insurance facilities were extended by the company to guards, engine drivers and stokers.

By the end of 1850 the company was operating on thirty-two railways including the London and North Western, Eastern Counties, Great Western, Midland, Lancashire and Yorkshire, and Great Northern. The number of Periodical Tickets issued that year totalled 2,808 and the number of Single Journey 110,074. In addition to medical and surgical relief, 37 persons had been awarded sums varying up to £210. The company's activities had by this time attracted a great deal of attention and in its issue of October 19th, 1850, *Punch* indulged in some friendly banter about them:

> "We believe it is generally known—for the comfortable intelligence is placarded at nearly every terminus and station—that a passenger losing life or limb on a Railway can, if he goes his journey with the agreeable sensation that life and limb are in jeopardy, effect an

assurance before starting that will give him pecuniary damages for any personal damage that may be done to him. There is, in fact, a Railway Accident Assurance Company, which publishes from time to time a list of its bonuses on broken bones, and tries to tempt the public by showing them how 'a gentleman shaken was awarded six pounds'--no great shakes, by the by—in way of compensation; and how another gentleman, who received his mother-in-law unexpectedly and forcibly on the point of his nose, was adjudged one pound for the disagreeable proximity. Now, there is scarcely a married man who would consent to receive a mother-in-law so completely *chez lui* on these moderate terms; and one pound seems a very poor equivalent for rendering still closer a somewhat disagreeably close relationship. A wife's mother is not always the most desirable person to be brought literally face to face with by a railway collision, for there are in most families enough of domestic collisions to render this sort of contact quite superfluous."

Sir John Paul resigned from the company's Chairmanship in 1855 and was succeeded by James Clay, a politician who had been one of the original directors. Under Clay the company branched out into general personal accident insurance. In this widened field it continued on its pioneer way. There was, for instance, little or no reliable guidance on the subject of premium rates. W. J. Vian, the Secretary, undertook some exhaustive research into the subject and with actuarial advice eventually submitted his recommendations which were approved by the board in the following form :

| *Annual Premium* | | *Sum payable in* | *Weekly Compensation* |
|---|---|---|---|
| Class 1 | Class 2 | *case of Death* | *for Injury* |
| £ s. d. | £ s. d. | £ | £. s. d. |
| 10 0 | 16 0 | 100 | 15 0 |
| 1 0 0 | 1 12 0 | 250 | 1 10 0 |
| 1 15 0 | 3 3 0 | 500 | 3 0 0 |
| 3 0 0 | 5 5 0 | 1,000 | 6 0 0 |

the principle of limiting compensation to a period of 12 months for any one accident being agreed.

It is remarkable how accurate Vian's forecast proved to be and the basis laid down in this table was substantially followed in the company's personal accident schemes for almost one hundred years. Vian's business acumen, sound reasoning and common sense had devised a basis which was to stand the test of time.

Among holders of these personal accident policy holders was a military officer whose name now figures in the English dictionary. While serving in Ireland in 1880, a certain Captain Boycott received threats to his life and was placed under military protection. The company thought it necessary to warn Boycott that, if he remained in that country, his policy could only be renewed subject to the exclusion of assault.

That year of 1880 saw the passing of the Employers' Liability Act and the Railway Passengers Assurance was among the first offices to transact business in this new field. In 1897 it started to undertake fidelity guarantee work and insurance against illness, in 1900 burglary business, and in 1905 it introduced a form of comprehensive insurance covering sickness in addition to personal accident.

The nature of the Railway Passengers Assurance's work in its early years lent itself to a centralised organisation. This tradition lasted on even after it had launched out into other projects altogether. In the United Kingdom it used agents for local representation and its only branch was one in London's West End which had a brief existence from 1863 to 1880.

It seems strange that it never took advantage in its early years of the great interest aroused abroad by its pioneer work on British railways. James Batterson, for example, who founded that well-known American office, The Travelers, in 1863, admitted that he conceived the idea of starting accident insurance in the United States as the result of a train journey between Leamington and London a few years earlier. On that occasion he had been persuaded to buy a "Railway Passengers Journey Ticket". It was not until 1883 that the "Railway Passengers" entered the foreign market. This was through an agency in Amsterdam. Nearly a decade passed before it went further afield, this time to India through a firm in Bombay. In 1901, however, it launched out successfully in South Africa and repeated there its outstanding achievements of earlier days over railway passenger insurance. A year later it started activities in Canada, meeting with great success and developing an extensive organisation, which came to deal with every new development of accident business.

In its own particular sphere the Railway Passengers Assurance was unrivalled when it threw in its lot with the North British &

Mercantile in 1910. But it had not extended itself into the fire, life and marine markets. It was too late to turn itself into a composite company and it was equally too dangerous to continue an independent existence in face of the rapidly growing incursion of the composite companies into its own domain. So much value did its new owners place on its record and experience that the whole administration and development of the North British Group's accident work at home and abroad was thenceforth centralised in the offices of the Railway Passengers Assurance at 64 Cornhill.

6

Between 1910 and the start of the First World War the size and shape of the North British & Mercantile showed perceptible change both at home and abroad, signifying a rapidity of all-round growth. The home organisation was enlarged. Expansion of the overseas fire organisation was even more pronounced. Already, in 1910, the company was well represented in Australia with branches in all the principal cities of the Commonwealth—Melbourne, Sydney, Adelaide, Brisbane and Perth—the administrative control being centralised in Melbourne. South African activities were being managed from Johannesburg. In Canada the branch in Montreal had now become a central office co-ordinating affairs further afield in the Dominion. A new branch for the North West Provinces had recently been established at Winnipeg and a smaller office under resident agents at Toronto. The central office in New York was now supervising a network of agencies scattered through the United States. In South America, the company's interests had recently become represented by a branch for the Argentine in Buenos Aires. In Europe, the Berlin and Vienna offices were extremely active and flourishing, and a new branch had recently been established at Budapest.

These overseas interests of the company were to be extended to the Far East in 1911 through a branch opened at Shanghai and to Newfoundland the following year through a branch at St. John's. Meanwhile, the organisation in India had become an extremely well integrated business with a central office and a board of directors in Calcutta's Clive Street, whence branches in Calcutta, Bombay and Colombo, under local committees of management, were controlled.

It is of some interest that, as a composite insurance office, the North British & Mercantile was continuing to deal with its work through an administrative pattern that differed from most of its contemporaries. The parent company of a group which it had now become, it dealt directly in fire and life business only. Here it may be recalled that up to 1908 these remained its exclusive fields of activity, except for a very small and tentative excursion into the accident sector over employers' liability. With its acquisition of the Ocean Marine, it entered into entirely unfamiliar waters and wisely decided to leave its new subsidiary, with its distinctive name and prestige, to conduct such transactions as independently as possible. Likewise, in 1910 it left the Railway Passengers Assurance, with its immense experience of accident underwriting, to control its own destinies within the group, even transferring to it its employers' liability portfolio. No attempt, in fact, was made to absorb either office to the extent of converting them into the marine and accident departments of the North British, though in actual functioning that is what they became.

In view of all these developments, which had begun to tip the balance of influence within the organisation away from Edinburgh and towards the City of London, some reorganisation of structure had become necessary. So the shareholders could scarcely have been surprised at an announcement made to them on the occasion of the annual general meeting in 1915 by the company's Chairman, C. J. Cater Scott:

"Now you know the North British & Mercantile has a somewhat anomalous position. I think it is the only Company which has a Head Office in Edinburgh and a Head Office in London. These two Head Offices have divided the world between them for the conduct of their business, each having its own particular sphere. But the business does sometimes overlap and constantly questions come up affecting both Boards, which it is very desirable should be dealt with promptly. We have found some of the inconveniences of our anomalous position in the past, and after a considerable amount of consideration we have thought that an Advisory Committee without any executive powers, to consist of certain members from Edinburgh and certain members from London, would be of great assistance in regulating the relations of each Board. That Advisory Committee was formed last year, and I am pleased to say . . . that it has done very good work."

7

The creation of the Advisory Committee was to be only a temporary solution of this particular problem, as we shall see in due course. Meanwhile, the far greater problems of war had come to envelop the Boards and management. The experiences of the North British in the First World War were to some extent similar to those of the Commercial Union. In some respects, however, it found itself having to weather even more serious set-backs during the early period of the conflict. Its German and Austrian fire business was much larger than that of any other British insurance office. In addition to the loss of very considerable income from these sources, it was compelled to liquidate its liabilities in each country.

Over one particular war-time event the company's experience was almost certainly more unfortunate than that of any other office, British or foreign. Towards the end of 1915 an Anglo-French force was landed at Salonika in Eastern Greece and pushed inland towards Monastir, the intention being to bring relief to Serbia which had been invaded by Bulgaria. This was the beginning of the Allies' Balkan campaign which after a long stalemate eventually ended in a victorious advance. Throughout that campaign Salonika remained the base of operations and it was there that in 1917 the famous "Salonika Fire" occurred. This disaster started in a small house on the outskirts of the city. Salonika's water supply would have been quite adequate under normal conditions to counter the fire. But conditions were far from normal. The city and its surroundings were packed with British and French soldiery whose demands on the water supply system were too great to leave any reserve for a crisis like this. To add to this piece of misfortune a high wind arose and carried the flames from the suburbs into the heart of the business quarter. Nearly the whole of this district and much besides were destroyed. In the end the fire was only arrested by the waterfront.

At the time there were strong rumours that the conflagration was the work of enemy agents. These were never confirmed, but the disaster was a serious temporary set-back for the Allies. Also, the loss of property amounted to more than £4 million, about half of which fell on British offices. The North British & Mercantile was more heavily involved than any other company, losses paid under its policies totalling nearly £1,200,000.

Despite these vicissitudes the North British & Mercantile Group emerged from the war as a much more powerful business than when it entered it. Its total income in the final year exceeded £7 million. From board level to junior clerks its record of service in the forces had been notable. 892 of its members, from offices at home and overseas, joined the fighting forces; 112 lost their lives and 118 received decorations for gallantry and distinguished conduct. Casualties among directors included the President of the parent company, the Duke of Roxburghe, wounded on active service in 1914, and Major Vincent Hoare, killed in Flanders in February 1915; later casualties included the Hon. C. T. Mills, a member of the London Board, and Lord Ninian Crichton Stuart, a director of the Railway Passenger Assurance, both of whom were killed in fighting on the Western Front.

8

In the decade following the war the North British & Mercantile Group greatly extended its activities at home and overseas. At home it had enhanced its position in 1917 by acquiring the Fine Art and General Insurance Company. Established in London nearly thirty years earlier, the Fine Art, as its name implied, had started by specialising in the underwriting of pictures, *objets d'art* and art exhibitions. It had in the process achieved traditions and experiences of a somewhat unique and unusual kind. To this activity it had subsequently added more general work in the fire and accident fields. It was exclusively a home business and of moderate size. But it proved an admirable acquisition which, as the years went by, was to return a yearly growth of profits to its new owners.

T

In 1918 the group established its first branches in New Zealand—at Wellington and Auckland. In the following year it augmented its Canadian organisation by converting its agency-operated office at Toronto into a fully fledged branch and by opening another branch at Vancouver. In 1921 it established a branch at Singapore where it had worked through an agency since 1862. It broke new ground in Australia a year later by purchasing 85 per cent of the holdings in the Insurance Office of Australia, a company incorporated in New South Wales twelve years earlier.

So far as Central Europe was concerned, the parent company made no attempt to resuscitate its branches there. It did, however, return to the German market through an ingenious series of transactions. In 1924 it purchased a large proportion of the shares of the Sedina Versicherungs A.G., a business founded in 1920 at Stettin to undertake fire, marine and burglary insurance. It was not interested in the marine portfolio of this concern which it passed on to another Stettin office under a special agreement. In the same year it also acquired a controlling interest in the Nürnberger Feuer Versicherungs A.G. In 1925 it acquired complete control of the Stettin company, changed its name to the Allgemeine Feuer Assekuranz Aktien Gesellschaft, and transferred it to Hamburg. At the end of 1927 it merged the Nuremburg business into its Hamburg organisation. The one other important excursion of the Group into the continent of Europe in the post-war years was to establish a branch for Belgium at Brussels.

These various developments, especially those overseas, were the essential part of the programme for an insurance business, however large it had become, to maintain progress in a disturbed and highly competitive world.

In 1926 the directors decided to combine the London and Edinburgh Boards into a single Court of Directors and to centralise executive control of the business in London under one General Manager, Sir Arthur Worley. At the same time Lord Lawrence of Kingsgate, Chairman of the London board, was elected Chairman of the new Court. 64, Princes Street, Edinburgh, remained the registered office and the annual general meetings continued to be held in Edinburgh. The decision had been unanimous, but on grounds of sentiment it was reached with reluctance on the north side of the

Border. It was left to Lord Novar, a Scottish director and an eminent man of affairs—a former Governor-General of Australia and one-time Secretary of State for Scotland—to voice this sentiment:

"Personally I regret the tendency, which has become marked of late, to transfer centres of financial control from Edinburgh to London, and I believe that insurance can be run every whit as effectively outside of London as it is in the United States outside of New York. In our case, however, the conditions are such and the reasons for amalgamation so unanswerable that I see no alternative course."

9

To meet up with its new requirements the London head office in Threadneedle Street was rebuilt in 1926. In the following year Sir Arthur Worley was elected to the Court of Directors and for the first time in its history the North British & Mercantile had a Managing Director. Lord Lawrence died within a few months of assuming Chairmanship and his place was taken by Sir Alexander Kleinwort. It was in that year of 1927 that the Group expanded its organisation in the United States. A decade earlier it had increased its fire interests there by acquiring a moderate sized office with a history dating back to 1825—the Pennsylvania Fire Insurance Company. It now formed in New York the Homeland Insurance Company of America.

The decision to unify the Group's work was more than justified. 1928 turned out to be a prosperous year, with satisfactory progress in the Life Department and fire premiums that created a new record. In quite remarkable style the Group passed through the period of financial crisis that started in 1929. "A wonderful result in a year of universal depression" was its Chairman's description of activities in 1930. Despite some fluctuations in accident and marine results the record of success continued, with an almost unbroken growth from year to year of life and fire business. Sir Arthur Worley retired in 1936 and was succeeded by H. S. Milligan as the chief executive. Under Milligan the Group continued to flourish and it was only the advent of a Second World War that brought a temporary check to continuous progress.

During that war 1,097 members of the Group's staff, at home and overseas, served in the armed forces and other wholetime national services; 60 died on active service; 58 earned decorations or were mentioned in despatches. In addition, large numbers of the staff joined in various part-time duties like the Home Guard, A.R.P. and fire services.

An interesting episode in the history of the business was the evacuation to the country for the duration of the war of the majority of its London staff. Like many other large businesses with considerable numbers of employees in the London area, the North British started to search, after the Munich crisis, for a place to house its London staff, should conditions require this. In the spring of 1939 it purchased a mansion at Chalfont St. Giles in Buckinghamshire, known as Newland Park. The mansion had extensive grounds, but was inadequate to provide for the needs of such a large number of people. Immediate steps were, therefore, taken to instal working huts, canteen facilities, living accommodation, air-raid shelters and other auxiliary services such as a hydrant system. The work was so well advanced that by the last week-end in August, 1939, the move to Newland Park was made and the war-time head office was established. With relatively minor modifications it successfully fulfilled its functions throughout the war. Newland Park was subsequently sold to the Buckinghamshire County Council for use as a teachers' training college—a function which it still fulfills.

10

Once again the North British & Mercantile emerged successfully from a long period of stress. Milligan, who had ably led it through the struggle, retired in 1946 and became Deputy Chairman. He was succeeded by Sir Thomas Frazer, the Deputy General Manager and Secretary, who had recently been knighted for war-time services to the Government in numerous financial capacities. That year of 1946 was a red-letter year in the group's history; the new life business registered a record; the Fire Department's income showed large increases, the Accident Department an increase of 28 per cent; the marine results were more than satisfactory. Through the late forties and the early fifties, firstly under the general management of Edward Lansdowne, who succeeded Sir Thomas Frazer on the latter's retirement in 1949, and then under R. G. Harman, who succeeded Lansdowne in 1954, the Group's progress continued to gather way.

In 1955 the North British & Mercantile entered into casualty business for the first time in the United States through an outright purchase of the Central Surety and Insurance Corporation of Kansas City, Missouri. By then it was running into some heavy weather, like other offices on the North American continent. It merged the Homeland Insurance into the Central Surety at the end of 1957. This had been a serious year for the Group, with considerable losses in the United States and Canada. But by 1958 the position was being well retrieved. The trading results were generally better than those of the preceding year, especially in fire underwriting. The life results constituted a record. Indeed, the Group had recovered remarkably well despite continued difficulties in North America.

The principal reason, in fact, for the amalgamation with the Commercial Union in 1959 was that stated at the beginning of this chapter—the importance of consolidating and developing fire and casualty business in the United States, the problems and potentialities of which have so frequently figured in the history of British insurance overseas.

# CHAPTER XXI

## Recent Events

### I

EXPANSION of the Group's organisation and operations at home and overseas during the last three years has been so rapid and considerable that prominence of attention must be reserved for major developments in this concluding chapter. However, there is one particular event, affecting the Group's services to clients in London's West End, which commands a reference for its own intrinsic interest. This was the purchase from the Crown of the head lease of Schomberg House, Pall Mall, in May, 1959, and its subsequent conversion into the Group's West End office.

At the time of the purchase Schomberg House was one of the finest examples of Restoration architecture that still adorned the West End. Its superb façade had, however, been partially defaced by ugly alterations made in the fifties of the last century. Cecil H. Elsom, F.R.I.B.A., was engaged to direct the restoration of the building's exterior, which now resembles as nearly as possible its appearance when it was completed in 1666. The work of converting the interior of the building into modern offices was also carried out under his direction, and in such a way as to conform to the general style and tradition of the original structure.

Schomberg House had seen the coming and going of a strangely varied assortment of occupants before, in the second half of this century, it was to become tenanted by an insurance business. Originally known as Portland House, it was owned by the Countess

278

of Portland, who resided there till 1694. For a year or so subsequently the Duke of Leinster lived there, but in 1697 it was reconstructed for the Duke of Schomberg, was renamed Schomberg House and has retained that name ever since. This occupant was the second Duke of Schomberg, then "General of the Forces in England". His father was among the ablest soldiers of his day and lost his life fighting by the side of William of Orange at the Battle of the Boyne.

The Schomberg family continued to occupy the house until 1719, when it was taken over by the Earl of Holderness. Later, it passed into the tenancy of a succession of further peers of the realm. Then, in the second half of the eighteenth century, some famous painters followed the peers as tenants, John Astley taking over the main tenancy and sub-dividing the house. His most illustrious sub-tenant was Thomas Gainsborough, who moved from Bath to London in 1775 and rented the west wing, remaining there till his death in 1780.

Among subsequent occupants the most notorious was a certain Dr. Graham, who converted the central portion of the building into "The Temple of Health or The Temple of Hymen, Pall Mall". This was in 1781, but the preachings and practices of the learned "doctor" earned him such a reputation that he eventually had to flee to Scotland.

Later tenants included a picture dealer, an auctioneer, and also the famous bookseller, Thomas Payne, who moved to Schomberg House from his former shop, where now stands the National Gallery, in 1806. Shortly after the Crimean War the whole building was taken over by the War Office. In 1908 part of the War Office was demolished for the erection of the Royal Automobile Club.

2

The merger which brought together the Commercial Union and North British Groups was quickly followed by other developments. They were developments that reflected change and progress in overseas insurance markets, especially in the English-speaking countries of the Commonwealth.

The emergence in recent years of the former Dominions into

nations of world importance is well exemplified by the Common-wealth of Australia whose population now stands at around ten million. The opening up of new mineral resources and new indus-tries, and the growth of agricultural activities, accelerated by vast schemes of irrigation and other measures, have made the sub-continent infinitely more self-sufficient and have attracted from Europe and elsewhere a steadily increasing influx of immigrants. These changing circumstances have promoted continuous advance in the country's commercial life and, consequently, in its insurance activities.

In 1959 the Board and management in Cornhill gave careful consideration to certain trends and sentiments in the Australian market and the General Manager, F. E. P. Sandilands, studied them on the spot during a lengthy tour throughout the various States. This was to result in a major reorganisation of the Group's Australian business.

The history of the Commercial Union's associations with Aus-tralia, it may be recalled, went as far back as 1865. Since then the Commercial Union's own interests there had been greatly extended. But this was only part of the picture, because its acquisitions of other British businesses—the British General, the Edinburgh Assurance, the Palatine, the Ocean Accident and Guarantee, and the Union Assurance Society, all of which had established themselves on Australian soil—had still further enlarged its connections with fire, accident and marine business in Australia. The Commercial Union had also established a direct link with indigenous under-writing through the Australian Mutual Fire Insurance Society.

There had been another, and a most successful factor, in the Group's relationships with Australia. This had been its progressively close associations through agency arrangements with a number of leading woolbroking and pastoral agency houses, which constitute a unique and vital element in the agricultural and commercial life of the country. These comprised Dalgety and Company Ltd., Elder Smith and Co. Ltd., the New Zealand Loan and Mercantile Agency Co. Ltd., the Queensland Primary Producers Co-operative Associa-tion Ltd., and Roberts Stewart and Company Ltd. of Tasmania.

Taking into account on the one hand the general structure of the Australian business, which had materialised from these various associations, and on the other the increasingly conscious Australian aspirations towards independence in the operation of the nation's commercial affairs, it was recognised in Cornhill that the time was ripe for change. What was required was a reorganisation that would more fully integrate a somewhat loose-knit fabric and at the same time conform with the marked growth of national prosperity and prestige.

The outcome of this recognition was a decision to form a new company in Australia to take over all the Group's interests there and to permit the important pastoral agencies, as well as the Australian public, a considerable measure of participation in it by way of shareholdings and independent management. With these ends in view, the Commercial Union Assurance Co. of Australia Ltd. was established in July, 1960. The basis of its capital structure consisted of a £A 2 million holding by the Commercial Union in 5/- shares and a £A 550,000 holding by the pastoral agencies in similar shares. A further £A 450,000 in 5/- shares was subsequently issued in Australia and taken up by Australian subscribers before the end of the year.

The new company's Board of Directors is predominantly Australian and its chairman is Sir Edgar Coles. Its chief executive officer is C. F. W. Oakley, formerly the Commercial Union's Resident Manager in Australia. The head office is in Collins Street, Melbourne, on the site owned by the Commercial Union since 1882, and it is from there that the new company controls the Australian activities not only of the former British parent company, but also of its six associated companies, already mentioned, which have been transferred to its ownership.

3

A feature of post-war underwriting has been a movement towards linkage between life assurance and general insurance. This is yet another development that has brought change to the Group's activities in the English-speaking nations of the Commonwealth.

In recent years this tendency has become increasingly apparent in New Zealand and Canada. In New Zealand neither the Commercial Union nor any of its subsidiaries entered life business after taking up other insurance work there. But in 1960 a decision was made to add life assurance to the Group's activities through the acquisition of the Dominion Life Assurance Office of New Zealand Ltd. This was effected by a proposal to purchase the company's 38,550 issued cumulative preference shares and its 211,450 ordinary shares at a price of £5 and £3 each respectively. These offers were soon accepted by a large majority of the shareholders and the company became a member of the Group in September of that year.

This has been an interesting and valuable accession. The Dominion Life, founded in 1928, had built up a high reputation in the short period of its independent career as a progressive life office, transacting its business wholly within New Zealand. When formed in 1928, it was found convenient to register it as a company under the laws of New South Wales. But as its activities were confined to New Zealand, the New Zealand Parliament passed a special act in 1931, which provided that the office "should be deemed to be registered under the New Zealand Companies Act".

Though the causes for entering the Canadian life assurance market were similar to those experienced in New Zealand, they were considerably accentuated by the very large post-war growth of Canada's population, which now well exceeds sixteen million. In a sense this step has been a return to a former sphere of work; it may be recalled that under the Morland Watson agency, appointed by the Commercial Union in 1863 at Montreal, life business was extended through various parts of the Province of Quebec. However, it was given up within a fairly short period and never seems to have been practised widely by the company in the other provinces. For this reason some historic interest attaches itself to the revival of earlier associations with life assurance in Canada, which has taken place on April 1st of this year, 1961. On that date a life branch under the manager for the Group was created at Montreal.

4

There have been new men at the helm of the Commercial Union Group in these recent years. The Board itself has seen several changes. In 1958 Colonel John Leslie retired from its Chairmanship after presiding successfully over its affairs through a decade in which the business made remarkable progress despite the aftermath of war. He was succeeded by Ronald C. Brooks, who has continued as Chairman since then.

For many years now the Board of the Commercial Union has been distinctive in its composition. It continues to show the same character and tradition today, its membership representing both the City of London—in all which that conveys by way of financial and commercial influence—and the world of public affairs. Its present membership, listed in an appendix, clearly illustrates this characteristic. But any reference to the Board would be incomplete without a particular reference to the two present Vice-Chairmen—Sir Mark Turner, well known for his many connections with banking and commerce, and Cyril H. Kleinwort, Chairman of the North British and Mercantile, with the long career of which his family has been prominently connected.

Under the present General Manager, F. E. P. Sandilands, the shape and size of the Group at home, and even more so overseas, have already seen wide-scale change and reorganisation. This has been reflected in additions to the higher management and in other alterations at the centre, including the co-ordination of the Group's overseas fire and accident operations under a single Overseas Manager. There has also been a dispersal of the principal departments of the Group to individual premises in various parts of the City, and 24 Cornhill has become specifically a headquarters of direction and management.

## 5

Early in 1960 the Board of the Commercial Union decided to seek further capital. It will be remembered that less than a year earlier the Group's nominal capital had been raised to £13,187,500. The need for still further augmentation will have become obvious from the record of developments in this and the preceding chapter. What may be less obvious were some of the particular financial involvements necessitated by expansion. The acquisition of the North British had been effected mainly through a share exchange, but there was also a cash consideration amounting to £2,750,000. Moreover, at the time of the merger, the North British was considering the need to raise its capital in order to augment its free reserves held in London—a need arising from the tendency in overseas countries to introduce legislation immobilising local resources. The North British derived an even larger proportion of its business from overseas than the Commercial Union and it was, therefore, scarcely surprising that the enlargement of the Group resulting from the merger promoted even greater requirements for free reserves held in London. If one also takes into account the additional commitments involved over the various other contemporaneous developments of the business, especially overseas, the requirements for fresh capital become more than ever obvious.

To implement its decision the Board convened an extraordinary general meeting of shareholders on July 4th, 1960, at which a resolution increasing the authorised capital of the company to £16,750,000, by the creation of 14,250,000 ordinary shares of 5/- each, was duly passed. A "Rights" issue of 11,225,500 of these shares was then offered to the existing shareholders at the issue price of 20/- each. By August 3rd acceptances of the offer had been received, covering more than 98 per cent of the issue, and the shares not taken up had been sold for the benefit of the shareholders concerned.

There could have been little doubt regarding the result of the "Rights" issue. In presenting the accounts for 1959 the Chairman had stated:

"With the inclusion of the business of the North British & Mercantile Insurance Company Ltd. and its associated Offices, our net premium income from the Fire, Accident and Marine Accounts now comfortably exceeds £100 million—a figure which truly reflects our position as one of the foremost groups of insurance companies in the world today. In the Life Department, also, record levels were achieved in 1959, new sums assured exceeding £57 million."

It may be recalled that the combined assets of the Commercial Union and North British Groups at the time of their fusion totalled some £319 million. By the end of 1959 they exceeded £336 million.

These are the latest figures available as we bring this history to a close, but assessment based on subsequent progress points to still further growth in assets during 1960 and 1961.

6

Achievement, however, cannot be assessed solely and simply in the cold light of financial figures. The economic aspects of the growth of insurance, as exemplified by the expansion of a single insurance office into a great complex of interests within a hundred years, are of decided interest. Some of these aspects have been dealt with in the introduction to this history. Of deeper and more human interest, however, are the contributions made by individuals, as well as groups of individuals working in close co-operation, to the wresting of progress out of adversity and to the advancement of a business throughout a century marked by international crises, world wars, vast social changes and industrial evolution. Of equal human interest is the continuously growing amelioration which the insurance industry has brought to bear on individual human misfortunes and on the results of events ranging from a single death or minor accidents to great disasters.

It has been said more than once in this record that insurance touches life in every field of human enterprise. This is particularly true of a large-scale composite insurance business encompassing activities in every corner of the globe. Even before the turn of the century the Commercial Union had come to play a distinctive part in British insurance both at home and overseas. From the turn of the century onwards it added accident insurance to its other activities and also transformed itself into a leading group of companies under the guidance of an enlightened Board and a succession of remarkably able General Managers, starting with Roger Owen in 1901.

This record of British achievement has attempted to let facts and events speak for themselves, and it is hoped that due tribute has also been paid to other leading offices in British insurance, with which the Commercial Union Group has come to work in close and friendly co-operation over major national and international developments. One particular impression, however, made on the writer of this history is that throughout its career the Commercial Union has shown an almost consistent resilience in the management of its affairs, a capacity to profit from mistakes and to anticipate change, to find the right men at the right occasion to direct its momentum, and to move forward constantly and rapidly with the times.

" New times demand new measures and new men.
The world advances and in time outgrows
The laws that in our fathers' days were best.

One age moves onwards and the next builds up
Cities and gorgeous palaces, where stood
The rude log huts of those who tamed the wild,
Rearing from out the forests they had felled
The goodly framework of a fairer state.

Truth is eternal, but her effluence
With endless change, is fitted to the hour;
Her mirror is turned forward to reflect
The promise of the future, not the past."

These lines written by the American poet, James Russell Lowell, some few years before the origin of the Commercial Union, seem applicable to its century of progress recorded in these pages and to the "promise of the future" in the second century on which it is now embarking.

# *Appendices*

# Commercial Union Assurance Company Limited

## PRESENT BOARD OF DIRECTORS

The Rt. Hon. Lord Aldenham
The Hon. David F. Brand
Ronald C. Brooks, O.B.E., M.C. (*Chairman*)
Sir Geoffrey Crowther
Sir Thomas Frazer, O.B.E., F.F.A.
E. W. Grazebrook, T.D.
Sir Edmund L. Hall-Patch, G.C.M.G.
W. W. H. Hill-Wood, C.B.E.
Robert Hollond
Cyril H. Kleinwort

Roger Leigh-Wood
Lt. Col. John Leslie, D.S.O., M.C., D.L.
R. K. Lochhead, F.I.A.
Sir John Makins
A. D. Marris, C.M.G.
The Rt. Hon. Lord Pender, C.B.E.
J. G. Phillimore, C.M.G.
The Rt. Hon. Lord Plowden, K.C.B., K.B.E.
Sir Mark Turner

## MEDICAL OFFICERS

| | |
|---|---|
| 1862–1899 | Sir Thomas Smith, Bart., F.R.C.S. |
| 1862–1895 | John Syer Bristowe, M.D., F.R.C.P. |
| 1895–1949 | Sir William Hale-White, K.B.E., M.D., F.R.C.P. |
| 1899–1902 | John Wychenford Washbourn, C.M.G., M.D., F.R.C.P. |
| 1902–1937 | John Fawcett, M.D., F.R.C.P. |
| 1913–1920 | Herbert French, C.B.E., M.D., F.R.C.P. |
| 1920–1958 | Hector Charles Cameron, M.D., F.R.C.P. |
| 1939– | John Maurice Hardman Campbell, O.B.E., M.D., F.R.C.P. |
| 1939– | Arthur Cecil Hampson, M.C., M.D., F.R.C.P. |
| 1956– | Ralph Kauntze, M.B.E., M.A., M.D., F.R.C.P. |

# PRESENT MANAGEMENT

*General Manager*
F. E. P. Sandilands

*Deputy General Managers*
V. E. Masters    R. P. F. Smallwood

*Assistant General Managers*
L. H. Hewens    A. B. Kempton    C. H. Miller    A. W. White

*Controller of Accounts*
A. D. Clark, LL.B.

*Investment Manager*
R. A. Bodey, F.I.A.

*Actuary and Life Manager*
N. R. Gatenby, F.I.A.

*Marine Underwriter*
G. W. Hogsflesh, O.B.E., T.D.

*Accident Manager*
R. L. Hervey, LL.B.

*Home Fire Manager*
A. J. Yardley

*Overseas Manager*
M. H. R. King

*Assistant Managers*
C. I. W. Ibbotson    E. Orbell    L. N. Wills

*Secretary*
L. S. Cooper

# CHAIRMEN

| | |
|---|---|
| 1861–1863 | Henry W. Peek |
| 1863–1865 | Henry Trower |
| 1865–1866 | Samuel Hanson |
| 1866–1867 | John Kemp Welch |
| 1867–1869 | John Boustead |
| 1869–1870 | Alexander Sim |
| 1870–1871 | Jeremiah Colman |
| 1871–1872 | Francis Hicks |
| 1872–1873 | Alfred Giles |
| 1873–1874 | Frederick W. Harris |
| 1874–1875 | William Leask |
| 1875–1876 | Sir Henry W. Peek |
| 1876–1877 | A. J. Mundella |
| 1877–1878 | Henry Trower |
| 1878–1879 | Alexander Sim |
| 1879–1880 | A. J. Mundella |
| 1880–1881 | Robert Barclay |
| 1881–1882 | Thomas Russell |
| 1882–1883 | W. Middleton Campbell |
| 1883–1884 | W. R. Arbuthnot |
| 1884–1886 | Andrew R. Scoble |
| 1886–1887 | John Holms |
| 1887–1888 | Alfred Giles |
| 1888–1889 | Frederick W. Harris |
| 1889–1890 | W. Middleton Campbell |
| 1890–1891 | Robert Barclay |
| 1891–1892 | W. R. Arbuthnot |
| 1892–1893 | Jeremiah Colman |
| 1893–1896 | John Trotter |
| 1896–1897 | Sir James F. Garrick, Q.C., K.C.M.G. |
| 1897–1899 | Gen. Sir Henry W. Norman, G.C.B. |
| 1899–1900 | William C. Dawes |
| 1900–1901 | W. Middleton Campbell |
| 1901–1902 | Sir James F. Garrick, K.C., K.C.M.G. |
| 1902–1903 | Jeremiah Colman |
| 1903–1904 | W. Murray Guthrie |

| | |
|---|---|
| 1904–1906 | John Trotter |
| 1906–1907 | P. Bence Trower |
| 1907–1908 | Robert Barclay |
| 1908–1909 | Sir Jeremiah Colman, Bt. |
| 1909–1910 | W. Murray Guthrie |
| 1910–1911 | W. J. Thompson |
| 1911–1912 | W. Middleton Campbell |
| 1912–1913 | C. R. G. Hoare |
| 1913–1914 | Sir Jeremiah Colman, Bt. |
| 1914–1915 | J. Carr Saunders |
| 1915–1916 | C. D. Seligman |
| 1916–1917 | H. Tabor Brooks |
| 1917–1918 | Warrington Laing |
| 1918–1919 | Sir Jeremiah Colman |
| 1919–1920 | Hon. A. H. Holland-Hibbert |
| 1920–1921 | E. Roger Owen |
| 1921–1922 | Sir James Leigh-Wood |
| 1922–1923 | A. B. Williamson |
| 1923–1924 | Sir Austin E. Harris, K.B.E. |
| 1924–1925 | Robert L. Barclay, C.B.E. |
| 1925–1926 | C. D. Seligman |
| 1926–1927 | H. Tabor Brooks |
| 1927–1928 | J. F. G. Gilliat |
| 1928–1929 | Hon. W. D. Gibbs |
| 1929–1930 | Sir Percy W. Newson |
| 1930–1931 | Sir Robert Horne |
| 1931–1935 | Sir James Leigh-Wood |
| 1935–1938 | Herbert Lewis |
| 1938–1943 | Sir Bertram Hornsby |
| 1943–1948 | J. F. G. Gilliat |
| 1948–1959 | Lt. Col. J. Leslie, D.S.O., M.C., D.L. |
| 1959– | Ronald C. Brooks, O.B.E., M.C. |

# Commercial Union Group of Insurance Companies

## HOME AND OVERSEAS BRANCHES AND SUB-BRANCHES

### LONDON

*City*

24 Cornhill, E.C.3.
1 & 2 Royal Exchange Buildings, E.C.3.
2/3 Old Broad Street, E.C.2.
38 Moorgate, E.C.2.
35/36 Lime Street, E.C.3.
Chichester House, 278/282, High Holborn, W.C.1.
30 Great Tower Street, E.C.3.
8 Billiter Square, E.C.3.

*West End*

Schomberg House, 82 Pall Mall, S.W.1.

*Suburban*

Highbury Corner, N.5.
141 High Street, Southgate, N.14.
77/79 High Road, Wood Green, N.22.
128 Finchley Road, N.W.3.
227 Holland Park Avenue, W.11.
51 Borough High Street, S.E.1.
60 Borough High Street, S.E.1.
147 Rushey Green, Catford, S.E.6.
57 Hill Road, Wimbledon, S.W.19.
1/1A Wyatt Park Road, Streatham Hill, S.W.16.
15/16 The High Parade, Streatham High Road, S.W.16.
48/50 Hartfield Road, S.W.19.

# ENGLAND AND WALES, ISLE OF MAN AND CHANNEL ISLANDS

Aberystwyth
Ashford, Kent
Ashton-under-Lyne
Aylesbury
Banbury
Bangor
Barnoldswick
Barnsley
Barnstaple
Barrow-in-Furness
Basingstoke
Bath
Bedford
Berwick-on-Tweed
Birkenhead
Birmingham
Blackburn
Blackpool
Bolton
Boston
Bournemouth
Bradford
Bridgend
Bridlington
Brighton
Bristol
Burnley
Burton-on-Trent
Bury
Bury St. Edmunds
Caernarvon
Cambridge
Canterbury
Cardiff
Carlisle
Carmarthen
Chelmsford
Cheltenham

Chester
Chesterfield
Chichester
Cirencester
Colchester
Colwyn Bay
Coventry
Crawley
Crewe
Croydon
Darlington
Derby
Devizes
Dewsbury
Doncaster
Dorchester
Douglas, Isle of Man
Dudley
Eastbourne
Evesham
Exeter
Farnham, Surrey
Folkestone
Gloucester
Gravesend
Grimsby
Guernsey, C.I.
Guildford
Halifax
Harrogate
Harrow
Hastings
Haverfordwest
Haywards Heath
Hereford
Huddersfield
Hull
Ilford

Ipswich
Jersey, C.I.
Keighley
King's Lynn
Kingston-upon-
   Thames
Launceston
Leeds
Leicester
Lincoln
Liverpool
Luton
Maidenhead
Maidstone
Manchester
Mansfield
Margate
Middlesbrough
Morecambe
Newbury
Newcastle-upon-
   Tyne
Newport, Mon.
Northallerton
Northampton
Norwich
Nottingham
Oldham
Oxford
Peterborough
Plymouth
Portsmouth
Preston
Reading
Rochester
Romford
Rothbury
Rotherham

# ENGLAND AND WALES, ISLE OF MAN AND CHANNEL ISLANDS—(*cont.*)

St. Albans
St. Helens
Salisbury
Sandown, Isle of
  Wight
Scarborough
Scunthorpe
Sheffield
Shrewsbury
Slough
Southampton
Southend-on-Sea
Southport

Stafford
Stockport
Stoke-on-Trent
Sunderland
Swansea
Swindon
Taunton
Torquay
Truro
Tunbridge Wells
Wakefield
Wallingford
Walsall

Watford
Weston-super-Mare
Whitchurch, Shrop-
  shire
Whitehaven
Wigan
Wolverhampton
Worcester
Worthing
Yarmouth
Yeovil
York

## SCOTLAND

Aberdeen
Ayr
Dumfries
Dundee
Edinburgh
Elgin

Galashiels
Glasgow
Greenock
Hamilton
Inverness
Keith

Kilmarnock
Kirkcaldy
Perth
Stirling
Wick

## IRELAND

Armagh
Athlone
Belfast
Cork
Drogheda
Dublin

Galway
Kilkenny
Limerick
Londonderry
Newry
Sligo

Tralee
Tullamore
Waterford
Wexford

## OVERSEAS

| | | | |
|---|---|---|---|
| ARGENTINA | Buenos Aires | CANADA *(cont.)* | Saint John N.B. |
| | | | Toronto |
| AUSTRALIA | MELBOURNE | | Vancouver |
| | Adelaide | | Winnipeg |
| | Ballarat | | |
| | Bendigo | CEYLON | Colombo |
| | Brisbane | | |
| | Darwin | DENMARK | Copenhagen |
| | Fremantle | | |
| | Geelong | EAST AFRICA | NAIROBI |
| | Hobart | | Dar es Salaam |
| | Kalgoorlie | | Kampala |
| | Launceston | | Mombasa |
| | Maryborough | | Moshi |
| | Newcastle | | |
| | Perth | FEDERATION OF | SALISBURY |
| | Shepparton | RHODESIA AND | Bulawayo |
| | Sydney | NYASALAND | Kitwe |
| | Toowoomba | | Lusaka |
| | Townsville | | |
| | | FRANCE | Paris |
| AUSTRIA | VIENNA | | |
| | Dornbirn | HOLLAND | Amsterdam |
| | Eisenstadt | | Haarlem |
| | Graz | | Rotterdam |
| | Innsbruck | | The Hague |
| | Klagenfurt | | |
| | Linz | HONG KONG | |
| | Salzburg | | |
| | | INDIA | CALCUTTA |
| BELGIUM | BRUSSELS | | Ahmedabad |
| | Antwerp | | Bangalore |
| | Bruges | | Bombay |
| | Charleroi | | Lucknow |
| | Ghent | | Madras |
| | Liège | | New Delhi |
| | Louvain | | |
| | | INDONESIA | DJAKARTA |
| CANADA | MONTREAL | | Surabaia |
| | Calgary | | |
| | Hamilton | MALAYA | KUALA LUMPUR |
| | Ottawa | | Ipoh |
| | Quebec | | Penang |

| NEW ZEALAND | WELLINGTON | SOUTH AFRICA | Newcastle |
| | Auckland | *(cont.)* | Pietermaritzburg |
| | Christchurch | | Pietersburg |
| | Dunedin | | Port Elizabeth |
| | Hamilton | | Pretoria |
| | Invercargill | | Queenstown |
| | Palmerston North | | Springs |
| | | | Vereeniging |
| PAKISTAN | KARACHI | | Witbank |
| | Chittagong | | Worcester |
| | Lahore | | |
| | | SPAIN | Barcelona |
| SINGAPORE | | | |
| | | UNITED STATES | NEW YORK |
| SOUTH AFRICA | CAPE TOWN | OF AMERICA | Atlanta |
| | Benoni | | Chicago |
| | Bloemfontein | | Detroit |
| | Durban | | Kansas City |
| | East London | | Los Angeles |
| | Graaf Reinet | | New York Metro- |
| | Grahamstown | | politan |
| | Johannesburg | | Philadelphia |
| | Kingwilliamstown | | San Francisco |
| | Kroonstad | | St. Louis |
| | Krugersdorp | | |

# Commercial Union Assurance Company Limited

## GENERAL AGENTS OVERSEAS IN CORRESPONDENCE WITH LONDON

ADEN
: Cowasjee Dinshaw & Bros. (Aden) Ltd.,
Steamer Point.

ANGOLA
: Hull Blyth (Angola) Ltd.,
Caixa Postal 100, Lobito.
Hull Blyth (Angola) Ltd.,
Caixa Postal 1214, Luanda.

BELGIUM
: Stanislas H. Haine,
Rempart Kipdorp 42, Antwerp.
Ch. Le Jeune (Assurances) S.C.R.L.,
Bureau d'Europe,
17 rue d'Arenberg, Antwerp.

BERMUDA
: L. P. Gutteridge,
Harold Hayes Frith Building,
Hamilton.

BOLIVIA
: Gibbs, Williamson (Bolivia) Ltd.,
Casilla No. 957, La Paz.

BRAZIL
: Frank May & Cia. Ltda.,
Rua Portugal No. 11, Sala 902,
Salvador, Bahia.
John A. Thom,
Rua do Bom Jesus 226,
Recife, Pernambuco.
Sociedade Sulina de Administracao e
Representaçao Ltda.,
Rua Uruguay 155, Porto Alegre.

BRAZIL *(cont.)*    Representaçoes Pryor S.A.,
Av. Pres. Vargas No. 502—14.0,
Rio de Janeiro.
J. Speers-Seguros Ltda.,
Caixa Postal No. 604, Sao Paulo.

BRITISH GUIANA    Sprostons Ltd.,
3–9 Lombard Street, Georgetown.

BRITISH
HONDURAS    W. H. Courtenay, O.B.E.,
174 Church Street, Belize.

CANADA    Dale & Co. Ltd.,
710 Victoria Square, Montreal.

CEYLON    Shaw Wallace & Hedges Ltd.,
363 Kollupitiya Road,
Colpetty, Colombo.
The Ceylon Trading Co. Ltd.,
P.O. Box No. 161, Colombo.
The Ceylon Insurance Co. Ltd.,
69 Queen Street, Colombo.
Harrisons & Crosfield Ltd.,
Prince Building, Colombo.

CHILE    Sociedad Comercial Cominsa Ltda.,
Casilla 178–D, Santiago.

COLOMBIA    Tracey & Cia. S.A.,
Calle 13 No. 12–42,
Apartados $\begin{cases} \text{Nacional 1196} \\ \text{Aereo No. 3597} \end{cases}$
Bogota.
Gustavo Posada & Cia. Sucs. Ltda.,
Apartados $\begin{cases} \text{16 Nacional} \\ \text{630 Aereo} \end{cases}$
Medellin.

CONGO    Ch. Le Jeune (Assurances) S.C.R.L.,
Building Forescom,
Boite Postale No. 178,
Leopoldville.

CUBA    Sr. Don Santiago V. Perez,
Calle de Lealtad 564,
Havana.

CURACAO    Julius L. Penha & Sons Inc.,
Heerenstraat No. 1.

| | |
|---|---|
| CYPRUS | Francoudi & Stephanou Ltd.,<br>85 Evagorou Avenue,<br>Famagusta.<br>Z. D. Pierides,<br>P.O. Box No. 25, Larnaca. |
| DENMARK | A. Frederiksen & Co.,<br>Ved Stranden 8, Copenhagen. |
| ECUADOR | Sociedad General,<br>Guayaquil. |
| FINLAND | Avbrottsförsäkringsaktiebolaget OTSO,<br>Bulevarden 10,<br>Helsingfors. |
| FRANCE | Maurice Gombaud & Fils,<br>24 Cours du Marechal Foch, Bordeaux.<br>R. Landais,<br>3 rue de la Bourse, Paris. |
| GAMBIA | Maurel Frères S.A.,<br>P.O. Box No. 269,<br>Bathurst. |
| GERMANY | Mund & Fester,<br>Trostbrücke 4, Hamburg. |
| GIBRALTAR | Barclays Bank D.C.O.,<br>83/89 Irish Town. |
| GREECE | A. & G. Plytas,<br>23 Stadium Street, Athens 1. |
| GUATEMALA | Serrano, Matheu y Cia. Ltda.,<br>Apartado Postal No. 485,<br>Guatemala City. |
| HOLLAND | Blom & Van der Aa,<br>Prins Hendrikkade 33,<br>Amsterdam.<br>Langeveldt Schröder,<br>514 Herengracht, Amsterdam.<br>Bicker Caarten & Obreen,<br>Schiedamse Vest 48/50, Rotterdam.<br>W. J. Havelaar,<br>Coolsingel 65, Rotterdam.<br>Tulleners & Brummer,<br>Coolsingel 58, Rotterdam. |

| | |
|---|---|
| INDONESIA | Harrisons & Crosfield Ltd.,<br>Kali Besar Timur 25, Djakarta-Kota.<br>Harrisons & Crosfield Ltd.,<br>P.O. Box No. 155,<br>Medan. |
| ISRAEL | The Levant Bonded Warehouses Co. Ltd.,<br>P.O. Box No. 36,<br>Haifa.<br>The Levant Bonded Warehouses Co. Ltd.,<br>119 Allenby Street (Blue House),<br>Tel Aviv. |
| ITALY | Bevington Vaizey & Foster Ltd.,<br>Via Borgogna No. 2,<br>Milan. |
| JAPAN | British Insurance Group,<br>Room 849 (8th Floor),<br>Kokusai Kanko Kaikan,<br>1 Marunouchi 1-chome,<br>Chyoda-Ku,<br>Tokyo. |
| MALAYA | Harrisons & Crosfield (Federation of Malaya) Ltd.,<br>70 Ampang Road,<br>Kuala Lumpur. |
| MALTA | A. & V. Von Brockdorff,<br>14 Zachary Street,<br>Valletta. |
| MAURITIUS | Adam & Co. Ltd.,<br>1 Queen Street, Port Louis. |
| MOROCCO | Wm. E. Calver & Co. Ltd.,<br>18 Rue Tolstoi, Tangier. |
| NEW CALEDONIA | Etablissements Ballande, S.A.<br>Rue de l'Alma, Noumea. |
| NEW HEBRIDES | Les Comptoirs Francais des Nouvelles Hebrides,<br>Port Vila,<br>Efate. |
| NORWAY | Sev. Dahl's Assurancekontor A/S,<br>Kronprinsesse Märthas Plass No. 1,<br>Oslo. |

| | |
|---|---|
| PHILIPPINE ISLANDS | Conrad & Co. Inc., Shurdut Building, General Luna, Intramuros, Manila. |
| | The Findlay Millar Timber Co., A. Magsaysay Building, San Luis, Ermita, Manila. |
| | Smith Bell & Co. (Philippines) Inc., Trade & Commerce Building, 215 Juan Luna Street, Manila. |
| | Warner, Barnes & Co. Ltd., Hongkong Bank Building, Manila. |
| PORTUGAL | Rawes & Co. Ltd., 2 Rua da Nova Alfandega, Oporto. |
| PUERTO RICO | Albert E. Lee & Son Inc., 4/6 Nueva Street, San Juan 13. |
| | Mendez & Co. Inc., 6 Deposito Street, San Juan 14. |
| SALVADOR | F. D. Gibson, 2a Avenida Sur, San Salvador. |
| | H. de Solae Hijos S.A., San Salvador. |
| SIERRA LEONE | Paterson Zochonis & Co. Ltd., Wilberforce Street, Freetown. |
| SINGAPORE | Harrisons & Crosfield (Singapore) Ltd., P.O. Box No. 865. |
| SUDAN | Mitchell Cotts & Co. (Middle East) Ltd., Kasr Avenue, Khartoum. |
| SURINAM | West India Trading Company, Benz & Co. Ltd., Paramaribo. |
| SWEDEN | Charles Tottie & Co., Nybrokajen 7, Stockholm C. |

| THAILAND | The Anglo Thai Corporation Ltd.,<br>Bush Lane,<br>Bangkok. |
| --- | --- |
| URUGUAY | Bunge & Born Ltda. S.A.U.,<br>Plaza Independencia 811–2° Piso,<br>Montevideo. |
| WEST INDIES | Oswald Moseley,<br>Nassau, New Providence,<br>Bahama Islands.<br>C. F. Harrison & Co. (Barbados) Ltd.,<br>P.O. Box No. 304,<br>Bridgetown, Barbados.<br>Geo. F. Huggins & Co. (Grenada) Ltd.,<br>St. George's,<br>Grenada.<br>Manton & Hart (Insurance) Ltd.,<br>34 Duke Street,<br>Kingston, Jamaica.<br>Cargill & Graham,<br>4 Duke Street,<br>Kingston, Jamaica.<br>Robert L. Merwin & Co. Inc.,<br>Frederiksted,<br>St. Croix,<br>Virgin Islands of the United States.<br>Gordon, Salles-Miquelle, McNamara & Co<br>Castries,<br>St. Lucia.<br>Geo. F. Huggins & Co. Ltd.,<br>Colonial Building,<br>70/74 South Quay,<br>Port of Spain, Trinidad.<br>Geo. F. Huggins & Co. Ltd.,<br>19/21 St. James Street,<br>San Fernando, Trinidad. |

# BIBLIOGRAPHY

## PUBLISHED SOURCES

*Australian Encyclopaedia.* (Various relevant articles.) Angus & Robertson, 1958.

*Cambridge History of the British Empire.* (Volumes relevant to the former Dominions.)

CLAPHAM, SIR JOHN. *An Economic History of Britain.* Parts 2 and 3. (As reprinted in 1952 and 1951.) Cambridge University Press.

CLOUGH, S. B. and COLE, C. W. *Economic History of Europe.* Part Three —Chapters XXI to XXVI. D. C. Heath & Co., Boston, U.S.A., 1952.

CONRAD, JOSEPH. *The Mirror of the Sea.* Seventh Edition, 1917. Methuen.

CRUTWELL, C. R. M. F. *A History of the Great War. 1914–1918.* Clarendon Press, 1934.

*Encyclopaedia Britannica.* Fourteenth Edition. (Various relevant articles.)

*Encyclopaedia Canadiana.* (Various relevant articles.) Canadian Encyclopaedia Co., 1957-1958.

*Encyclopaedia of the Social Sciences.* Edited by E. R. A. Seligman. Vol. 8. Article on Insurance. Macmillan, New York, 1935.

GIBB, D. E. W. *Lloyd's of London.* Macmillan, 1957.

HARDWICK, ARTHUR. *Memorable Fires in London. Past and Present* Post Magazine, 1926.

LARKWORTHY, FALCONER. *Ninety-one years.* Edited by Harold Begbie. Mills & Boon, 1924.

LLOYD, CHRISTOPHER. *The Nation and the Navy.* Cresset Press, 1954.

MACKENZIE, COMPTON. *Realms of Silver*—One Hundred Years of Banking in the East. A History of the Chartered Bank. Routledge & Kegan Paul, 1954.

MARTIN, FREDERICK. *History of Lloyd's & Marine Insurance.* London, 1876.

RAINBOW, EDWIN D. *The St. Lawrence Seaway*—Shipping and Marine Insurance Aspects. Witherby, 1957.

RAYNES, HAROLD E. *A History of British Insurance.* Pitman, 1950.

ROSKILL, CAPTAIN S. W., D.S.C. R.N. (Retd.) *The Navy at War. 1939–1945.* Collins, 1960.

RICHARDS, D. and HUNT, J. W. *An Illustrated History of Modern Britain.* Longmans, Green & Co., 1950.

SIEGFRIED, ANDRÉ. *America Comes of Age.* Translated from the French by H. H. Hemming and Doris Hemming. (As published in Life and Letters Series, 1930.) Jonathan Cape. *England's Crisis.* By same translators. Jonathan Cape, 1931.

THOMSON, DAVID. *England in the Nineteenth Century.* (1815–1914). Penguin Books, 1950.

TRAILL, H. D. and MANN, J. S. *Social England.* Volume VI. Cassell, 1904.

TREVELYAN, G. M. *English Social History.* Chapter XVIII. (Second British Edition, 1946.) Longmans, Green & Co.

WALFORD, CORNELIUS. *The Insurance Encyclopaedia.* (Compiled in the Seventies of the last century.) Layton.

## UNPUBLISHED SOURCES

(In Archives of Commercial Union Assurance Co., Ltd.)

*Board Minutes, and Supporting Documents* from 1861 to 1945.
*Minute Books of:*
  1. Fire Department Committee from 1861 onwards.
  2. Life Department Committee from 1862 onwards.
  3. Marine Department Committee from 1924 onwards.
  4. Accident Department Committee from 1901 onwards.
  (These Minute Books were consulted, as and when necessary, for fuller details not included in the Board Minutes.)
*Annual Reports of:*
  1. Fire Department.
  2. Life Department.
  3. Marine Department from 1930 onwards.
  4. Accident Department.
*Marine Department's loss Report Books* from 1898 onwards and *Casualties Books* from 1911 onwards.
*Reports on Overseas and European Visits by Senior Officials* from 1871 onwards.
*Similar Reports Presented by General Managers* from 1903 onwards.
*Prospectus* including list of Provisional Directors, 1861.

X

*Letter* sent out with prospectus under the name of the Chairman, Henry Wm. Peek, August 17, 1861.

*Deed of Settlement* of the Company, September 28, 1861.

*Papers* relating to the Company and its acceptance of the London Mercantile Tariff, 1863.

*Record Books* of early foreign agencies and branches (one undated; the second dated 1887).

*Notes* drawn up by H. Mann, July, 1924, on the constitution and early history of the Company.

*Transcript of Speech by Sir Jeremiah Colman Bt.*, at a dinner at Savoy Hotel, October 21, 1935, to celebrate his fifty years on the Board of the Company.

# DOCUMENTS RELATING TO SUBSIDIARY COMPANIES

Booklet, containing history of the West of England Fire and Life Insurance Co., to celebrate opening of new offices of the Exeter Branch, January 10, 1952.

The Origin and History of the Hand-in-Hand Fire and Life Insurance Society. Booklets issued in 1883 and 1888.

Bi-Centenary Notice of the Hand-in-Hand Fire and Life Insurance Society, issued in 1896.

*Union Assurance Society Bi-Centenary*—A Short History of the Society since its formation in 1714, issued in 1914.

*Union Assurance Society*—A further historical account issued in 1939.

Board Minutes of Union Assurance Society, and Supporting Documents, 1914 to 1919. (For references to interests in Germany affected by First World War.)

Prospectus of the Accident Insurance Co., 1883.

*A Hundred Years, 1823 to 1923*—An Outline of the History of the Edinburgh Life Assurance Co.

Minutes of the Festive Meetings of the Directors of the Edinburgh Life Assurance Co., 1836 to 1943 (mostly recorded in manuscript).

Edinburgh Life Assurance Company's New Building at Newcastle-upon-Tyne—Booklet issued to celebrate its opening in 1908.

Notes on history of the West of Scotland Insurance Office, compiled by C. R. Prosser, 1937.

*The Ocean Accident and Guarantee Corporation*—The First Forty Years. Outline of history compiled by F. E. P. Sandilands.

National Insurance Co. of Great Britain. Historical note compiled by its Manager, 1937.

Twenty-One Years' Progress of the British General. Twenty-first Birthday Brochure, 1925.

*The Spirit of 1906.* An account of the San Francisco Earthquake and Fire by G. W. Brooks. Issued by the California Insurance Co., 1921.

*The California Pays.* Brochure issued by the California Insurance Co., 1933.

*The Hardest Years.* Centenary Booklet issued by the American Central Insurance Co., 1953.

North British & Mercantile Insurance Company Centenary, 1809 to 1909. Booklet issued in 1909.

Railway Passengers Assurance Co. Centenary, 1849 to 1949. Booklet issued in 1949.

## MISCELLANEOUS DOCUMENTS

Annual Reports and Chairmen's Statements, Commercial Union Assurance Co. Ltd., from 1861 onwards.

Articles in *The Link*, Staff Magazine of the Commercial Union Group, 1926 to 1960.

Reports, printed in 1924 and 1925, relating to legal actions against insurance companies in regard to the Smyrna Conflagration of 1922.

Booklet issued by the Commercial Union in 1930 and describing its new Head Office Building.

*Bequests by Sir William Dunn, Bt.*—Privately printed report containing observations by Sir Jeremiah Colman, Bt., Chairman of the Dunn Trust Committee.

Report by Sub-Committee of the Committee of Imperial Defence on the Insurance of British Shipping in time of War. Presented to Parliament, August, 1914.

Various White Papers etc. relating to Parliamentary Acts and Government measures concerning insurance in the First and Second World Wars.

Annual Reports and Chairmen's Statements, North British & Mercantile Insurance Co. Ltd., from 1910 onwards.

## NEWSPAPERS AND PERIODICALS

Frequent recourse has been made to relevant articles and reports in the *Times*, the *Financial Times*, and other newspapers.

Considerable use has been made, throughout the history, of the *Post Magazine* and *Post Magazine Almanack*; as also in recent years of the *Fire Protection Association's Journal*.

Information has been extracted from specific articles in trade and technical publications as hereunder:

1. Description of the Commercial Union's building in Cornhill in *The Builder*, May 28, 1895.

2. Article on the King's Arms Tavern, Cornhill in the *The Marine Magazine*, February, 1932.

3. Articles in *The Policy Insurance Weekly*, January 21, 1954, on the History of the Commercial Union Assurance Group in Australia and New Zealand.

4. Article on the *Commercial Union-Ocean Group* in America and some of its chief agencies in *The Eastern Underwriter* (New York), October 22, 1954.

# Index